AGAINST BETTER JUDGMENT

Winner of the Walker Cowen Memorial Prize
for an outstanding work of scholarship
in eighteenth-century studies

AGAINST BETTER JUDGMENT

Irrational Action and
Literary Invention in the
Long Eighteenth Century

THOMAS SALEM MANGANARO

UNIVERSITY OF VIRGINIA PRESS
Charlottesville and London

University of Virginia Press
© 2022 by the Rector and Visitors of the University of Virginia
All rights reserved
Printed in the United States of America on acid-free paper

First published 2022

9 8 7 6 5 4 3 2 1

Library of Congress Cataloging-in-Publication Data

Names: Manganaro, Thomas Salem, author.
Title: Against better judgment : irrational action and literary invention in the long
    eighteenth century / Thomas Salem Manganaro.
Description: Charlottesville : University of Virginia Press, 2022. | Includes
    bibliographical references and index.
Identifiers: LCCN 2021043726 (print) | LCCN 2021043727 (ebook) |
    ISBN 9780813947297 (hardcover) | ISBN 9780813947303 (paperback) |
    ISBN 9780813947310 (ebook)
Subjects: LCSH: English literature—18th century—History and criticism. |
    English literature—Early modern, 1500 to 1700—History and criticism. | Act
    (Philosophy) in literature. | Philosophy of mind in literature. | Philosophy,
    English—17th century. | Philosophy, English—18th century.
Classification: LCC PR448.P5 M35 2022 (print) | LCC PR448.P5 (ebook) |
    DDC 820.9/005—dc23/eng/20211013
LC record available at https://lccn.loc.gov/2021043726
LC ebook record available at https://lccn.loc.gov/2021043727

Cover art: David Garrick as Macbeth. Copperplate engraving from John Bell's
edition of Shakespeare, 1776. (Alamy Stock Photo)

To Lidia, Salem, and Bowie

CONTENTS

AGAINST BETTER JUDGMENT

INTRODUCTION

MOLL FLANDERS WENT THROUGH with it anyway. It is true, she was now "in good circumstances" and out of the state of poverty that had previously warranted her stealing, but, as they say, old habits die hard. Stealing was fun, the acquisition of riches immensely satisfying. Pangs of regret were sure to follow, she knew that, especially when taking from those in need. When, in an earlier encounter, the thought had crossed her mind to murder the young child she had stolen from, she had also begun to wonder what kind of a person she was becoming. This wasn't a good sign. Nonetheless, these worries could be shrugged off. Plus, she had built a sort of business for herself, and wouldn't it be a shame to throw away the skills she had accumulated? In the end, Moll "could not forbear": she returned to the trade.[1]

The above is a rewriting of the consciousness of the titular character from a late scene in Daniel Defoe's 1722 novel *Moll Flanders*. Defoe didn't write it in quite this way. In my reconstruction, provided in third-person omniscient narration, I have made use of free indirect discourse, a technique that allows the narrator to momentarily perform the consciousness of the character while still in the guise of the third-person narrator. This has allowed me (the narrator) to present some of the falsity of the character's reasoning without explicitly drawing attention to it ("wouldn't it be a shame . . . ?"). Defoe's novel, meanwhile, is told in first-person retrospective narration, which offers us different angles for understanding Moll's sense of her own guilt. In Defoe's version of the scene, Moll the narrator tells us, repentantly, "O! . . . I had still leisure to have look'd back upon my Follies, and have made some Reparation." This perspective leaves the reader with some ambiguity—namely, it is unclear whether the repentant attitude is that of the character at the time of the scene or that of the narrator. Did Moll in the midst of the scene wish she could reverse her course, or is it just the narrator expressing that wish for her former self? Defoe's narrative differs too in its introduction of the devil as an entity that tempts and holds Moll in a state of wickedness. In a similar scene focused on a theft, she tells us, "The busie Devil that so industriously drew me in, had too fast hold of me to let me go back."[2] This way of writing Moll's criminality implies a sense of compromised freedom: the devil keeps her stuck doing the bad things she is doing. In other moments, though, the psychology of Moll is presented in a mode closer to free indirect discourse, which helps to portray her strategizing as freely pursued. As she tells us at one point, "The Resolution I had formerly taken of leaving off this horrid Trade, when I had gotten a little more, did not return; but I must still get farther, and more."[3] In the last part of this phrase, the narration seems to shift to perform the consciousness of the character ("I must still get farther, and more"), which, as in my rewriting of the scene, momentarily reveals her greedy mentality.

These different techniques used by Defoe and myself all, in different ways, to greater or lesser extents, contribute to conveying something specific about Moll: that she acts against her better judgment. By this I mean, on the one hand, she knows what would be the best thing to do, but, on the other hand, she freely doesn't do it, or she pursues another course of action. She proceeds intentionally but also wearily. In this sense, she exemplifies what the ancient Greeks called the condition of *akrasia* (pronounced in English as /əˈkreɪziə/). For Aristotle, the "akratic" man is he who knows the virtuous action but does not act on it due to a state of "incontinence" or "weakness." This person acts badly, but not because of ignorance. He has the knowledge part down; the problem is the follow-through. The concept arises again in a Christian framework as "weakness of the will," examined most famously by St. Augustine in the fourth-century *Confessions*. Augustine's meditations draw upon the condition of the Apostle Paul, who says, "For I do not do the good I want to do, but the evil I do not want to do—this I keep on doing." It is a difficult condition to write out: it sounds like a paradox, but it is the task of the writer to represent it as a plausible fact.

As the above two versions of writing Moll may begin to suggest, for a piece of writing to portray this condition—what I will be calling this "akrasia"—it needs to be careful about phrasing, about the perspectives it takes, about the level of psychology it describes, about the metaphysical paradigms it upholds, about its attention to time, and even about its use of rhythm. The core difficulty lies in the fact that the piece of writing needs to maintain two seemingly contradictory truths at once: first, that the person believes that there is an available course of action that is better to pursue, and second, that the person freely and intentionally pursues a different course of action. As philosopher Donald Davidson has defined it, "In doing x an agent acts incontinently [akratically] if and only if: (*a*) the agent does x intentionally; (*b*) the agent believes there is an alternative action y open to him; and (*c*) the agent judges that, all things considered, it would be better to do y than to do x."[4] For the writer, the person's action needs to be portrayed as *in spite of* the person's own beliefs, pursuing x despite knowing it would be better to pursue y. We might say that the portrayal's success hinges around its mode of conveying the *"and yet"* or the *"anyway."* It is ultimately a portrayal of an undermotivated character. The trick is to depict this undermotivated quality in a way that feels right or true.

This book will argue that this condition is especially difficult to write in Daniel Defoe's time—or, more broadly, in the period we can refer to loosely as "the long eighteenth century." This is a period in European history that has long been associated with questions surrounding autonomy and self-governance. Interestingly, however, this same period also witnessed profound transformations in philosophy when it came to explaining, understanding, and depicting human action—changes that put constraints on the ability to make sense of or even articulate akrasia. For the older paradigms that had long informed philosophy and literature—Aristotelian, Augustinian, Scholastic—action is intrinsically connected to the moral, teleological, or normative realm. In those frameworks, to "explain" action means to situate it in relation to a moral state or condition. Although akrasia/weakness of will is puzzling for philosophers like Aristotle or Augustine, these thinkers were nonetheless able to articulate the condition as an example of weak or failing agency. However, with the influence of Baconian and Newtonian premises in the seventeenth century, and specifically the elimination of teleological forms of explanation from philosophical inquiry, we get an altogether different sense of what it means to explain action. In the influential trajectory of philosophers that includes Thomas Hobbes, Benedict de Spinoza, John Locke, and David Hume, action is increasingly understood as an event to be explained by proximate causes, by what we might call strictly *efficient* rather than *formal* or *final* causation. This epistemological shift presents particular challenges to the philosopher who wants to account for akrasia, which, as we will see, leaves literature in a uniquely privileged position to take it up.

Indeed, as will be discussed more fully in chapter 1, during the period known as the Enlightenment, the old concept of akrasia/weakness of will all but disappears from philosophy. From Hobbes through Hume, when the possibility of akrasia comes up, it is promptly dismissed as a contradiction in terms and so disallowed as unreal. Operating under the terms of explanation as explicating (efficient) causes, if you have written out a scene like that from *Moll Flanders* and maintained a contradiction, then you simply have not been precise enough in your writing. At some level of psychological or bodily explanation, you have gotten something wrong. In the various treatments of the example of the person who acts against their better judgment in the work of these philosophers, we see two types of dismissals. First, we see a revival of Socrates's old position (put forward in Plato's *Protagoras*) that akrasia is not possible, for belief is always convertible with action: if a person freely acts, then that action corresponds with the person's most strongly held belief. One always does what one believes is best, full stop. Second, we see a revival of what we might call an Epicurean or Lucretian view: actions must be credited to the overwhelming blind power of subpersonal entities or processes—for the Enlightenment philosophers, these are desires (Hobbes), affects (Spinoza), states of uneasiness (Locke), or passions (Hume). In all cases, there can be no conflict, no blip in the causation of agency.

As this book will argue over the course of five chapters, for those who want to take seriously this concept of akrasia in the period of the long eighteenth century—for those who want to preserve the possibility that people do in fact (we might even say regularly, in boring and banal ways) freely contradict themselves and do so knowingly, regretfully, mournfully, unhappily, and intentionally—for these writers, if they do not want to rely upon the spiritual terminology of the "perverse will" or the machinations of the devil, a new linguistic toolkit will need to be built. Language will need to be better equipped to convey the ways that people procrastinate, fail to follow through on their beliefs, dupe themselves strategically, and resist their capacities to account for themselves. People will need to be portrayed in the mode of *in spite of,* as acting with a trace of regret, as undermotivated, and plausibly so. As I will argue, authors in the eighteenth century and Romantic era consider these conceptual difficulties as opportunities for literary experimentation and invention. Forms of ironic expression take on new importance. Free indirect discourse becomes particularly useful. Interpretation—rather than causal explication—becomes an essential value when it comes to representing and understanding people in texts. Contradiction is held up as a fundamental expressive asset, rather than a flaw, for writing.

In showing how literature engages akrasia in ways Enlightenment philosophy does not, this book traces versions of irrational action in a range of literary works in eighteenth-century and Romantic-era English literature, from novels and personal essays to autobiographies and lyric poetry, from the 1710s through the 1810s. For example, we find a version of akrasia in Laurence Sterne's Yorick from *A Sentimental Journey* (1767), who adopts modes of ignoring his conscience while pursuing what he wants. We see it in Samuel Johnson, who, in his periodical essays from the 1750s, seeks to make sense of his maddening habits of procrastination. We see it in a character like Jane Austen's Emma Woodhouse from *Emma* (1815), who knows better even as she indulges in a needlessly unkind comment. We see it in the poetry of indolence by William Wordsworth and John Keats (1805–10s), both of whom as poets know the work they want to do but delay and fret and fret and delay. In these instances and others we find that authors develop and rely upon an array of writing strategies—techniques, styles, ideas—that are not parts of philosophy proper.

More specifically, I will argue that the difficulty of writing akrasia in this period results in several developments that we can understand as distinctive to the domain of "literary writing." First, in chapters 2 and 3, we see a new emphasis on *the ironic sentence* in prose narratives. This type of sentence knowingly presents a false statement as a way of disclosing the falsity of the character in question. Rather than exhibiting conflicting thoughts in a linear progression, allowing different states of mind to be ultimately explained or elucidated in a coherent train of connections, the ironic sentence can present conflict as unresolved within a single formulation. This strategy allows prose narrative—the novel form in particular—a way of exhibiting a person's knowing and self-incurred failure in a way a more linear (causal) mode of narration cannot. In my rewriting of Moll Flanders's condition above, I have made use of sentences in free indirect discourse, one version of the ironic sentence, which I consider in depth in chapter 3. A second literary development this book identifies (in chapter 4) is that of a new epistemological priority on *interpretation* over causal explanation when it comes to understanding people and texts. The condition of akrasia demands a recurrent rereading and re-treating of a person's conflict, rather than seeking to understand the person through a factic or fixed solution or resolution. In personal essays and in an autobiography concerned with akrasia, we can see the privileges of the former mode of knowing when it comes to texts concerned with the representation of people. Lastly, in chapter 5, we find in Romantic-era poetry that engages with akrasia a new poetic prioritization of the principle of *maintaining contradictions*. This allows poetry distinct privileges in conveying the mode of holding divided and conflicting intentional attitudes and going ahead with what is ill considered. This principle of poetic construction also distinguishes what poetry is and what poetry can do: it can itself enact the stance of intentional irrationality.

These developments can be thought together in the sense that they arise out of a motivation to express what causal explication cannot. In this sense, they can be understood as together contributing to an emergent idea of "literary writing" as a domain that is epistemologically privileged in exploring human irrationality—which is to say, human experience. In this historical context, the mode of writing that maintains irony, interpretation, and contradiction as core principles of its construction may be particularly well suited to credit and examine some fundamental things about what it is like to be a person. In seeking to express a condition increasingly important to writers in England in this period—this experience of knowingly failing to act or proceed upon knowledge, belief, and considered judgment—these authors look for ways to express the absences, blanks, confusions, and failures of the living person and do so through the absences, blanks, confusions, and failures of language itself.

Akrasia would seem to be both right at home and out of place in discourses surrounding the long eighteenth century. For this reason, it may seem both surprising and unsurprising that it has escaped sustained consideration in critical studies on the period—surprising given eighteenth-century and Romantic-era literature's close associations with the dynamic between reason and the passions, the upheavals of sentimentalism and sensibility, and broader discourses around autonomy and self-governance, and unsurprising given the concept's nontreatment in the philosophy of the period itself. Indeed, akrasia has likely not been taken up in this context because studies centered on literature and the philosophy and sciences of mind, action, or the passions in the long eighteenth century have understandably stayed focused on the terms of the operative explanatory paradigms in that period. For example, Adela Pinch's *Strange Fits of Passion* (1998) interrogates the usurping power of emotions in sentimental and Romantic literature through the framework of Hume's philosophy of the blind passions, which "do not always belong to individuals," but are rather "impersonal," "transpersonal," and "autonomous entities."[5] In a slightly different vein, looking earlier in the eighteenth century, Helen Thompson's *Fictional Matter* (2017) demonstrates the significance of Robert Boyle's and John Locke's theory of corpuscles—understood as "variably qualified, divisible, and real" while also "imperceptible"—to the realist epistemology of the eighteenth-century novel, including the writing of characters.[6] Humean philosophy and corpuscular philosophy stand out as important explanatory paradigms that influence and seep into a range of discourses from the literary to the political and indeed pave the way to some of our own contemporary theoretical preoccupations, from affect theory and neuroscience to new materialism and theories of plasticity. For roughly the same reasons, all of these paradigms are unable to credit the reality of akrasia: in their terms, any seeming disruption in the causation of human agency can be explained by recourse to a fuller account of the subpersonal entities and processes that bring about actions. For their modern outlooks, "akrasia" would appear to be an outdated formulation that insists upon a nonexistent problem; as a result, for critics, it might seem to be the wrong formulation for interrogating distempered subjects in this historical context.

Relatedly, in two notable studies interested in causation, action, and questions surrounding blame and responsibility in the eighteenth century—Sandra Macpherson's *Harm's Way* (2010) and Jonathan Kramnick's *Actions and Objects from Hobbes to Richardson* (2010)—we can see critical attention to epistemological frameworks (materialist and "externalist") which likewise are not well suited for addressing akrasia. Both studies invite us to see how literature and philosophy (and, for Macpherson, law) from the Restoration period and eighteenth century stay committed to a view of causation in which human action plays no metaphysically privileged or unique role. For Macpherson, focusing on strict liability in eighteenth-century novels means turning away from notions like "person" and "will and its analogues (intention, consciousness, sovereignty, freedom)"; the emphasis is not on people acting against their better judgments but the ways "persons [are] causes of harms that go against their best intentions but for which they are nonetheless accountable."[7] For Kramnick, similarly, attending to "the largely unacknowledged role of external factors in the period's conception of mind" means that in the writers considered, "the ostensible privacy or interiority of mental states is often not an issue."[8] These studies provocatively defamiliarize eighteenth-century literature by emphasizing this period's distinctive interest in an "outside" perspective when it comes to questions of action, intention, blame, and exculpation. This also means that akrasia is necessarily out of the purview of such an outlook, for human action, like all other events in the universe, is best explained by reference to a discernible proximate cause and so cannot be understood as "undermotivated."

I want to suggest that there are distinct advantages to attending to the lack or incoherence of a philosophical concept in this time period, particularly when it comes to considering the distinctive qualities of literary writing—that there are advantages to looking at the philosophy and science for what they do *not* credit and identifying a conceptual hole in order to draw connections between that empty shape and literary form. To say more about what it might mean to focus on such an absence in the philosophy of action in particular, it will be useful to distinguish my own approach a bit more from that of Kramnick's *Action and Objects,* a book that is specifically focused on philosophy of action and engages a wide range of philosophical topics in depth and with particular ingenuity. Because its aim is to trace various topics across literature and philosophy and not exactly to distinguish the formal advantages of one over the other, *Actions and Objects* does not set out to find problems, strains, or difficulties in the philosophical paradigms in question.[9] On the contrary, it helpfully goes to great lengths to elucidate and rationalize the relevant philosophical views. An example can be seen in the book's attention to the origins of "compatibilism"; Kramnick writes, "One major contribution of seventeenth- and eighteenth-century theories of action was . . . *not* to pose freedom and responsibility against necessity. It was rather to show how the two could be compatible. Traditionally credited to Hobbes, compatibilism of this kind has had great influence up to this day."[10] Kramnick spells out in detail how Hobbes's view is supposed to work, noting that "freedom turns out to be a particular kind of causal relation, one in which reasons are able to become actions."[11] This explainer takes Hobbes on his own terms and, as such, makes it possible to draw connections to narrative and poetry. However, one can also choose to frame Hobbes's philosophy of action a little differently. Hobbes's influence in the sense described cannot be denied, but we can also observe that this collapse of the notion of freedom to "a particular kind of causal relation" redefines the idea of freedom entirely and, in doing so, helps precipitate a more or less permanent crisis for modern philosophy—one identified a century

and a half later by Immanuel Kant through the antinomy between Enlightenment philosophy's treatment of the will as mechanistic (as in the
realm of natural philosophy) and its treatment of the will as spontaneously
free (as in the realm of moral philosophy). This division in turn produces
subfields of "philosophy of action" and "ethics" that are no longer clearly
related to each other, producing a range of new puzzles for philosophy.
If Hobbes offered explanatory advantages through these new premises,
in other words, he also helped to accelerate a shifting of tectonic plates
that would leave future philosophers struggling to keep both legs planted.

My aim is to take up a more critical vantage toward the philosophy
of the period and, more specifically, to the history of the philosophy of
action—one that stays attuned to the sorts of trouble produced by the
new premises of Hobbes (and Spinoza, Locke, and Hume). Significantly,
this vantage entails a different view toward the relationship between
philosophy and literature in the period. The nature of this relationship
changes, as we will see, when we put some pressure on the former. Taking
interest in this period's philosophy of action for its destabilizing effects
puts us in a unique position to emphasize the privileges of various forms
of properly literary writing when it comes to certain (classically) philosophical questions, and thus, literature's *distinctive* role in an age of not
just philosophical advancement but also philosophical crisis.[12]

The "long view" of the history of the philosophy of action that I take
is one that I draw from various philosophical accounts and intellectual
histories focused on broad transformations in epistemology and metaphysics in the early modern and modern periods. These include G. E. M.
Anscombe's "Modern Moral Philosophy" (1958), Hannah Arendt's *The Life
of the Mind* (1978), Alasdair MacIntyre's *After Virtue* (1981), Susan James's
Passion and Action (1997), J. B. Schneewind's *The Invention of Autonomy*
(1998), and Thomas Pfau's *Minding the Modern* (2013). Although there
is no single study that identifies a dissolution of akrasia for philosophy
in the seventeenth and eighteenth centuries, some of these intellectual
histories briefly address akrasia in the midst of their accounts of the
transformations of theories of human agency in the modern period.[13]
The most concise formulation that articulates the nature of the shift in
philosophy of action that concerns this book can be found in MacIntyre's

After Virtue; there MacIntyre writes, "In the seventeenth and eighteenth centuries the Aristotelian understanding of nature was repudiated," and we find a new sense of what it means to "explain action," one in which "the explanation of action is increasingly held to be a matter of laying bare the physiological and physical mechanisms which underlie action." This change produces long-term consequences in philosophy, resulting in a split between notions like "intention, purpose, reason for action and the like on the one hand and the concepts which specify the notion of mechanical explanation on the other"—a split that "becomes part of the permanent repertoire of philosophy." MacIntyre continues, "The former notions are however now treated as detached from notions of good or virtue; those concepts have been handed over to the separate subdiscipline of ethics. Thus the disjunctions and divorces of the eighteenth century perpetuate and reinforce themselves in contemporary curricular divisions."[14] Susan James has put it similarly: the developments of Descartes, Hobbes, Spinoza, and Locke, she writes, lead to "the conditions for the emergence of the twentieth-century orthodoxy that actions are to be explained simply by evoking beliefs and desires."[15] Thus we no longer think of questions of action within the realm of "moral philosophy," but rather within a more discrete domain of "philosophy of action," which talks in terms of the causation of beliefs, desires, and reasons.

One can argue about whether or not this transformation marked an improvement in philosophy—that is, whether such a change more correctly understands action—but that question is not my focus here. Nor is it my aim to revive, recuperate, or restore older models of agency, Aristotelian, Augustinian, or Thomistic. Instead, I am interested in the fact that a cataclysmic shift like this one does not occur without some casualties (incoherences) and that these, in turn, present new linguistic possibilities for literature.[16]

In its attention to akrasia, this book joins other recent work on eighteenth- and nineteenth-century literature interested in the limits of systematic or logical thinking. Different kinds of human conditions appear resistant to tidy conceptual categorization, for instance in Anne-Lise François's *Open Secrets* (2008; "a mode of recessive action that takes itself away as it occurs") and in Wendy Anne Lee's *Failures of Feeling* (2019; the "insensible" character that "oscillates between impassivity [no feeling] and contempt [bad feeling]").[17] Enlightenment systematic thinking reaches its impasses in long-eighteenth-century literature in Andrew Franta's *Systems Failure* (2019), and, looking at a slightly later period, logical thinking is thwarted by the vagaries of desire in the Victorian novel in Daniel Wright's *Bad Logic* (2018). Although akrasia is not a subject of inquiry for these critics, they bring out some related insights regarding the affordances of literary form in light of the period's explanatory challenges.[18] In Patrick Fessenbecker's *Reading Ideas in Victorian Literature* (2020), on the other hand, akrasia is taken up directly, although that study takes a different approach with regards to philosophy and literature. Fessenbecker shows how novels themselves espouse theories of moral psychology and akrasia and that their contributions can thus be adjudicated philosophically in relation to theories of akrasia found in philosophy proper.[19] My book does not treat akrasia in quite this way; my goal is not to ask how we can glean content from different formal projects but rather how the content in question affects, indeed transforms, form. Put differently, my focus is not on the explanatory takeaways of the authors' depictions of akrasia; rather, it is on the linguistic acrobatics they undertake in order to preserve the trope at all.[20]

In order to examine literary developments vis-à-vis shifts in philosophy of action that accompanied the seventeenth and eighteenth centuries, this book moves between "eighteenth-century" and "Romantic-era" literature without taking the periodic distinction as especially significant. Indeed, neither "the age of reason" nor "the age of the passions" is especially well equipped to make sense of akrasia insofar as the models of thought that privilege the one or the other are similarly reliant upon an understanding of action as "explained" by temporally prior mental or bodily states. As we will see, the conceptual transformations around human agency in the seventeenth and eighteenth centuries produce implications that spill over both periods as traditionally conceived, motivating formal innovations in each. Consequently, the book is roughly equally divided between treatments of "eighteenth-century" and "Romantic-era" English literature: chapters 2 and 4 are focused on eighteenth-century authors (chapter 2 on Daniel Defoe, Eliza Haywood, and Laurence Sterne, and chapter 4 on Samuel Johnson and Jean-Jacques Rousseau—our only non-English author), whereas chapters 3 and 5 are focused on authors typically considered in the context of the Romantic era (chapter 3 on William Godwin and Jane Austen, and chapter 5 on William Wordsworth and John Keats).

Similarly, this book moves between different genres of literary writing (novels, life writing, and poetry) in order to examine the various ways that what we today call "literature" increasingly built or emphasized particular techniques, outlooks, and styles in response to the challenge of writing akrasia. The goal is to show how a single philosophical problem motivated multiple kinds of literary responses across different types of literature in the long eighteenth century. At no point is it the book's aim to produce holistic theories of the origins of these respective forms—on the rise of the novel or Romantic lyric poetry—nor does it seek to offer wholly new or innovative definitions of the notions important for literature (e.g., irony, interpretation, contradiction), but it does ask us to see some of these forms and their innovations differently, in light of a historically specific difficulty with representing action. The novel's technology for conveying failure through ironic expressions, life writing's value on interpretation, and the priority of contradiction in poetry—these can all be understood as linguistic responses to new challenges that arose with changing paradigms for understanding human agency. As I hope will become clear in the chapters that follow, these distinctively literary qualities of writing interrelate: they all refuse standards of exactitude and disaggregation when it comes to representing people, privileging instead certain kinds of silence, whether in its ironic mode of unsaid implication, in its refusal of a final or fixed explanation, or in its allowance of a state of unresolved antinomy. Telling the story of these literary developments amid the backdrop of these philosophical transformations is the task at hand.

Some notes on the terminology are in order. By and large, I have chosen to use the term "akrasia" over "weakness of will." In the original Aristotelian sense of the word, "akrasia" is correlated with "outward" action and does not explicitly refer to inactive conditions like indolence, which may be more naturally described by "weakness of will." However, "weakness of will" requires that we accept the ontological category of "the will," a notion Christian in its origins, and this may restrict us in thinking broadly about practical reason as it appears in a range of contexts. In the last half-century, the word "akrasia" has been used to encompass a broader variety of phenomena. I choose it instead of "weakness of will" throughout not only because it is more concise, but also, at least in recent philosophical analyses, considered to be the more capacious. I follow philosopher Amélie Rorty's lead in identifying "akrasia" as the more inclusive and less misleading term of the two, and indeed as able to encompass "a psychological action, like perceiving or deciding."[21] Hence we can speak of "akrasia of belief," which is a species of akrasia. As Rorty writes, "A person believes akratically when he believes that *p,* being implicitly aware that *p* conflicts with the preponderance of serious evidence or with a range of principles to which he is committed. Just as an akratic agent must be capable of acting in accordance with his judgment about what is best to do, so an akratic believer must be capable of forming and maintaining a belief that is in accordance with his judgment about what is appropriate for him to believe."[22] Adjacent to this notion is that of self-deception, which can often be identified as a strategy *for* akrasia: "Akrasia is often—though not necessarily—accompanied by self-deception: the person rationalizes his action or belief."[23] There is overlap here too with Jean-Paul Sartre's notion of *mauvaise foi* (bad faith): akrasia is often bad faith in action.[24] This book thinks of akrasia in these various ways—outward (visible) akrasia, akratic inaction (laziness), and akrasia of belief, which are often coupled with the phenomenon of self-deception.

"Akrasia" is not a word that is widely used within literary studies (it is more likely to be found in philosophy, classics, and theology),[25] but, when it is, the focus is most likely to be on medieval or early modern literature such as Spenser's *Faerie Queen* ("Acrasia's bower") or one of Shakespeare's dramas that feature weak-willed or undermotivated heroes or antiheroes.[26] Importantly, neither the word "akrasia" nor the expression "weakness of will" is used in the works I consider in the long eighteenth century. I use these expressions aware of their potential anachronicity, but they are interestingly anachronistic on both sides—in relation to both antiquity and the present. Focusing on what goes unrecognized and unnamed in the period means isolating cases that sufficiently replicate the condition as recognized in its exemplary types—Aristotle's akratic man, Euripides's Medea (or Ovid's, which is the primary example considered by the Enlightenment philosophers), Augustine's weak-willed self—and that satisfy the conditions identified by philosophers like Davidson, Rorty, and Agnes Callard.[27] In this book, we can find akrasia arising in different shapes. All seven sins are on the table: lust, greed, sloth, pride, wrath, gluttony, and envy. One could also observe gendered differences between "types" of akrasia. It could be said that one legacy of akrasia has its origins in the St. Augustine's masculine sexualized version of weakness of will in book 2 of his *Confessions,* and another legacy has its roots in the literary prototype of Medea, whose neglect of the good is taken up as associated with feminine "weakness," a word that, in eighteenth-century in medical textbooks, conduct books, and novels, is frequently associated with the female constitution.[28] It is not my goal to bring out such distinctions, but rather to stay attuned to the commonalities across these various versions in order to examine how they present challenges for writing belief, desire, intention, judgment, and action.

Throughout my discussions of literary works in chapters 2 through 5, I have tried to pick examples that most unambiguously resemble acting *knowingly* and *freely* against what the character holds to be (all things considered) for the best. Chapter 2 does focus on some borderline cases, which are interestingly unclear about whether this ought to be considered under the classic definition of akrasia, including Defoe's Moll Flanders, as already briefly considered. However, for the most part, I try to stay clear of cases that are ambiguously akratic. Cases of addiction, for example, are related, but less vividly convey the point, for there is a stronger reason for thinking of such cases as examples of physiological compulsion, and so they risk getting us into excessive caveats and qualifications. Necessarily this also means the focus is not on characters who do not know better— that is, whose guilt is associated with ignorance or bad principles. This book is less concerned with ignorance's equivalence with innocence than with knowledge's equivalence with guilt. There are inevitably more examples I could have emphasized, from Coleridge's ancient mariner, whose shooting of the albatross exemplifies an under-motivated act, to Robert

Lovelace in Richardson's *Clarissa,* whose relentless pursuits can at time be characterized as akratic ("'Tis a plotting villain of a heart . . . I so little its master!")[29] In selecting examples, I have primarily strived to minimize repetition in the argument while bringing out a set of distinct though interrelated ways this trope arises and motivates formal experimentation in this period in English literary history.

Further, it is important to clarify that the phrase "irrational action" (from the book's subtitle) is never meant to imply "irrational" as adjudicated by some external standard—the culture's, the author's, yours, or mine. The word "irrational" can easily be—and historically has been—used to heighten one or another standard of so-called "rationality" in order to denigrate a person or a class of people, which is indeed one of the most profound legacies of the "Enlightenment." Here the word only indicates irrationality by the standard of the person him or herself: these are cases in which it is difficult for the person to give an account of themselves, for the action is illegible, seemingly paradoxical, outside the bounds of articulation. This also means that "akrasia" is not necessarily to be read as bad (or as good); if for Moll Flanders it is associated with the wicked deed of stealing, for Keats it means the origins of poetic construction. The book's interest is in the challenges it produces for causal explanation and the opportunities it presents for literary experimentation.

Akrasia undoubtedly has the potential to take on broader significance—cultural, national, economic—in this period or, indeed, for a theory of "modernity" more broadly. Inevitably, akrasia "scales up." When the ancient mariner shoots the albatross, one could also discern Coleridge's reflections in the 1790s on the sin of the slave trade, pursued in full knowledge of its evil. Godwin's intemperate characters in his novels from the early 1800s speak to his own interests in intemperance in the context of the French Revolution. The versions of indolence and procrastination we see in Johnson, Wordsworth, and Keats speak to the condition experienced by a new middle class that, more than ever before, is afforded the capacity for leisure, which also means the capacity to be lazy and "waste time." A different book could be written on the akrasia of the State or of a national culture, and an analogy could be drawn between the irrational (knowingly self-defeating) dynamics of that broader collective entity and those same dynamics that reside on the scale of the person. Indeed, a book could be written on the origins of our own forms of cultural, economic, political, and ecological akrasia.[30] For the purposes of this book, those analogies can only be made suggestively. They are relevant insofar as the connections to the cultural or national scale are important for the authors in question, for the ways their characters' actions are motivated by or represent broader problems. However, throughout, my primary focus will be on the challenges and opportunities when it comes to writing akrasia in a person, one person at a time, for it is this scale that presents particular troubles to philosophical explanation.

The following five chapters are split so as to focus on literary developments across distinct genres of writing. We start with philosophy (chapter 1) in order to lay the groundwork for the conceptual changes that entail an elimination of akrasia from the philosophy of the period. Chapters 2 and 3 shift to novels and novellas, then chapter 4 moves to life writing, and chapter 5 focuses on poetry. The breakdown of these chapters is not strictly chronological and, of the forms considered, not all encompass the full scope of "the long eighteenth century." The novels and novellas of chapters 2 and 3 cumulatively stretch across the eighteenth century (chapter 2's narratives are from 1719 to 1767) and the Romantic era (chapter 3's novels are from 1799 to 1815), while the essays and autobiography of chapter 4 are exclusively written in the mid-eighteenth-century (1750s–70) and the poetry of chapter 5 is exclusively from the Romantic era (1805–19). We might note that these latter two chapters consider slightly different time periods because of the asynchronicity of the development of these respective forms (life writing and poetry) when it comes to representing mundane experience through neither overtly allegorical nor religious paradigms. Although different forms respond to the problem of representing akrasia at slightly different periods, they all arise in response to the same conceptual difficulties that accompany the Enlightenment. The aim is not to suggest that all of these developments occurred simultaneously, but to demonstrate that they all can be seen in relation to the same source. What follows is a slightly more detailed overview of each chapter.

Chapter 1 ("Akrasia and Explanation in Enlightenment Philosophy") argues that the older notions of "akrasia" and "weakness of will" from

Aristotle and St. Augustine, respectively, disappear as coherent concepts in key works of Enlightenment philosophy by Thomas Hobbes (1651), Benedict de Spinoza (1677), John Locke (1694), and David Hume (1740). It examines how and why philosophy changed in the seventeenth and eighteenth centuries such that akrasia could no longer be articulated and is instead replaced by models of irrational action as based in either compulsion or ignorance. This chapter thus prepares us to recognize the distinctive epistemological capacities of writing that dwells in silences, absences, nonexplanations, and contradictions. In the latter portion of the chapter, I turn to the treatments of akrasia in two twentieth-century philosophers, Donald Davidson and Iris Murdoch, which help to demonstrate the importance of style, perspective, and voice in giving shape to akrasia within the context of philosophy.

Chapter 2 ("Some Encounters with Akrasia in Eighteenth-Century Prose Fiction: Defoe, Haywood, Sterne") moves from Enlightenment philosophy to eighteenth-century fiction by drawing parallels between philosophy's difficulties representing akrasia and those of early English novels and novellas. Select instances in Daniel Defoe's *Robinson Crusoe* (1719) and *Moll Flanders* (1722) as well as Eliza Haywood's *Fantomina* (1725) and *The History of Betsy Thoughtless* (1740) reveal tensions in representing akrasia that are similar to the explanatory tensions detected in philosophy. These tensions parallel those found in philosophy insofar as they maintain formal interest in causal psychological description on the one hand, but moral interest in akrasia on the other. The chapter then turns to Laurence Sterne's *A Sentimental Journey* (1767) to show one self-conscious method of portraying akrasia—specifically, by abstaining from psychological description in favor of ironically performing the failures of causal narration. A variation of this type of ironic sentence can be observed in the novels discussed in chapter 3.

Chapter 3 ("Akrasia and Free Indirect Discourse in Romantic-Era Novels: Godwin and Austen") continues to pay attention to novelistic strategies for portraying undermotivated and seemingly inexplicable action by turning to William Godwin's novels *St. Leon* (1799) and *Fleetwood* (1805) and Jane Austen's *Emma* (1815). Godwin's novels concern characters with intemperate psychological states and, in this sense, explore phenomena that his earlier mechanistic philosophy was unable to parse. I show that Godwin develops an early version of free indirect discourse in his novels as a formal solution to this representational problem. We can see the particular epistemological benefits of free indirect discourse in evoking knowingly guilty action by centering on Austen's Emma Woodhouse. In *Emma,* free indirect discourse functions as a representation of a character's strategy to foreground a third-person view of a self in order to absolve oneself of responsibility for one's actions. In this way, free indirect discourse helps to represent the mode of self-excuse inherent to akrasia in a way causal psychological description cannot.

Chapter 4 ("Akrasia, Life Writing, and Interpretation: Johnson and Rousseau") moves us toward the experience of akrasia in authors who wrote about themselves. In Samuel Johnson's periodical essays of the 1750s and Jean-Jacques Rousseau's *Confessions* (written in 1769–70, published in 1782), we see a growing self-consciousness about the impossibility of devising a formally complete analysis of one's own contradictory behaviors. As these authors puzzles over their erratic and procrastinatory tendencies as authors, they both articulate a new conception of "interpretation" as an open-ended mode of understanding oneself and a literary work of writing. It is worth noting that Rousseau is the sole non-English author considered, but the inclusion of his *Confessions* is justified, given its profound significance to English literary history—particularly to authors Godwin and Wordsworth—and its stark and telling contrasts with Augustine's *Confessions.*

The final chapter, chapter 5 ("Akrasia and the Poetry of Antinomies: Wordsworth and Keats"), turns to these two Romantic poets' engagements with indolence and procrastination, which they understood as constitutive of the poet's experience. It argues that the puzzles of self-contradicting inaction are at the basis of the historically specific understanding of poetry as that which contains contradictions—the capability of being negative, or what Keats called "negative capability." In contrast to Samuel Taylor Coleridge's approach to the problem in his philosophical prose, William Wordsworth engages his own procrastination by performing it in *The Prelude* (1805), exemplifying a stylistic poetics of antinomy. Likewise, John Keats, borrowing William Hazlitt's notion of human agency as "disinterested," understands indolence and poetry alike as able to contain contraries in a gestational if disappointed state of abeyance. In his letters and poems including "On Seeing the Elgin Marbles" (1817), "Ode to a Nightingale" (1819), and "Ode on Indolence" (1819), indolence figures as a form of paradoxical agency that symbolizes and performs his notion of the disinterested stance. For these poets, literature is unproductive and irrational and, for that very reason, a privileged domain for understanding human life.

As for literature after the long eighteenth century and outside of the English context, these are necessarily beyond the scope of this book. However, I hope that a reader, after taking in the story told here, can turn to literary depictions of people who act against their better judgments in different literary traditions or historical periods and identify there the (similar or related) representational difficulties akrasia produces, the opportunities it presents, and the legacies it has inherited from the authors I have examined. One could also bring these arguments to the practice of reading philosophy, where I believe we can recognize the essential roles of formal decisions and stylistic tendencies—slips in perspective, amplifications of tone, attention to rhythm—that provide not just ornament or elegance, but epistemologies in and of themselves.

1

AKRASIA AND EXPLANATION IN ENLIGHTENMENT PHILOSOPHY

HOW CAN AN ACTION be simultaneously intentional and irrational—that is, freely pursued but also knowingly in pursuit of an outcome understood to be for the worse? In the analysis of philosopher Agnes Callard, historically there have been two dominant ways of discrediting the reality of such an action, as can be considered through the following example:

> He goes to the party, though he thinks he should stay home and study. What explains a weak-willed (or *akratic*) action like this one? One answer is that he is a pseudo-akratic: he doesn't *really* believe he ought to study. Either he never fully believed that he should study, or perhaps he believed this once but temporarily forgets or suppresses it at the moment of action. Another answer is that he is an unintentional akratic: his desire to go to the party is so strong that it compels him, carrying him against his will like a strong wind.[1]

An akratic action, Callard writes, could thus be explained away by clarifying that the person's *real* belief (deep down) did in fact correlate with the action at the time of the action; alternatively, it could be explained away by clarifying that the person's action was not in fact free and so was not really an intentional action at all. In the first kind of account, the action is not irrational; in the second, it is not intentional. However, the philosopher who wants to defend the reality of akrasia—that the person in question both *believed* going to the party was ultimately for the worse, and that his action was *voluntary*—needs some other kind of explanation.

The difficulty would seem to lie in the desire to both eliminate logical conflict (presumably one of the goals of "explanation") and still preserve the kind of conflict inherent to the idea of akrasia. In the passage above, the conflict is felt through the dramatic tension of a narrative: "He goes to the party, though he thinks he should stay home and study." It is brief, but it is a narrative nonetheless, complete with a character, an event, and the drama of a psychological problem. There is an inclination in one direction ("he goes") and another in the reverse direction ("though he thinks"). The drama lies in this conflict. What kind of an explanatory account, then, can preserve the drama of the narrative while also illuminating or clarifying what has occurred?

Callard suggests that the most common way philosophers have provided an account of akrasia has been to maintain that the akratic agent acts upon "the weaker reason"—a curious phrase, and an account that Callard ultimately argues is wrong, but her diagnosis of its usage through history is helpful for showing us how philosophers have grappled with this phenomenon.[2] It is an approach, as we will see, that allows philosophers to maintain the reality of akrasia while preserving the sense in which a person fails him or herself. It also offers an expression that can be helpful for us as readers of literature when we seek to identify how literary works attempt to represent acting against better judgment. Callard elaborates on what she means by "the weaker reason": "Having determined that he ought to do one thing, the weak-willed agent does another. On the standard view, he fails to act on his all-things-considered (i.e., what he considers his best) reason, but he acts on a reason nonetheless. He acts on his *weaker reason,* his (outweighed) reason to perform the akratic action."[3] In other words, for most philosophers who want to maintain the reality of akrasia, the akratic person does act upon a reason (so the act is intentional); however, it is a reason that he or she sees is "weaker," indeed "outweighed" (this makes it irrational). Another way to say this is to say that the action is *undermotivated*: the person acts upon a reason, but it is not a *good* reason, and the person knows it. So one might explain the partygoer's state by saying that he sees the stronger reason (that he should stay home and study) and the weaker reason (it would be fun to go out), and he acts upon the weaker reason. The action is undermotivated, because he knows the reason is unjustified. It is not a good reason for going out, but he's acting on it anyway.

However, this sort of explanation also creates questions. How to account for the practice of *neglecting* a stronger reason for the sake of the weaker? As we will see, for philosophers like Aristotle and Augustine, this type of failure—the lack of follow-through, the disconnect, the ignoring or purposeful forgetting—becomes an important part of their theories of human agency. It is to be understood from within the intrinsically moral realm of practical reason that understands a trajectory from man-as-he-is to man-as-he-ought-to-be. This realm is, however, largely eliminated from the major strands of Enlightenment philosophy. As we will see, in the seventeenth- and eighteenth-century philosophy in question, if reasons are to be understood as causes, then there is no weaker or stronger; if a reason brought about an action, then it is, by definition, not weak.

This chapter provides a condensed intellectual history of akrasia in order to help us see how agential weakness—failing in action—is pushed out of the space of philosophical inquiry during the age of the Enlightenment. I focus on Callard's phrase "the weaker reason" as a way to stay focused on what exactly becomes disallowed in philosophical explanations of action—a neglect, a silencing of what is known to be justifiable—and then, as I will consider in chapters 2 through 5, what finds new forms of articulation in literary writing. The end of this chapter will also briefly step outside of the historical trajectory in order to consider treatments of akrasia in essays from the 1960s by philosophers Donald Davidson and Iris Murdoch. This will help us see more clearly some of the epistemological privileges of literary strategies when writing about akrasia, except here we will consider those privileges not within literature (as will be the focus in chapters 2 through 5) but within more recent works of philosophy. Although this portion of the chapter does not explicitly contribute to the historical argument of this book, it lends to its theoretical argument by helping us see the importance of taking narrative, perspective, and character seriously for those who want to write about akrasia outside of the teleological/moral paradigms of human agency.

The chapter is split into four sections: the first centers on the cases of Aristotle and Augustine, the two philosophers who have bequeathed conceptions of akrasia/weakness of will unto philosophy; the second examines the elimination of akrasia in Thomas Hobbes, Benedict de Spinoza, and David Hume; the third looks at the somewhat more complicated case of John Locke, who both eliminates akrasia but also tries to preserve it through his use of narrative; and the fourth considers the privileges of the literary in writing akrasia in essays by Davidson and Murdoch.

The story told here rests upon much broader accounts regarding the transformations away from classical worldviews in the seventeenth and eighteenth centuries—specifically, around the idea of "explanation," and the impacts of those transformations on theories of human agency. It is not my goal to try and provide that fuller story. My more limited focus here is on what happens to the concept of akrasia when teleological and moral modes of characterizing and explaining action are out of the picture, as with Hobbes, Spinoza, Locke, and Hume. To go deeper into the past to set the stage for these changes to conceptions of "will" might mean turning to the University of Paris's censuring of Aristotle's treatises in the thirteenth century and in the writing of William of Ockham in the early fourteenth century, which resulted in the institutional strengthening of voluntarist theology; as told in the account of Thomas Pfau, it is in that period that we see a "momentous shift from the Thomistic synthesis of Aristotelianism and Augustinianism toward a Franciscan (voluntarist) theology—one wherein agents, situations, and meanings are no longer connected to an underlying rational order or substantial form but, instead, prove inherently discontinuous."[4] Alternatively, one could trace the growth and spread of Lucretian thought in "modernity," suggested through Stephen Greenblatt's story of Poggio Bracciolini's discovery of Lucretius's *On the Nature of Things* in 1417.[5] Or one could follow Charles Taylor's characterization of the invention of a form of "inwardness" that is tied to "disengaged reason" in Descartes.[6] What will be especially significant to our investigation of

Hobbes and his legacy, however, is the identification of the elimination of teleological and moral frameworks from philosophy. Alasdair MacIntyre brings out this change through the figure of Blaise Pascal in particular, in whom he perceives a synthesis of "a Protestant-cum-Jansenist conception of reason" on the one hand and "the conception of reason at home in the most innovative seventeenth-century philosophy and science" on the other. MacIntyre argues that this synthesis leads to an embrace of a new model of reason that "does not comprehend essences or transitions from potentiality to act; . . . it can assess truths of fact and mathematical relations but nothing more. In the realm of practice therefore it can speak only of means. About ends it must be silent."[7] Another way to see the loss of teleological reasoning might be to focus on Isaac Newton, who, as Louis Dupré has written, "himself avoided using teleological arguments, not in the first place because they interfered with mathematical deduction, but because they escaped observation";[8] his empirical method then "forbade him to introduce metaphysical speculations about a transcendent cause."[9] As we will see in the Enlightenment philosophers discussed here, if reasoning and explanation are strictly focused on what can be empirically perceived or rationally determined as immediately prior, resulting in a commitment to "cause" understood strictly as "efficient cause," with teleological and moral explanations out of the picture, then human action becomes quite a different thing.

Before we get there, we will need to have a clearer grasp of what it means to explain action in moral and teleological terms, and what it might mean to say that someone who acts against better judgment acts upon "the weaker reason." For this we turn to Aristotle and Augustine.

AKRASIA AS FAILURE IN ACTION: ARISTOTLE AND AUGUSTINE

Aristotle and Augustine are often considered to be the two most fundamental early pillars that bequeath to a Western philosophical tradition the understanding of human agency as a domain that is separate from the domain of the merely intellectual. Their distinct paradigms have been broadly understood as combined in medieval Scholasticism and with the thought of Thomas Aquinas in particular, so it is worthwhile to examine the Aristotelian model as well as the Augustinian model as having originally formulated ideas that would be dominant (in different ways) within and through medieval and early modern philosophy and theology. For both, the notion of acting weakly or incontinently is an important possibility for human beings, and an essential consequence of this view is that the domain of agency is not strictly correlated with the domain of thought or reason.

Although Augustine did not know the work of Aristotle, both wrote in response to the claims put forward by Socrates in Plato's *Protagoras*. In that dialogue, Socrates maintains that if a person acts freely and knowingly, then it is always in accordance with what he believes to be best. "No one who either knows or believes that there is another possible course of action, better than the one he is following," Socrates says, "will ever continue on his present course when he might choose the better. . . . Then it must follow that no one willingly goes to meet evil or what he thinks to be evil. . . . When faced with the choice of two evils no one will choose the greater when he might choose the less."[10] For the Socrates of the *Protagoras* (it is less clear whether we ought to attribute this position to Plato), action is convertible with belief.[11] If a man gives in to the rush of passion and commits a violent act, we simply say that he believed that act was the greater act. If he did not believe it was the greater act, then we must say he did the act blindly, ignorantly, or was compelled in some way to act in this manner.

Here is where we can identify Aristotle's uniqueness as a philosopher focused on becoming (action, praxis) as separate from being, and on "practical" reason as separate from "theoretical" reason. As Hannah Arendt has put it, "The starting-point of Aristotle's reflections on the subject [of the will/purposive choice] is the anti-Platonic insight that reason by itself does not move anything."[12] For Aristotle, akrasia serves as a central example that disaggregates reasoning from doing and allows him to deny that action is necessarily convertible with belief or knowledge.

Aristotle's most prolonged discussion of akrasia can be found in book 7 of the *Nicomachean Ethics*. He defines the "enkratic man" (or the "continent man") as he who feels the afflictions of contrary passions or appetites, but is able to control them. The enkratic man experiences inner conflict even as he does the right thing and for this reason is not considered perfectly virtuous. The "akratic man" (the "incontinent man"), however, is he who not only possesses passions and appetites that draw away from what is good, but he also succumbs to them in action despite knowing the correct action.[13] How is this so? At one point, Aristotle puts it this way: "When appetite happens to be present in us, the one opinion bids us avoid the object, but appetite leads us towards it (for it can move each of our bodily parts); so that it turns out that a man behaves incontinently under the influence (in a sense) of a rule and an opinion, and of one not contrary in itself, but only incidentally—for the appetite is contrary, not the opinion—to the right rule."[14] This is a curious and heavily debated description, for the phrase "leads us towards it (for it can move each of our bodily parts)" seems to imply determinism and lack of freedom. But this interpretation is misleading, for the man, according to Aristotle, acts upon "the influence (in a sense) of a rule and an opinion" correlating to the appetite—in other words, it is a free and voluntary action that follows a rule or opinion correlated with the appetite. In an important sense, akratic action in Aristotle is *voluntary:* the incontinent man, he tells us later, "acts *willingly* (for he acts in a sense with knowledge both of what he does and of the end to which he does it)" (emphasis mine).[15] However, crucially, the akratic does not act in accordance with what he calls "choice."[16] Indeed, this example serves to distinguish "the voluntary" from *prohaeresis*—namely, purposive choice (or judgment, deliberation, commitment).[17] It is also for this reason that Aristotle calls the incontinent man "half-wicked," for if he acted badly in accordance with choice, that would be wicked action. (To this extent, he is interestingly soft on the akratic, morally speaking.) It then makes sense to say that the akratic man in Aristotle is he who acts upon a reason of a sort, a "weaker reason," going off of a certain *kind* of knowledge: "For he acts in a sense with knowledge both of what he does and of the end to which he does it."

What is this "knowledge in a sense"? Aristotle describes the "practical syllogism" that governs the production of action, in which there is a universal premise (like "dry food is good for every man") and a minor premise (like "this food is dry"). In the case of the incontinent man,

Aristotle writes, "there is nothing to prevent a man's having both prem-isses and acting against his knowledge, provided that he *is using only* the universal premiss and not the particular" (emphasis mine).[18] Thus Aris-totle maintains that the akratic can fail to "exercis[e] the knowledge" of the minor premise; he *allows* the weaker reason to prevail. He describes it a bit differently somewhat later. The akratic, Aristotle writes, should be understood as "having knowledge in a sense and yet not having it, as in the instance of a man asleep, mad, or drunk."[19] The reference to the mad or drunk person would seem to imply compromised intelligence, suggest-ing that akrasia is only possible when belief or knowledge is unclear. As the discussion proceeds, however, Aristotle affirms that the akratic has knowledge, but specifies what kind of knowledge this is: "It is not in the presence of what is thought to be knowledge proper that the affection of incontinence arises (nor is it this that is dragged about as a result of the state of passion)," he writes, "but in that of perceptual knowledge."[20] "Perceptual knowledge" appears to be a weaker kind of knowledge that can motivate action. Risto Saarinen writes that the most common inter-pretation of this passage is that "the details of the minor premise remain to an extent ignored."[21] The domain of *ignoring, neglecting, failing* to exercise the stronger reason—this is the domain of practical reason and where the "akratic break" takes place.[22]

It is important for Aristotle that we be able to talk about action not just in causal terms but also in moral terms. The soul, the object of study in the *Nicomachean Ethics,* is defined by virtue of its telos, and the goal of the *Ethics* is to study the soul by virtue of "examin[ing] the nature of actions, namely how we ought to do them; for these determine also the nature of the states of character that are produced."[23] The *Ethics* is a study not merely of what actions *are* in a theoretical sense, but also always what actions *ought to be*. To this extent, any study of actions is always a study in the terms of the good toward which action aspires. To ask the question "What is an action?" and expect a merely causal answer would seem strange to Aristotle: action is a subject that is intrinsically situated within the teleological scheme of study that is moral philosophy (ethics). Action can fail; otherwise, theoretical reason would be all that is required for virtuous action. MacIntyre puts it this way: "Within that teleological scheme [of the *Nicomachean Ethics*] there is a fundamental contrast between man-as-he-happens-to-be and man-as-he-could-be-if-he-realized-his-essential-nature. Ethics is the science which is to enable men to understand how they make the transition from the former state to the latter. Ethics therefore in this view presupposes some account of potentiality and act, some account of the essence of man as a rational animal and above all some account of the human *telos*."[24] For this reason, an explanation of action would need to be able to account for the fact of man's failings. An explanation strictly in the terms of efficient causation would elide that intrinsically moral dimension of action.

In the writings of St. Augustine, too, there is no separating a study of action or agency without the underlying framework of "the human *telos*." Like Aristotle, Augustine's writings can be understood in contrast with (indeed, as responding to) the intellectualism in Plato's writings—that is, Plato's aspiration to attaining the good by intellect alone.[25] In this sense, Augustine can be seen as paralleling Aristotle in forming a philosophical framework for agency, although his response to Platonism was more informed by some of the philosophical equipment of Stoicism.[26] What is new with Augustine, however, is the concept of "will" (*voluntas*).[27]

While Aristotle's most extensive discussion on acting against better judgment appears in a philosophical treatise, Augustine's comes in the midst of his autobiographical *Confessions*.[28] The early portrayal of what he would call "weakness of will" is presented in book 2, when he describes stealing pears from a pear tree as a young boy. This well-known episode, so fundamental for later theorizations of sin and weakness of will alike, also provides the groundwork for literary narratives of akrasia we will find in the eighteenth century and Romantic era (especially in Defoe, Rousseau, and Wordsworth):

> There was a pear tree in the orchard next to ours, laden with pears, but not ones especially appealing either to the eye or the tongue. At dead of night, after messing around on some empty plots in our usual insalubrious manner, a group of us young delinquents set out, our plan being to shake the tree and make off with the pears. We carried off a vast haul of them—but not in order to feast on them ourselves; instead, we meant

to throw them to the pigs. And though we did eat some of them, we did so only for the pleasure we had in tasting forbidden fruit. Such was my heart, O God; such was my heart, on which you showed your pity in the depths of the abyss. Let my heart now tell you what its purpose was; why I was gratuitously evil, and why there was no reason for my evil save evil itself. My evil was loathsome, and I loved it; I was in love with my own ruin and rebellion. I did not love what I hoped to gain by rebellion; it was rebellion itself that I loved. Depraved in soul, I had leapt away from my firm foothold in you and cast myself to my destruction, seeking to gain nothing through my disgrace but disgrace alone.[29]

The first-person narrative form immediately offers us different possibilities for understanding the condition than that provided in Aristotle. The narrative format ties description to confession, an inherently moral mode of writing, and the repetition of seeming tautologies serves to reinforce the sense of logical contradiction as moral contradiction. Essential here is the knowing sense of the act as ultimately undermotivated: "It was not poverty that drove me to conceive the desire to steal, and to act upon that desire. . . . What I stole, I already had in abundance, and of much better quality too."[30] In other words, there is no good or strong reason to steal; rather, he stole "to enjoy the theft itself, and the sin." It was contrariness— the rebellion—that he wanted. The lack of a good reason here connects to the scriptural sense of sin, and there is no missing the allusions to scripture—the "forbidden fruit," and the lines from Paul's conversion in Romans 7:15–20: "I do not understand what I do. For what I want to do I do not do, but what I hate I do. . . . For I have the desire to do what is good, but I cannot carry it out. For I do not do the good I want to do, but the evil I do not want to do—this I keep on doing."[31]

These first-person musings culminate into a philosophical meditation on the will in book 8. Here, as in book 2, the first experience is puzzlement, but then the narrator seems to be articulate and give a name to this condition: it is the will as "divided" and "weak":

Whence is this strange situation? and why is it so? The mind orders
the body, and the body obeys; the mind orders itself, and it resists. The

mind orders a hand to be moved, and this is accomplished with such ease that its authority can scarcely be discerned from that of a master over his slave. The mind orders the mind to will; it is only one mind, but it does not do as ordered. Whence is this strange situation? and why is it so? I repeat: the mind that gives the order to will could not give the order if it did not will to do so; but it does not do what it orders. It does not will with its whole being, therefore it does not order with its whole being. The mind orders in so far as it wills, and its orders are not obeyed in so far as it does not will them; for it is the will and nothing else that gives the order that the will should exist. If the will were a full will, it would not give the order that the will should exist, since it would already exist.[32]

The first few sentences repeat the paradox that justifies the expressions of puzzlement: "Whence is this strange situation? and why is it so?" By a bit of rephrasing, he arrives at the understanding that "it does not will with its whole being" and then, subsequently, "if the will were a full will, it would not give the order that the will should exist, since it would already exist." This leads to the recognition that the will is not indeed "full": "It is not, therefore such a strange situation" if we understand the condition as "a sickness of the mind, which, even when uplifted by the truth, does not fully arise, being weighed down by its habit." If in Aristotle the better reason is not "exercised" and is "ignored," in Augustine it is "weighed down."

This dynamic, however, does not mean that there are merely two forces tugging Augustine in different directions. His condition is a product of having a "divided will" (*duae voluntates*): "My *two wills, the old, carnal will, and the new, spiritual will* (cf. Eph. 4.22, 24, Col. 3.9–10), were *at war with one another* (Rom. 7.16–17), and in their discord rent my soul in pieces."[33] This does not mean he has two wills, but one will that is divided. Augustine is turning against the Manichean thought that had previously enticed him—that is, the Manichean notion that there are "two wills at war with each other, that there is a conflict between two opposing minds, one good and one bad, springing from opposing substances and opposing Principles."[34] This resistance to a notion of the compartmentalized "faculties," which reflects Stoicism's influence, is essential for distinguishing the reality of akrasia/weakness of will, and it is also this kind of compartmentalization that we will see again with Enlightenment philosophy that eliminates akrasia.

Augustine's framework for understanding will and action, then, must be understood within the context of acting in accordance with God's will or acting sinfully. So, when Augustine writes, "It was *no longer I that did this, but the sin that dwelt in me* (Rom. 7.17, 20)—that sin itself being part of the punishment for a sin more willingly committed, since I was a son of Adam," he does not mean that he has been determined to sin.[35] The capacity to act in accordance with God's will is a capacity fully available to sinful man, and "the sin" that "did this" is constituted within the "I."[36]

As with Aristotle, for Augustine the condition of acting against better judgment is a matter of man failing himself. Aristotle's model of syllogistic practical reason according to which man may follow the knowingly worse minor premise made available through perceptual knowledge has important differences from Augustine's model according to which man acts knowingly against the good as a result of a weak, sick, and divided will based in sin. Nonetheless, both, reacting against Platonic intellectualism, join in the view that a difficulty to explain action must be discussed in terms that grant a moral dimension to action. When Aristotle and Augustine suggest that the akratic or weak-willed person acts upon something like "the weaker reason," they mean that the person does so because, in their frameworks, what a person can assent to do and intend to do in practical reason can be different from what they believe or judge theoretically is best to do—and that this disjunction is to be understood as failure.

THE ELIMINATION OF AKRASIA: HOBBES, SPINOZA, AND HUME

"Philosophical explanation" in the work of Thomas Hobbes, according to Michael Oakeshott, "is concerned with things caused. A world of such things is, necessarily, a world from which teleology is excluded; its internal movement comprises the impact of its parts upon one another, of attraction and repulsion, not of growth or development."[37] In an intellectual landscape in which teleological explanation is out of the picture, a new world appears before our eyes. The clearest sense of how the idea of human action changes in this new world can be found in the *Leviathan* (1651).[38] Hobbes's introduction begins, "For what is the *Heart,* but a *Spring;* and the *Nerves,* but so many *Strings;* and the *Joynts,* but so many *Wheeles,* giving motion to the whole Body, such as was intended by the Artificer?"[39] The old moral senses of good and evil are out of the picture: here good and evil are aligned descriptively (and empirically/behavioristically) with what a person wants most: "Whatsoever is the object of any mans Appetite or Desire; that is it, which he for his part calleth *Good;* And the object of his Hate, and Aversion, *Evill;* . . . For these words of Good, Evill, and Contemptible, are ever used with relation to the person that useth them: There being nothing simply and absolutely so."[40] These notions of good and evil are ascribed after the fact—not transcendent but always dependent upon the use of the object in question.

What happens, then, to the old idea of "the Will"? Hobbes denies this possibility of "Will" as *"Rational Appetite"* from the outset by turning to the example of the person who acts against his better judgment. For, if the will was a rational appetite, then "there could be no Voluntary Act against Reason." That is to say, the idea of will as rational and intentional immediately presents the paradox of akrasia, and so it cannot be allowed. Instead, we need the idea of will as sheer appetite, which can help explain irrational action in terms of a series of unthinking appetites. *"Will* therefore," he tells us, *"is the last Appetite in Deliberating"* or "the last Appetite, or Aversion, immediately adhaering to the action."[41] He continues, "And though we say in Common Discourse, a man had a Will once to do a thing, that neverthelesse he forbore to do" (here he is referring to the concept of akrasia) "yet that is properly but an Inclination, which makes no Action Voluntary; because the action depends not of it, but of the last Inclination, or Appetite."[42] This view, then, is a wrong one, because the will is just an inclination, "which makes no Action Voluntary."

Hobbes approaches it similarly in *Of Liberty and Necessity* (1654), here explicitly citing the line from *Medea*—a line that recurs, as we will see, in discussions by Spinoza, Locke, and Hume as well—*"Video meliora, proboque,/Deteriora sequor"* ("I see and approve the better, but I follow the worse"). It is a nice little story, Hobbes tells us, but it is wrong: "But that saying, as pretty as it is, is not true; for though Medea saw many reasons to forbear killing her children, yet the last dictate of her judgment was, that the present revenge on her husband outweighed them all, and thereupon the wicked action *necessarily* followed."[43] Because Medea's temporally final judgment was that she ought to inflict revenge on her husband, it prevailed. Hobbes's framework disallows akrasia because it is inclined toward removing any discrepancies in the explanation of action through the implementation of a monocausal system. All actions, reasonable or unreasonable, are alike reduced to the same causal laws, in terms of which every action can be explained. Oakeshott has described Hobbes's philosophy as, "in all its parts, preeminently a philosophy of *power*," and this is so "precisely because philosophy is reasoning, reasoning the elucidation of mechanism, and mechanism essentially the combination, transfer, and resolution of forces."[44] This also necessarily completely reconfigures what counts as moral philosophy. A "philosophy of action"—which concerns itself with what actions are—will need to be re-thought as a different discipline.

Spinoza's approach to akrasia in the *Ethics* (written between 1661 and 1675, published in 1677) can be seen as largely in line with that of Hobbes. In similar fashion, Spinoza did not believe that the "soul" could properly be understood as outside of the laws of nature: "We are acted on, insofar as we are a part of Nature," he writes.[45] Again, this requires that moral philosophy be something quite different than it had been for Aristotle or Augustine. "Good" and "evil" are no longer transcendent or ideal notions but, rather, adjectives for describing use: "by good I shall understand what we certainly know to be useful to us," and "by evil . . . I shall understand what we certainly know prevents us from being masters of some good,"[46] and, likewise, "the knowledge of good and evil is nothing but an affect of joy or sadness."[47] There are differences between "actions" and "passions," insofar as actions are brought about by the agency of the mind (when ideas are "adequate" they can allow the mind to "do certain things [acts]"), and passions are brought about by the body's affects.[48] However, both can ultimately be explained by deterministic causal laws.

This framework allows no difficulty in explaining Medea's condition of acting against better judgment—that is, "why men are moved more by opinion than by true reason, and why the true knowledge of good and evil arouses disturbances of the mind, and often yields to lust of every kind. Hence that verse of the Poet: . . . video meliora, proboque, / Deteriora sequor."[49] Part 4 of the *Ethics* ("Of Human Bondage") articulates "man's lack of power to moderate and restrain the affects."[50] In the case of Medea, "knowledge of good and evil" is easily overpowered by mere opinion, because this is a case of "bondage": "For the man who is subject to affects is under the control, not of himself, but of fortune, in whose power he so greatly is that often, though he sees the better for himself, he is still forced to follow the worse."[51] The case of Medea is not a matter of the person ignoring or neglecting or failing oneself, but, rather, one of compulsion: he is "forced" to follow the worse. Action is no longer described in inherently moral terms but on a more reductionistic level, as a matter of the latter affects simply being stronger than the former. The condition is no longer puzzling.[52]

One more representative instance of Enlightenment philosophical engagements with akrasia can be seen in the writings of David Hume, for whom, famously, "reason is the slave of the passions." Hume's model of the passions is well known for its skeptical outlook, which minimizes the dominance of the faculty of reason; however, there is no escaping a different kind of rationalism in his philosophy, that which undergirds his metaphysics.[53] The direct causal relationship between passions and action leaves Hume, in the words of John Rawls, as "lack[ing] altogether what some writers think of as ideas of practical reason and of its authority."[54] Somewhat like Hobbes and Spinoza, Hume defines the will as an epiphenomenal aftereffect of predetermined forces: "By the *will*," he writes in the *Treatise of Human Nature* (1740), "I mean nothing but *the internal impression we feel and are conscious of, when we knowingly give rise to any new motion of our body, or new perception of our mind*."[55] As for reason's impact on the will, it is ultimately subservient to the nonrational: "Reason alone can never be a motive to any action of the will," because "reason is, and ought only to be the slave of the passions, and can never pretend to any other office than to serve and obey them."[56] Further, it is a category error to suggest that reason and a passion might conflict. As ideas are representations or copies of objects, and passions are not, "'tis impossible, therefore, that this passion can be oppos'd by, or be contradictory to truth and reason; since this contradiction consists in the disagreement of ideas, consider'd as copies, with those objects, which they represent."[57] This means that passions can only be considered "contrary to reason" if they are themselves *accompany'd* with some judgment or opinion." Impulses can be contrary to each other, which is easy to explain, but to say that an irrational passion is contrary to reason would require that the passion be accompanied by a judgment or opinion, assented to incorrectly or wrongly.

Whether it is a matter of the brute passions simply overpowering each other or an incorrect judgment/opinion winning out, a person's irrationality can be explained as a matter of shifting power relations. Hume writes,

> 'Tis not contrary to reason to prefer the destruction of the whole world
> to the scratching of my finger. . . .'Tis as little contrary to reason to prefer
> even my own acknowledg'd lesser good to my greater, and have a more
> ardent affection for the former than the latter. A trivial good may, from
> certain circumstances, produce a desire superior to what arises from
> the greatest and most valuable enjoyment; nor is there anything more
> extraordinary in this, than in mechanics to see one pound weight raise
> up a hundred by the advantage of its situation.[58]

What one might call an irrational action is in fact perfectly rationally explicable: preferring "the destruction of the world" is a matter of a more ardent affection taking hold. While it may look at first like a weaker reason, if you look a little more closely, that reason, which is actually powered by a passion, must be understood as stronger. Thus, human rationality is displaced and replaced with a broader metaphysical rationalism. The result is an unambiguously mechanistic metaphor: the person who acts against her or his better judgment is like a balance that has been tilted so that one passion or judgment outweighs the other passion or judgment.[59]

Desire, affect, passion: in distinct though similar ways, action is explained as a product or effect of a previous state. As a result, the study of action is not a study of agency in an intrinsically moral sense, but as a physical event with an efficient cause. Although akrasia offers us a "pretty phrase," as Hobbes put it, when we look at the human frame and find springs, wheels, or the necessitating power of affects or the blind passions, one is forced to conclude that there is in no there there. The problem is no longer a problem once you remove the action's intentionality, or, as the case may be, its irrationality.

NARRATING VERSUS EXPLAINING AKRASIA: THE CASE OF LOCKE

Locke deserves some more careful discussion. While his model largely fits within the trajectory just discussed between Hobbes and Hume, his treatment of the problem is more complicated and revealing for the ways it tries to accommodate the causal sense of will as noncognitive force along with a notion of will as *self*-determining. His account of acting against better judgment in the second edition of the *Essay Concerning Human Understanding* (1694) reveals how the philosophical standards of systematic causal explication run contrary to the possibility of crediting akrasia proper. It is here that we see the importance of a *narrative* expression of personhood for maintaining the structure of the concept. In this sense, Locke will help prepare us to consider some twentieth-century philosophy that reveals the significant role of word choice and narrative in writing about akrasia.

The will proved to be a particularly troubling issue for Locke, so much so that he significantly revised his first edition, adding twenty-six sections in chapter 11, "Of Power," in order to revise his original framework.[60] In the first edition from 1690, Locke defines "will" as the power to prefer one thing over another and adds that preference "[is] always determined by the appearance of Good, greater Good."[61] As a result, the will always follows perception of the greater good. When man acts against the greater good, then, it can only be because of false perception: what *"determines the choice* of the Will, and obtains the preference . . . is also only the Good *that appears,"* and appearances are affected by perceptions, including false perceptions. This highly rational picture of the will, then, can be said to recall that of Socrates.

However, the second edition from 1694 offers a more complicated and strained account of the will, which results in an account of akrasia that moves between a Hobbesian-Spinozian-Humean eliminativist account on the one hand and an account that credits the possibility of failing volition on the other. "But yet upon a stricter enquiry," he writes in the revised version, "I am forced to conclude, that *good,* the *greater good,* though apprehended and acknowledged to be so, does not determine the *will*"—that is, actions are not always reducible to the person's most recent sense of what is the greater good, for a person can consciously act contrary to the greater good.[62] This change involves a new definition of the will, not as defined by following the person's automatic preference, but as something rather self-determining. As Stephen Darwall writes, "Locke's new view is that will consists not in a preference an agent *has* for an act but in the agent's power *himself* self-consciously to 'direct,' 'command,' or 'order' these."[63] The will is now described as the faculty or power to command oneself: "To the Question, what is it determines the Will? The true and proper Answer is, The mind. For that which determines the general power of directing, to this or that particular direction, is nothing but the Agent it self exercising the power it has, that particular way."[64] This would seem to move Locke further away from Socrates and closer to an Augustinian model of the will: one that operates itself and so can function in a way divorced from reasoning about the greater good.

But Locke does not leave the matter there, for he insists that some may not be satisfied with this way of putting it, so he offers a redescription: "If this Answer satisfies not, 'tis plain the meaning of the Question, *what determines the Will?* Is this, What moves the mind, in every particular instance, to determine its general power of directing, to this or that particular Motion or Rest? And to this I answer, The motive, for continuing in the same State or Action, is only the present satisfaction in it; The motive to change, is always some *uneasiness.*"[65] Thus, through a series of subtle steps, Locke shifts from saying that the will is determined by "the Agent it self" toward saying that it is determined by "some *uneasiness.*" We might say that the first is based in the person, the second in a noncognitive state—something closer to Hobbes's "desire," Spinoza's "affect," or Hume's "passion." Indeed, it is a sort of desire: "This *Uneasiness* we may call, as it is, *Desire;* which is an *uneasiness* of the Mind for want of some absent good."[66] It appears that the description of will as self-directed by the mind does not suffice for the standards of systematic causal explication, and that ultimately the will can be redescribed as caused by a subpersonal state.

Locke's characterization of the man who acts against better judgment reveals this ambivalence between will as self-directing and will as automatically following the sensation of uneasiness. Although it is a result of a person's *failure* of directing the will properly, it is also causally unavoidable and a natural consequence of a physical-mental state. Interestingly, it is at this intersection between a pro-akrasia view and an eliminativist anti-akrasia view that we can also find in Locke's discussion a clash between the value of having a good narrative and the value of a conclusive explanation—which we might also call a clash between the values of *literary* writing and *explanatory* writing. One way to understand this is to perceive it as a difficulty between crediting the lived reality of knowingly acting against better judgment and seeking to explain that reality in the reductionistic terms of mental and bodily states. As Pfau has written in his discussion of Locke, "Locke appears caught between a strictly occasional conception of the will that Ockham and Hobbes had bequeathed him, and his manifest need to retain some phenomenological evidence of the will *in actu*," observing a certain clash between an adherence to philosophy as both concerned with physical causation and beholden to some phenomenological reality.[67]

Locke's primary example of akrasia is that of a drunkard—an interesting example, for this choice already implies a compromised conscious state, thus potentially diluting the intensity of the akrasia in question. Locke nonetheless wants to maintain the *drama* of the akratic person as failing himself:

Let a Drunkard see, that his Health decays, his Estate wastes; Discredit and Diseases, and the want of all things, even of his beloved Drink attends him in the course he follows: yet the returns of *uneasiness* to miss his Companions; the habitual thirst after his Cups, at the usual time, drives him to the Tavern, though he has in his view the loss of health and plenty, and perhaps the joys of another life: the least of which is no inconsiderable good, but such as he confesses, is far greater, than the tickling of his palate with a glass of Wine, or the idle chat of a soaking

Club. 'Tis not for want of viewing the greater good: for he sees, and acknowledges it, and in the intervals of his drinking hours, will take resolutions to pursue the greater good; but when the *uneasiness* to miss his accustomed delight returns, the greater acknowledged good loses its hold, and the present *uneasiness* determines the *will* to the accustomed action; which thereby gets stronger footing to prevail against the next occasion, though he at the same time makes secret promises to himself, that he will do so no more; this is the last time he will act against the attainment of those greater goods. And thus he is, from time to time, in the State of that unhappy complainer, *Video meliora proboque, Deteriora sequor:* which Sentence, allowed for true, and made good by constant Experience, may this, and possibly no other, way be easily made intelligible.[68]

In order to recognize the philosophical implications of this passage, I believe, a little literary analysis is called for. Indeed, the pacing matters. The storytelling choices matter. One way to analyze this passage is to identify where there is dramatic tension and where there is not. The following phrases carry elements of dramatic tension, because they offer the setup of man's awareness and hence prepare us for his eventual weakness and tragic fate: "Though he has in his view the loss of health and plenty, and perhaps the joys of another life." It matters a great deal what Locke means by "he has in his view." The man appears to recognize his health and financial condition as a matter of importance, but, to add to this, we see that the man is capable of aspiration. He is no bundle of mechanisms, but is imaginative and forward-looking. Likewise: "'Tis not for want of viewing the greater good: for he sees, and acknowledges it, and in the intervals of his drinking hours, will take resolutions to pursue the greater good." Borrowing from *Medea,* Locke tells us "he sees, and acknowledges" the greater good. He adds to the emphasis by shifting the narrative to "the intervals of his drinking hours," whether at home or elsewhere, when he takes his resolutions to act differently. The tension is heightened before the awaited event: "The greater acknowledged good loses its hold." This is where Locke comes closest to expressing akrasia in its most familiar— and most classical, Aristotelian or Augustinian—form. The verb "loses its hold" is undoubtedly meant to be expressive such that we readers can recognize to what he is referring. We can picture a hand. The verb "loses" carries the sense of failure ("loss")—it is a teleological verb. Also, interestingly, it is not the man that "loses its hold," but the "acknowledged good," bringing to mind a transcendent sense of "good" that pulls man toward it and holds it, or loses hold of it. The drama continues: "Though he at the same time makes secret promises to himself, that he will do so no more." We are given a glimpse of the man's "secret promises" made presumably in private quarters: the greater reasons left ineffective or muted by the predominance of the weaker reason.

However, this reading of Locke's passage is only partial. Let us now shift to the philosophical language that forecloses the drama and pushes the passage from a narrative into a solution to a problem. These phrases can be read as leaning toward the *explanatory:* "Yet the returns of *uneasiness* to miss his Companions; the habitual thirst after his Cups, at the usual time, *drives* him to the Tavern"; "the present uneasiness *determines* the will to the accustomed action" (emphasis mine). Here the source of the action is unambiguously drawn back to states that are prior to the subject: "The returns of *uneasiness* . . . the habitual thirst . . . *drives* him to the Tavern," "the present *uneasiness* determines the *will*." The example ceases to be about a person failing and turns into an explanation of subpersonal forces that cause an action in question, shifting from a picture of will as self-determining to a picture of the will as determined by states of uneasiness. At the same time, the dramatic tenor of the scene dissipates: the explanation eliminates the qualities that made it a compelling problem as well as a compelling narrative. In the end, Locke's *Essay* seeks an explanation, not a narrative. Given the changing nature of "explanation of action" in the period, the two are mutually exclusive.

AKRASIA AND THE LITERARY IN TWENTIETH-CENTURY PHILOSOPHY: DAVIDSON AND MURDOCH

Before turning to literary works that take up this trope, it will be useful to expand upon the discussion of Locke in order to say some more about some privileges of literary elements when it comes to writing akrasia in an era that has done away with teleological/moral frameworks of human agency. We can do this by considering a pair of philosophical works from the 1960s—one by Donald Davidson and one by Iris Murdoch—which can in different ways clarify the importance of questions of narrative, perspective, voice, and character when it comes to writing about divided or conflicted agency. Making this chronological jump is not a way of continuing a historical narrative about akrasia after Hume. Giving a fuller history of the concept might require discussion of its sparse and indistinct treatment in Kant, its continued disappearance in Schelling and Schopenhauer, and its nonexistence in the linguistic and quasi-behaviorist philosophies of Ludwig Wittgenstein and Gilbert Ryle. Rather, focusing on Davidson and Murdoch allows us to step a bit outside of the historical argument in order to flesh out the broader theoretical argument on literature and philosophy; this will come to be useful as we consider the authors in chapters 2 through 5.

Donald Davidson is arguably the philosopher most responsible for the set of terms and questions that structure the subfield of philosophy of action—and akrasia specifically—in contemporary analytic philosophy. His 1963 essay "Actions, Reasons and Causes" influentially argued that reasons for actions should be treated as causes of actions—a view that has come to be known as "causalism" within philosophy of action.[69] Davidson's argument has had profound effects; as Stewart Candlish and Nic Damnjanovic write, "Not only did it reshape the philosophy of action, it also contributed directly to forming the new consensus view in the philosophy of mind that psychological events or states are physical, spatially internal, and capable of standing in causal relations."[70] This in turn helped to "invigorat[e] the project of providing a complete naturalistic account of the mind" in a way that would imply a compatibility between philosophy of action and computational or otherwise naturalistic philosophical models of the mind. In this sense, Davidson's outlook can be understood as in some ways continuous with the outlook of the Enlightenment philosophers discussed already.[71]

However, from our standpoint, one important difference stands out: Davidson also wants to preserve the phenomenon of akrasia. Indeed, he thinks akrasia presents philosophy of action with one of its most difficult but pressing puzzles. Davidson revived akrasia as a topic for mainstream philosophy with his well-known 1969 essay, "How Is Weakness of the Will Possible?" Akrasia, he argues, is a particularly curious concept because it does not fit into a widely accepted paradigm of the relations between judgment, motivation, and action; specifically, it conflicts with the seemingly inarguable view that "if an agent judges that it would be better for him to do x than to do y, and he believes himself to be free to do either x or y, then he will intentionally do x if he does either x or y intentionally."[72] If that outlook on action is correct, he says, then it would appear to be categorically false that there are incontinent (akratic) actions. The sticking point is that he believes incontinent actions are real: "There is no proving such actions exist," he writes, "but it seems to me absolutely certain that they do."[73] As in Locke, the mode of systematic reasoning needs to adjust in order to do justice to a strong phenomenological sense of the reality of akrasia.

The philosophical dilemma is made especially acute when he separates it from any moral questions. In this way, quite unlike Aristotle and Augustine, Davidson advocates thinking about philosophy of action outside of a moral or teleological framework. He writes, "As a first positive step in dealing with the problem of incontinence, I propose to divorce that problem entirely from the moralist's concern that our sense of the conventionally right may be lulled, dulled, or duped by a lively pleasure."[74] One might observe that this insistent split from any moral question is what has made akrasia an especially difficult problem for analytic philosophy of action since Davidson. We might also observe that, in the midst of this causalism and the discounting of a sense of moral weakness that underlies weakness-in-action, we can discern a lurking need for the writing to convey this failure, disconnect, absence, neglect, or betrayal through careful manipulations of language.

Like Locke's discussion in the *Essay,* Davidson's writing allows us a glimpse into this lurking need for special aspects of storytelling and modes of expression in the writing of akrasia. We can see this in a narrative example he gives, which provides us with a somewhat opposite example to that which we saw with Locke. If Locke's narrative minimizes the drama for the service of an explanation in terms of states of uneasiness that determine the action (and thus eliminate the sense of akrasia), Davidson's narrative works hard to *uphold* the sense of akrasia, preserving the sense of drama, and this comes at the expense of offering a satisfying explanation. Indeed, the example is offered as a way to demonstrate the difficulty and reality of the problem of akrasia:

> I have just relaxed in bed after a hard day when it occurs to me that I have not brushed my teeth. Concern for my health bids me rise and brush; sensual indulgence suggests I forget my teeth for once. I weigh the alternatives in the light of the reasons: on the one hand, my teeth are strong, and at my age decay is slow. It won't matter much if I don't brush them. On the other hand, if I get up, it will spoil my calm and may result in a bad night's sleep. Everything considered I judge I would do better to stay in bed. Yet my feeling that I ought to brush my teeth is too strong for me: wearily I leave my bed and brush my teeth. My act is clearly intentional, although against my better judgement, and so is incontinent [akratic].[75]

The akrasia appears counterintuitive: his "better judgment" is that he should stay in bed, which will allow him a better night of sleep, but his impulse to brush his teeth gets the better of him, even if it is not well justified, so he rises to brush his teeth. Does this example effectively demonstrate the reality of akrasia? I think to some extent this depends on whether you think it is a good story. Let us pause over some of the literary choices here.

What if we think a little more about the character Davidson is building here, who I will call DD? Is it not possible that DD, a little deeper down, wants to maintain a *routine* of brushing teeth?[76] Perhaps there is a backstory—that, in some other area of his life, DD has understood that consistency is fundamental to upholding a value. For instance, maybe he has taken on the view that he should wash the dish he has just used in the kitchen regardless of whether later will be a better time to do it, because holding to a principle in the long term is the best way to assure order and clarity of mind with regard to his activities. Perhaps that same value of consistency is applied here, even though the matter is teeth-brushing rather than dish-washing, and that DD maintains the value of consistency for good reason—for a *better* reason than his judgment that he "would do better to stay in bed." Perhaps DD has these underlying views. If so, Davidson the author omits telling them for narrative effect—in order to preserve the sense of akrasia—and instead conveys through his story the dramatically compelling idea that he had no better reason for going to brush his teeth. This is an authorial choice, one that augments the conflict for the purposes of upholding the sensed reality of akrasia. Is this not a matter of a reader's interpretation? Is this not a question of writing character? Of reading character? Are these not inescapable dimensions of philosophy, even an analytic philosophy of action concerned with giving precise accounts of actions in the terms of beliefs, desires, and reasons?

Let us also note the way Davidson writes his action: "*Wearily* I leave my bed and brush my teeth." What is the philosophical function of an adverb? In the Hobbesian-Spinozian-Lockean-Humean models of action, adverbs of action cannot play any significant philosophical role, because adverbs can always be—and must always be—translated back into the action and its additions quantified. Actions must be treated logically as units that can be disaggregated from each other and systematized in symbolic language, capable of being clearly traced as objects of cause and effect. However, when I say "I do *x wearily*," I need to credit a quality to the action. This would imply that actions contain attributes that cannot be disaggregated from them, that they can be, for instance, heavy or weak.[77] It might appear that, in order to allow akrasia in a nonteleological framework, an adverb like "wearily" importantly serves to convey this type of action—action that follows "the weaker reason."

By the end of his essay, Davidson does not leave the problem of akrasia resolved. He concludes that the error of the akratic resides not in ignoring *y* while pursuing *x*, but in ignoring the relational judgment "*y* is better than *x*" while pursuing *x*: "The akrates does not, as is now clear, hold logically contradictory beliefs"; rather, the person is betraying a particular (different) principle—namely, the principle to "perform the action judged best on the basis of all available relevant reasons."[78] The problem is displaced a bit from a conflict in action to a conflict in belief, but it is the same sort of conflict. This leaves us in a rather similar place, for the person still acts without a strong enough defense of the reason for acting. Thus, we can, and

I think are meant to, perceive a silence in Davidson's account—a silence that reflects a broader silence about the difficulties of explanation when it comes to the matter of akrasia once we have departed from a moral view of agency. This silence is expressed with the essay's final sentence: "What is special in incontinence is that the actor cannot understand himself: he recognizes, in his own intentional behaviour, something essentially surd."[79] The word is short and sufficient: surd.

If Davidson is the most influential philosopher of akrasia from the mid-twentieth century onward, Iris Murdoch is arguably the twentieth-century English-language philosopher who most richly articulates the need for emphases on narrative and character as intrinsic parts of philosophical inquiry. In what is perhaps her most famous philosophical essay, "The Idea of Perfection" (1964), Murdoch examines the limits of philosophical frameworks that rely on public (behaviorist, empiricist) accounts to credit what is real about human action and morality. More specifically, her target is philosophy that is "behaviourist in its connection of the meaning and being of action with the publicly observable," "existentialist in its elimination of the substantial self and its emphasis on the solitary omnipotent will," and "utilitarian in its assumption that morality is and can only be concerned with public acts."[80] One consequence of the philosophical outlooks she describes is they do not credit qualities of "inner life" that could reveal change or, as the case may be, conflict. From the perspective of the behaviorist, Murdoch writes, "someone who says privately or overtly 'I have decided' but who never acts, however favourable the circumstances . . . has not decided."[81] Such a perspective, Murdoch insists, is seriously limiting. Life is not like this: decisions, thoughts, and intentions all exist, operate, change us, and do their work without manifesting in empirically perceivable output. For this reason, there are distinct epistemological privileges inherent to narrative.

Murdoch's central example is that of a figure we can loosely call a recovering akratic.[82] She is a mother, given the name M, who feels hostility toward her daughter-in-law, D; she "feels that her son has married beneath him," but at the same time she knows that her observations of D are unfair and ultimately unjustified. M can even be called "a very 'correct' person, behaves beautifully to the girl throughout, not allowing her real opinion to appear in any way."[83] It is something like an akratic belief. Over the course of some time, however, M changes.

> Time passes, and it could be that M settles down with a hardened sense of grievance and a fixed picture of D, imprisoned . . . by the cliché: my poor son has married a silly vulgar girl. However, the M of the example is an intelligent and well-intentioned person, capable of self-criticism, capable of giving careful and just *attention* to an object which confronts her. M tells herself: 'I am old-fashioned and conventional. I may be prejudiced and narrow-minded. I may be snobbish. I am certainly jealous. Let me look again.' Here I assume that M observes D or at least reflects deliberately about D, until gradually her vision of D alters. . . . D is discovered to be not vulgar but refreshingly simple, not undignified but spontaneous, not noisy but gay, not tiresomely juvenile but delightfully youthful, and so on. And as I say, *ex hypothesi,* M's outward behaviour, beautiful from the start, in no way alters.[84]

Nothing visible about M's behavior can be perceived as changing, but something has changed: her underlying attitude toward D was akratic and is no longer, for her beliefs now match up to the actions that are taken to reflect them. The purpose of Murdoch's example is to show that only a narrative like this one with interest in beliefs and actions in intrinsically evaluative (moral) frameworks can do justice to what is occurring. "Imprisoned" is the right word, because it is not just descriptive but also value-laden—indeed, it is how M might regrettably see herself. Most crucially, an empirical-behaviorist view "makes no sense of M as continually active, as making progress, or of her inner acts as belonging to her or forming part of a continuous fabric of being: it is precisely critical of metaphors such as 'fabric of being'. Yet can we do without such metaphors here?"[85] The transformation made available by a narrative and the kind of metaphor that makes sense of this transformation are both essential to crediting these elements of life, thought, intention, and action. The inner utterance "let me look again" indicates a quiet choice, a minor act, as real as M's outward behavior.

"And M's activity here," Murdoch continues, "so far from being something very odd and hazy, is something which, in a way, we find exceedingly familiar. Innumerable novels contain accounts of what such struggles are like. Anybody could describe one without being at a loss for words."[86] A woman holds on to a view of a family member that is knowingly unjustified; a man returns to the tavern despite his held resolutions to give up the habit; a woman continues to steal despite not needing the money. As Murdoch well knows, novels can work to give texture to these characters and their conditions: they can make the space for and find the phrases and formulations for the muted waverings and transitions, the absences, the failures, the surd. As becomes especially clear in the seventeenth and eighteenth centuries, in which paradigms for characterizing human thought and action have become separated from questions of "the good," how we write our people makes all the difference in how we do our philosophy.

The following chapter will shift our attention to literature and consider how eighteenth-century prose fiction maintained some standards for causal psychological explication in its depictions of characters that parallel some of the philosophical commitments to causal explication just discussed. To the extent that these fictions maintain this formal commitment, they also come up against representational tensions and paradoxes in evoking akrasia when the plot calls for it. After perceiving how some of those representational difficulties arise, the chapter proceeds to focus on a representational technique developed more self-consciously in order to portray akrasia—evoking it by failing to explicate it, thereby performing the contradiction itself.

2

SOME ENCOUNTERS WITH AKRASIA IN EIGHTEENTH-CENTURY PROSE FICTION

Defoe, Haywood, Sterne

"I KNOW NOT WHAT to call this," Robinson Crusoe tells us near the beginning of his narrative, "nor will I urge, that it is a secret over-ruling Decree that hurries us on to be the Instruments of our own Destruction, even tho' it be before us, and that we rush upon it with our Eyes open."[1] In this scene, Crusoe has just landed in Winterton after several weeks at sea in the midst of terrible storms. He had boarded the ship quickly, betraying his earlier considered judgments on the matter, including the clear warnings of his parents. Upon landing, he has the opportunity to return home to Hull. But instead, "tho' I had several times loud Calls from my Reason and my more composed Judgment to go home, yet I had no Power to do it," he tells us, at which point we arrive at the line provided above. What is this open-eyed destructive tendency? He suggests uncertainly that it is a "secret over-ruling Decree," and that he has "no Power" to do otherwise. But does he mean "no Power" in a strong metaphysical sense? Or is this a colloquial expression, meant to convey simply the fact that he did not do it? What is clear, above all, is that he does not know what to call it.

The line "I know not what to call this" stands out in a text that knows what to call nearly everything else. Indeed, *Robinson Crusoe* (1719) is a novel that can be distinguished by its emphasis on explication—of the names of objects, places, events, dates, thoughts, and actions. Ian Watt has described Crusoe as a character with a "book-keeping consciousness," visible in his dependence upon "contractual relationships" and his economic motives.[2] Watt meant it in the sense that Crusoe stood for *homo economicus* ("an embodiment of economic individualism"), but we can stretch that phrase to mean something more capacious: that Crusoe is a narrator who tabulates and enumerates elements of the world and of his mind. This is a world composed of things that can be named and counted. In this respect, Crusoe's condition of betraying his own judgment—the "this"—appears interestingly anomalous. It stands outside his capacity for book-keeping or articulation more generally; it creates a crisis of representation.

Indeed, as I will argue in this chapter, akrasia for a writer of prose fiction like Defoe stands out as a curiously challenging subject for narration in ways similar to those that we have seen for the Enlightenment philosophers in chapter 1. As in the cases of Hobbes, Spinoza, Locke, and Hume, the problem for Crusoe the narrator is that precise causal explication cannot suffice to give shape to the condition in question. What this means for the narrator is that perhaps it must be discussed in supernatural or spiritual terms—a "secret over-ruling Decree"—or perhaps there is just not much more one can say about it, the "this." Unlike in the philosophical texts examined, however, in Defoe's novels, this condition of akrasia is still significantly preserved, not completely explained away or dissolved, for it is a meaningful trope, thematically important, even if difficult to put into words.

This chapter examines various ways that eighteenth-century English novelists depict characters who act against their better judgments. It has two goals: first, to consider some of the representational challenges this trope presents to a storytelling form that is to an important degree, like the philosophy considered, committed to precise causal explication of people's thoughts and actions. As we will see, such moments produce curious formal ambiguities, as they do in the philosophy considered, which speak to this trope's broader difficulty: it demands that the writer either prioritize causal explication (and eliminate the sense of akrasia) or prioritize the moral dimensions of the trope (and thus give up the task of causal explication). A second goal is to consider some of the stylistic strategies in these works for preserving the condition in ways philosophy does not. To this end, the last part of this chapter will center on types of ironic formulations that convey akrasia self-consciously—in ways that we will see more consistently in the Romantic-era novels in chapter 3. The chapter will take on these aims by investigating a few instances collected from works by Daniel Defoe, Eliza Haywood, and Laurence Sterne—specifically, Defoe's *Robinson Crusoe* (1719) and *Moll Flanders* (1722), Haywood's *Fantomina* (1725) and *The History of Betsy Thoughtless* (1740), and Sterne's *A Sentimental Journey* (1767). The examples have been selected for the interestingly different ways they approach a scene of something like acting against better judgment. Together, they offer us some different approaches for either preserving the trope or nearly eliminating it. Through their differences, they also provide us a more general sense of the challenges faced by the nascent form of the novel when it comes to representing irrational action.

One way to think about akrasia's representational problem is to consider how the trope is held over from other literary forms—specifically, drama and spiritual autobiography. It is indeed quite a different thing to convey the weak-willed qualities of Macbeth or Hamlet. The mode of soliloquy in particular can express an akratic condition through a character's speech, which reflects, often repentantly, upon their contradictions and failures in ways that are intrinsically moral and never merely causal. Such expressions bear similarities to those we find in spiritual autobiography, also, where weakness of will is conveyed through a confessional mode. For eighteenth-century authors of works that we will come to call novels, the relevant inheritances for the trope of akrasia, then, are the works of Shakespeare (Brutus: "Between the acting of a dreadful thing / And the first motion, all the interim is / Like a phantasma, or a hideous dream"); Augustine ("I lost my firm foothold in you");[3] and seventeenth-century spiritual autobiographies like John Bunyan's 1666 *Grace Abounding* ("therefore I resolved in my mind, I would go on in sin").[4] For these novelists, however, new challenges arise, whether in the first-person retrospective prose narration of Defoe—indebted in different ways to the forms of the diary or business journalism—or the third-person omniscient narration of Haywood, indebted also to the form of the letter or amatory romance.

Although these are quite different kinds of works, they are to important degrees more distanced from spiritual frameworks and committed to explanatory thoroughness in relation to their characters.

Indeed, one way we can understand the tendency of keeping human actions coherent is through a more general principle of consistency and clarity when it comes to writing characters—namely, the principle of "conservation of character" as described by Henry Fielding in book 8 of *Tom Jones* (1749). As Fielding's narrator tells us, "Actions should be such as may not only be within the compass of human agency, and which human agents may probably be supposed to do; but they should be likely for the very actors and characters themselves to have performed." One consequence, the narrator continues, is that it would be a mistake to portray a character as acting against his nature: "Zeal can no more hurry a man to act in direct opposition to itself than a rapid stream can carry a boat against its own current. I will venture to say that for a man to act in direct contradiction to the dictates of his nature is, if not impossible, as improbable and as miraculous as anything which can well be conceived."[5] The principle would seem to imply that any depiction of akrasia ought to be revised such that the action is ultimately in line with the character's knowable qualities. For Fielding (as for Hobbes, Spinoza, Locke, and Hume), if an action appears akratic, it simply needs a little more clarification to ensure that the action can be understood, that it lines up with the character's nature. This is not to say that characters cannot do things that you or I might judge to be "irrational" (outside of what you or I believe to be the sensible thing to do); it simply means that we ought to be able to comprehend the nature of that irrationality—the hows and whys of their flaws, mistakes, delusions, or compulsions.

This standard, as we will see, finds its limits in the kinds of cases under consideration in Defoe, Haywood, and Sterne. Whether in the mode of first-person retrospective or third-person omniscient narration, preserving the trope of akrasia means that the storyteller needs to decide when to stop explaining (thereby betraying "conservation of character") or, as the case may be, when to shift to the lexicon of a spiritual metaphysics with spiritual entities. Let us consider again the classical formulation of akrasia in the context of philosophy: "*P* [person] didn't think doing

A [action] was for the best, but *P* freely did *A* anyway." We saw how, for philosophy, one needs to maintain the right level in order to preserve the conflictual nature of the phenomenon, not getting too close to either physiological/physical explanation that turns the action into compulsion or psychological explanation that reexplains the action as ultimately rational. The same challenge presents itself to the storyteller who wants to preserve the condition of akrasia. Indeed, the question we will find for Defoe, Haywood, and Sterne is whether to lean into the moral import of the scene, preserving the akrasia and sacrificing causal explication, or to lean into the causal explication, sacrificing the moral import. If the storyteller maintains a stronger commitment to detailed causal presentation than to moral instruction, then she or he might be inclined to rewrite the above sentence like the Enlightenment philosophers did, adding more physiological or psychological background information. This might mean turning to the person's blind passions, affects, or autonomous entities, or it might require a narrator's recourse to the subconscious, which helps to illuminate the deep-down beliefs that make sense of the action. A great deal of explanation would seem necessary, so much explanation that it could ultimately eliminate the drama of the person failing him or herself. This type of narration might indeed require a narrator who was so omniscient—whether first-person retrospective or third-person—that the story's perspective feels far removed from the lived experience of that character, for it is an explanation of the character that the character themselves would not have access to. On the other hand, if the storyteller maintained a stronger commitment to the moral than to descriptive dimensions of the story, then they might refer to the character's wickedness, cruelty, weakness, or giving-in to the workings of the devil. Here the classic sense of akrasia might be maintained, but in resorting to the lexicons of spiritual or classical frameworks, the story would risk trading in the conceit of a precise or plausible accounting of events in favor of a more overtly moral structure.

In this sense, the question of how to write akrasia speaks to a much larger dynamic long perceived as important for the development of the eighteenth-century novel: the dynamic between the goal of "neutral description" and the goal of providing an overarching moral structure, or between the novel's epistemological aims and its ethical ones. For Watt in *The Rise of the Novel,* "formal realism" is a mode of presentation that is by definition "ethically neutral" and so novelists that prioritize formal realism necessarily "subordinat[e] any coherent ulterior significance." In Watt's reading, in the longer picture of the rise of the novel, "the problem of the novel was to discover and reveal these deeper meanings without any breach of formal realism."[6] In *Origins of the English Novel,* Michael McKeon sees the dialectical history of the novel in terms of these dynamics between "questions of truth" and "questions of virtue," which ultimately synthesize in different ways in the novels of Richardson and Fielding.[7] Focusing on the question of akrasia illuminates this same conflict: how to tell a story so that it both maintains the veneer of truth *and* maintains a moral structure. It is not an easy task, for, as we see in the challenges of writing a mininarrative of an akratic, these two goals are not only not the same, but they often interfere with each other.[8] Write it explicitly (and eliminate the moral question), or write it morally (and eliminate the explicitness)?

Defoe, Haywood, and Sterne are quite different from each other as writers, so their versions of characters who act against their better judgments necessarily take different shapes. The examples from Defoe, for instance, tend to fit into questions around sin (filial disobedience, theft), whereas the examples from Haywood tend to be presented as examples of a character's blind passions or actions at odds with internalized social norms and expectations. In Sterne, matters of action-betraying-judgment are conveyed in the lexicon of passions and feelings, which are characterized (deceptively, as I argue) as the "causes" of his actions. In Defoe and Haywood, we will see various representational strategies taken to portray characters who go ahead with what they know they shouldn't do, including turning to overtly moral terminology (didactic or supernatural), reducing the action to mere compulsion, and merely abstaining from further explication. Instances of the latter seem to suggest the limits of explication in writing about people and indeed may suggest the opportunities of ironic expression. This interest in the limits of explication comes through most powerfully in several instances in Sterne, in which we find especially self-conscious ironic and negative uses of narration. Sterne's interest in performing the failures of causal narration allows his mode of prose fiction to convey through silence what it is like to be a problem to oneself.

DEFOE

After his first shipwreck, Robinson Crusoe is asked by an old man, *"What are you? and on what Account did you go to Sea?"*[9] It would benefit Crusoe to take both questions seriously. The first could be taken as simply inquiring into Crusoe's familial origins. But in its phrasing (*"What"* not *"Who"* are you?), it also seems to ask about his standing as a rational being. The second question retroactively gives meaning to the first question and lends to the second interpretation of it. When the old man asks, *"On what Account did you go to Sea?,"* he is asking Crusoe for an account of his action. Can he give an account of himself? To do so he would need to be able to list the reasons for acting, assuming that he has acted upon reasons. That would assume he was a rational actor.

In asking this question, the old man also puts forward a broader question that is vital for the structure of *Robinson Crusoe* and Daniel Defoe's other novels: What are the different ways one can "give an account" of oneself? There would seem to be two definitions of "account" operative in Defoe's time. One of them means something like "story." The preface to the novel introduces the text as an "Account," which reinforces this sense of the word as tale or sequence of events told through a narrative logic: *"If ever the Story of any private Man's Adventures in the World were worth making Publick, and were acceptable when Publish'd, the Editor of this Account thinks this will be so."*[10] If Crusoe were to give an "account" of himself in this sense of "story," then it might merely give the shape of a narrative, or "what happened." "I betrayed my father's advice" is a kind of account; it is a story; it tells us what happened. It is indeed this type of account he gives to the old man ("Upon that I told him some of my Story"). However, there is a second sense of "account" that is evoked here, one that demands a little bit more from the one who gives it. The second meaning is closer to the sense of "account" given by David Hume in his *Treatise of Human Nature,* when he writes that he intends to "give a particular account of ideas [and] impressions."[11] In this context, "account" means something more like "explanation." Can Crusoe give *this* kind of account of his actions? Can he articulate not just the "what" but the "why"?[12]

Defoe's fictions often operate on the pretense that these two modes of "account" can be conflated. In these novels, it often seems as if to tell a story *is* to explain by spelling out complex chains of causes and, conversely, to explain chains of causation is to tell the story. To give a narrative account *is exactly* to give an explanatory account and vice versa. And this is why akrasia stands out as an interesting trope in his fiction: it seems to pry apart these two types of account. Crusoe seems able and willing to give an account of himself going to sea in the sense that he tells us he betrayed his own mind; however, this is no longer the kind of (causally detailed) explanatory account that pervades the rest of his story. As discussed at the beginning of the chapter, *Robinson Crusoe* indeed assumes an explanatory logic throughout with its attention to enumeration. Here we can understand the structural logic of the work as "accounting" in the sense of "counting"—a tendency that extends to the way it lists thoughts, beliefs, intentions, and reasons for acting. When he reasons about the goods and evils of his shipwrecked state, Crusoe turns these thoughts into a chart, distinguishing, "like Debtor and Creditor, the Comforts I enjoy'd, against the Miseries I suffer'd."[13] In this sense, we can also think of "account" in a third financial or economic meaning, which gives it a similar function to the explanatory Humean meaning, in that both mean the items in it can be tabulated, counted up, and added together.[14]

So when Crusoe's father talks to him about why he should not leave for the high seas, the reasons put forth are clear and can be counted: 1) the life of the sea is for those of either "desperate Fortunes" or "aspiring, superior Fortunes," but not for those of the middling station of life; 2) the young Crusoe's current state of life is much envied by everyone; 3) he (the father) would do especially kind things for his son if he were to stay; 4) if Crusoe were to leave, he would be on track to follow in the footsteps of his elder brother, who had precipitously gone to war and died; and 5) God would neither bless him nor assist in his repentance if he were to leave. Our protagonist listens. He observes the tears trickling down his father's face. "I was sincerely affected with this Discourse," he tells us, "as indeed who could be otherwise? and I resolv'd not to think of going abroad any more, but to settle at home according to my Father's Desire."[15] Yet this resolution does not seem to hold for long. Here there is no "counting" or enumeration of reasons; instead we are told, "But alas! a few Days wore it all off; and in short, to prevent any of my Father's farther Importunities, in a few Weeks after, I resolv'd to run quite away from him."[16] We are thus provided the decision itself—"I resolv'd to run quite away"—without the reasons for the decision: the what but not the why. To put it another way, at this moment the phenomenon of akrasia necessitates nomological presentation (what is given to be the case, not as logically necessary, but just so) in place of logical presentation (which explicates *why* what happened happened).[17]

Crusoe is kept at bay this time, but a year later he goes through with it. Here as well we see the absence of a "good reason," as conveyed by the grammar:

> But being one day at Hull, where I went casually, and without any Purpose of making an Elopement that time; but I say, being there, and one of my Companions being going by Sea to *London,* in his Father's Ship, and prompting me to go with them, with the common Allurement of Seafaring Men, *viz* That it should cost me nothing for my Passage, I consulted neither Father or Mother any more, nor so much as sent them Word of it; but leaving them to hear of it as they might, without asking God's Blessing, or my Father's, without any Consideration of Circumstances or Consequences, and in an ill Hour, God knows.[18]

There is no positive verb in this sentence; the sense of the character *doing* something is completely concealed. First we have the repeated statement of his "being" ("being one day at Hull," "being there," "being going by Sea"); then we have the subject's verb: "I consulted." But it is in a negative formulation ("neither Father or Mother any more"), and the negatives keep coming ("nor so much," "without asking God's Blessing, or my Father's, without any Consideration of Circumstances or Consequences"). There is no sense of this as an action that is done for a good reason. The precepts have been ignored, dismissed, or neglected in some way. The avoidance of logical explanation speaks to the narrator's difficulty in presenting the condition in the terms of causal explication, for the act is underjustified; it has followed "the weaker reason."

Here we can observe akrasia necessitating that the narration move away from logical or causally precise explication of the relations between events. However, as we proceed, we can see that there is another way to understand the nature of this absence in explanation—namely, as evoking the blank causality and metaphysics of sin. Indeed, if such a moment means a departure from the economic-materialist-explicating mode of counting of causes, we can also see the importance of another (we might even say competing) epistemology: the Christian epistemology of the spiritual will. G. A. Starr has influentially argued that it is only in the mode of spiritual autobiography that we can make sense of Defoe's novels, including these early episodes in *Robinson Crusoe*. For Starr, this is a depiction of sin, which "consists in its violation of paternal, social, and divine order; . . . its wickedness is emphasized by the resemblance to similar acts of rebellion committed by Jonah and the Prodigal Son."[19] As J. Paul Hunter has argued as well, Crusoe in this first scene "plunges himself, through disobedience by reason of pride, into the universal predicament of fallen man."[20] We can see the Christian connotations of his act from his description of the "over-ruling Decree" in the passage and from the very beginning of the novel, when he tells us "that there seem'd to be something fatal in that Propension of Nature tending directly to the Life of Misery which was to befal me."[21] After he finally boards the ship at Hull, he tells us, "I was overtaken by the Judgment of Heaven for my wicked leaving my Father's House, and abandoning my Duty," and "my Conscience, which was not yet come to the Pitch of Hardness to which it has been since, reproach'd me with the Contempt of Advice, and the Breach of my Duty to God and my Father."[22] The violent storm afterward confers a strong sense of the punishment that follows from such an act of "rebellion." Taking the Christian worldview seriously here means also taking seriously a spiritual metaphysics of the will. Starr cites the minister Obadiah Grew who trained Defoe, and who wrote, "Every man by nature hath a lusting desire to leave God, and live at his own hand; . . . Thus it is with every man by Nature . . . Man would be at liberty from God and his Will, to follow and fulfill his own; . . . He hath a *principium laesum,* a devillish principle in his nature; an impulse to range about the earth, as Satan said of himself."[23] In this reading, Crusoe is a character with a *"principium laesum."* The abandonment of supplying a reason for the action then can be attributed to this mysterious principle.[24]

Historically, it has been difficult for scholars to settle on the question of whether Defoe ought to be thought of as a "formal realist" (more committed to neutral presentation) or a writer in the tradition of Puritan spiritual autobiography (more committed to moral presentation). It is not my purpose to try and settle that issue, but rather to observe that the ambivalence can be perceived in a particularly stark way through the figure of akrasia, which reveals the limits of one or the other epistemological framework.[25] If, after all, Crusoe's returns to the open seas are best "explained" by sin, then this is a very different sort of explanation than how we might "explain" Crusoe's decisions to build a fortress or hide from the natives. Here to explain Crusoe's sinful act is to call it contrary to his reason, following through on a less good reason, or perhaps it is to say that it was not intentional but rather followed the forces of fate (the "Propension of Nature") or the workings of the devil.

The clash between a materialist mode of explanation and a spiritual one in instances of something like akrasia comes through even more vividly in Defoe's second novel, *Moll Flanders* (1722). Also told in retrospective first-person narration, *Moll Flanders* tells the life of a woman who, as the title page reads, was "Born in NEWGATE, and during a Life of continu'd Variety for Threescore Years, besides her Childhood, was Twelve Year a *Whore,* five times a *Wife* (whereof once to her own Brother) Twelve Year a *Thief,* Eight Year a Transported *Felon* in *Virginia,* at last grew *Rich,* liv'd *Honest,* and died a *Penitent.*"[26] The perspective this novel takes and the stories it recounts overlap considerably with Defoe's other prose writings— specifically, his political tracts and journalism; indeed, it can be richly understood in the context of his other writings on crime in London. Moll can be read as a data point, whose trajectory illuminates real socioeconomic dynamics in a city that has seen a new influx of people of various classes, new roles for women, and new opportunities for and forms of criminal activity. If *Robinson Crusoe* offers a "book-keeping" epistemology of material causes in its tabulation of objects, calendar dates, and thoughts, then *Moll Flanders* offers a similarly materialist epistemology that is focused on how and why someone may descend into a life of crime.[27] When she first begins stealing, Moll can be understood from a sociological vantage: she needed to because she was brought to a state of poverty. "O let none read this part without seriously reflecting on the Circumstances of a desolate State," she tells us, "and how they would grapple with meer want of Friends and want of Bread; it will certainly make them think . . . of the wise Man's Prayer, *Give me not Poverty least I Steal*."[28] The implication here is that poverty would leave her in a place in which stealing would be necessary. Although it would be sinful, there is no causal mystery: the action would have a clear causal justification. In the bigger picture, the "evils" of her thefts would speak to the "evils" of society. Understood as a statistic, Moll's "actions" could be analyzed as events brought about by a set of conditions that can be counted and summed up.[29]

However, when Moll starts working as a thief, we see—indeed more explicitly than in *Robinson Crusoe*—the entrance of the devil as a central character, notable as the entrance of the first supernatural entity in the novel. The phrase *"Give me not Poverty least I Steal"* considered above also speaks to the possibility of temptation, which means that the causality of this novel is not just that of necessity, for it also hinges on the strength or weakness of a will. She goes on, "Let 'em remember that a time of Distress is a time of dreadful Temptation, and all the Strength to resist is taken away; Poverty presses, the Soul is made Desperate by Distress, and what can be done?"[30] In this line, we see a version of the temptation familiar from Augustine's *Confessions,* except the lack of strength appears to be more necessitated ("all the Strength to resist is taken away . . . and what can be done?"). However, the ontology of the will is difficult to parse here. The final words "and what can be done?" can also be read as a first-person utterance or an excuse for going ahead with it. Or the narrator may be asking us to see this as pure entrapment: she literally had no way out. In the first theft, then, we see the act explained through the character's state of *blindness* and *ignorance* and also as "pushed forward" through the spiritual agency of the devil:

> It was one Evening, when being brought, as I may say, to the last Gasp,
> I think I may truly say I was Distracted and Raving, when prompted

by I know not what Spirit, and as it were, doing I did not know what, or why; I dress'd me, for I had still pretty good Cloaths, and went out: I am very sure I had no manner of Design in my Head, when I went out, I neither knew or considered where to go, or on what Business; but as the Devil carried me out and laid his Bait for me, so he brought me to be sure to the place, for I knew not whither I was going or what I did. . . .

This was the Bait; and the Devil who I said laid the Snare, as readily prompted me, as if he had spoke, for I remember, and shall never forget it, 'twas like a Voice spoken to me over my Shoulder, take the Bundle; be quick; do it this Moment.[31]

The narration here is providing different means of helping us understand the act as causally justified: 1) she is brought "to the last Gasp," which means she is desperate for money; 2) she was "Distracted and Raving" and "had no manner of Design in [her] Head"; and 3) "the Devil carried me out," "laid the Snare," and "prompted" her as if with words.[32] Taken all together, Defoe has created a narration that seeks to provide an explanation for a knowingly guilty action by lessening both the amount of knowingness and the amount of freedom. At the same time, the sense of this scene as evidence of her weakness of will is augmented by having Moll play the part of Eve tempted by the serpent.

If these effects produce a sense of the action as explicable in terms of causes—material and spiritual—then some other moments that follow complicate this sense, as in the passage discussed briefly in this book's introduction. Indeed, less easy to explain are Moll's actions when she is no longer in a state of poverty. In these moments, the novel seems at certain points to preserve absences in explanation, evoking again the sense of acting upon a weaker reason. For instance, shortly after she steals valuables from a woman in need while her home went up in flames, Moll tells us, "I say I confess the inhumanity of this Action mov'd me very much, and made me relent exceedingly, and Tears stood in my Eyes upon that Subject: But with all my Sense of its being cruel and Inhuman, I cou'd never find in my Heart to make any Restitution: The Reflection wore off, and I began quickly to forget the Circumstances that attended the taking them."[33] How are we to understand a line like "I cou'd never find in my Heart to make any Restitution; The Reflection wore off"? Is this the same as saying "I never found in my Heart"? Was she literally incapable of making restitution? Or did she merely decline? Part of the ambiguity comes from the difficulty of discerning distance between narrator and character. Is the line "I could never find in my Heart" factually descriptive—sincere about the words "cou'd not"? Or is it in a sense performative of the condition of the character who merely *tells* herself she "cou'd not"?[34] Some of these ambiguities recur as the passage continues:

> Nor was this all, for tho' by this jobb I was become considerably Richer than before, yet the Resolution I had formerly taken of leaving off this horrid Trade, when I had gotten a little more, did not return; but I must still get farther, and more; and the Avarice join'd so with the Success, that I had no more thoughts of coming to a timely Alteration of Life; tho' without it I cou'd expect no Safety, no Tranquility in the Possession of what I had so wickedly gain'd; but a little more, and a little more, was the Case still.

As briefly discussed in the introduction, here we have the peculiar sense that her mental states were just things that happened ("the Resolution . . . did not return"), but we also have vocalizations or performances of the attitude of the past self ("but I must still get farther, and more," and "but a little more, and a little more"), which expose the greedy and strategic mentality of the character at the time. Moll's actions come through as more guilty in this scene as well because at this point we understand that her thefts are no longer justified. They are like the young Augustine's thefts from the pear tree described as "gratuitously evil": "It was not poverty that drove me to conceive the desire to steal, and to act upon that desire. . . . What I stole, I already had in abundance, and of much better quality too."

These instances in Defoe's novel, then, show some of the options available for the writer committed to some degree to causal explication in writing the trope of akrasia: we have (a) abstention from explanation to showcase the nomological over the logical (or a sense of the "account" given as account-as-story over account-as-explanation, the "what" rather than the "why"); (b) stipulation of the character's blindness and ignorance, which eliminates the akrasia; (c) the spiritual agency of the devil or "Propension of Nature" that drives the character forward and complicates the sense of akrasia; and (d) possible conflations of perspective in which the narrator evokes the greedy (and thus guilty) psychology of the character. The narrator then needs to either double down on the task of causal explication (as in [b]) or noticeably abstain from explication ([a] and [d]) or foreground the moral dimensions of the scene instead of "neutral description" (as in [c]). We see some similar options arise, though in quite different ways, in some of Haywood's fictions.

HAYWOOD

Certain moments from the prose works of Eliza Haywood reveal characters whose actions don't seem to match their beliefs or at least for whom the connection between belief and action cannot be perfectly or coherently explicated. But some important differences from Defoe stand out for our purposes. For one thing, because Haywood's fictions tend to take a third-person omniscient rather than first-person retrospective view, different formal questions necessarily arise when considering the matter of a given character's guilt or remorse. Moral assessments of a character are provided not through the retrospective considerations of the character herself but through the nameless and impersonal narrator. This makes it hard to see whether the moral view of a character is the character's own or the narrator's: If a character seems to act akratically, is the character acting against *her* own better judgment or merely against the narrator's judgment? Are the characters' behaviors bad because the character thinks so or because the narrator says so? In this way, the episodes in question maintain a distinct kind of ambiguity regarding whether or not a given action is to be considered akratic.

Another difference is more metaphysical: Haywood's works not only take particular interest in desire and the passions, but often do so in such a way that implies they are to be understood as blind subpersonal forces that determine action. A telling moment can be found in *Love in Excess* (1719) in which the narrator reflects upon the blamelessness of the subject under the power of the passions:

Passion is not to be circumscribed; and being not only, not subservient, but absolutely *controller* of the *will*, it would be meer madness, as well as ill nature, to say a person was blame-worthy for what was unavoidable.

When love once becomes in our power, it ceases to be worthy of that name; no man really possest with it, *can* be master of his actions; and whatever effects it may enforce, are no more to be condemned, than poverty, sickness, deformity, or any other misfortune incident of human nature.[35]

Thus, for good reason, various critics have examined Haywood's fictions in line with Hume or eighteenth-century physiological sciences. Margaret Case Croskery discusses the above passage in connection with Hume's notion that reason is the slave of the passions and describes *Fantomina* as "champion[ing] the primacy of passion as an essentially amoral, motivational force."[36] Likewise, Helen Thompson has read "Haywood's amorous plots [as] galvanized by a hydraulic physiology that vents or, for a time, smothers its passion. Like that of Willis's person, this passion can be shunted from 'part' to 'part,' but it cannot, finally be repressed."[37] If Defoe invites us to identify the metaphysics of the will from the spiritual autobiography, Haywood would seem to invite us to identify desire, the affects, and the passions more in line with the Enlightenment philosophers discussed in chapter 1. Driven by forces that determine and overpower the will, such characters would then not be acting intentionally. For Patricia Meyer Spacks, Haywood's heroines also do not act irrationally, per se, given that they are so often "unknowing"; reflecting on a separate scene in *Love in Excess*, Spacks writes, "Here, for a change, is a woman panting and heaving and confessing her wish to yield; but it's essential that she doesn't quite know what she's doing. That nightgown flies open without its wearer's conscious intent; her responsibility remains vague."[38] Ignorant and/or compelled, Haywood's characters would not seem to be of the sort to act knowingly and freely against what they believe.

However, precisely because such scenes seem to depict powerful passions or bad actions in ways that resist the classical category of akrasia, they invite us to find parallels to the accounts of the Enlightenment philosophers. As with Locke in particular, in moments where we find something like a character that does seem to know they are proceeding with an action about which they feel guilty, we can discern some carefully calibrated ambiguities concerning the presentation of intentionality, freedom, knowledge, and guilt. In such episodes, we see the results of either accommodating or evading the writing of such a condition, whether that means abstaining from further description in order to maintain ambiguity or writing more completely so as to eliminate the sense of akrasia.

Perhaps the most vivid (and discussed) presentation of the ambiguities in desire and action in Haywood's corpus can be found in *Fantomina* (1925). This short novel presents us with a stark example of a character who is, contra Spacks's description, explicitly "knowing" in most of her pursuits: throughout the narrative she proceeds intentionally and strategically in getting what she wants. Most of the narrative focuses on a young lady's machinations devised to dupe Beauplaisir into making love to her repeatedly while thinking that she is a different woman each time. Though she is a "knowing" character in this sense, it does not appear to be the case that, in these pursuits, she is betraying some deeply held moral sense of what is best for her. However, in a scene early in the novel, the young lady's beliefs and her actions appear to part ways or at least resist easy interpretation. This scene takes place after the lady first meets Beauplaisir, and he asks if she would like to accompany him to "some convenient House of his procuring" or "her own Lodgings." She is faced with the decision as to whether to oblige his requests or "confess her real Quality" as a lady "of distinguished Birth" rather than a prostitute, which would have removed her from the course of events that would follow.[39] While it is unclear whether she has a clear sense of what she believes to be best or what she wants in this moment, we are curiously told that she did not confess, because "the Influence of her ill Stars prevented it." This brief phrase is reminiscent of some of the language we found in *Robinson Crusoe* and *Moll Flanders* in their references to a mysterious "Propension of Nature" or the supernatural entity of "the Devil." In these cases, deployment of a phrase that indicates the intrinsically immoral quality of the act helps to indicate to the reader that the action is wrong. However, what is notable here is that it remains unclear whether the character sees it as such or not. Indeed, the phrase seems to imply moral judgment either on the part of the narrator or on the part of the character, though it is unclear which. Did she recognize that in neglecting to "confess her real Quality" she was giving in to "the Influence of her ill Stars," or is this the narrator's way of characterizing how a person may make a decision that is (in the narrator's view) bad for her? Is this narration a sort of performance of the character's consciousness, or is it an assessment of the scene by the moralizing narrator?

As the passage continues, these ambiguities persist, but the language shifts away from the supernatural terminology to more overtly causal— physical and physiological—language about the lady's thoughts and actions, which further muddles questions of agency and knowledge. At times she appears driven forward, but the grammar also implies that desire participates with conscious will. The young lady returns to her home to reflect on what to do next:

> But these Cogitations were but of a short Continuance, they vanished with the Hurry of her Spirits, and were succeeded by others vastly different and ruinous:—All the Charms of *Beauplaisir* came fresh into her Mind; she languished, she almost dy'd for another Opportunity of conversing with him; and not all the Admonitions of her Discretion were effectual to oblige her to deny laying hold of that which offered itself the next Night. . . . Strange and unaccountable were the Whimsies she was possess'd of,—wild and incoherent her Desires,—unfix'd and undetermin'd her Resolutions, but in that of seeing *Beauplaisir* in the Manner she had lately done.[40]

Here the lady is at the whim of "the Whimsies she was possess'd of." Indeed, more possessed than possessing, she is like one of Spinoza's or Hume's composite beings. Still, these do not entirely negate the sense that she is consciously "doing" or "willing." The grammar is particularly evasive in a phrase like the following: "Not all the Admonitions of her Discretion were effectual to oblige her to deny laying hold of that which offered itself the next Night." This concatenation of negative or passive formulations "not all the . . . ," "oblige her . . . ," and "to deny . . ." make it impossible to trace the agential sources and causal logic that results in the unnamed heroine's act. It appears that the source of moral judgment ("Discretion") is ineffectual in obliging (a passive verb) her (the object, not the subject of the sentence) to "deny laying hold." Amid an extended discussion on the complexities of will, mind, and consent in this scene, Jonathan Kramnick characterizes Haywood's language here as "loosening, often at the local level of sentence grammar . . . mental states from their ostensible subjects," so that it is not clear whether a subject or person is ultimately responsible for these disembodied thoughts.[41] Indeed, the grammar appears to be expressing the confusion that is being described.

However, if this characterization appears to stay on the level of disconnected mental and bodily states, Haywood's narration still seems to preserve a sense of moral failing in the passage. As in *Moll Flanders,* we can see this in the word "Spirits." Once again, we need to ask whether the word is functioning in the physiological or supernatural sense: Is the lady blindly led along? Or is she giving in to supernatural forces and entities? The following phrase magnifies this ambiguity: the Spirits "were succeeded by others vastly different and ruinous." How are we to understand the word "ruinous"? Is this an adjective attributed to the narrator's evaluation of the character, or is it the character's evaluation of herself? If the former, we might understand the passage as presenting a causal narration of the lady's mind, which is judged and criticized by the narrator; if the latter, it is a case of akrasia in which the character recognizes that she is proceeding to her ruin. With the final lines of the passage, we discern similar ambiguities around the sets of adjectives "strange and unaccountable," "wild and incoherent," "unfix'd and undetermin'd." If these are the narrator's articulations, then the character can be understood as blindly led on, unaware of the implications of her action; if they are the character's, this is more clearly a sense of the lady proceeding knowingly toward what she knows is bad for her.[42] In its shifting perspectives and its committed ambiguity, the novel appears to resist fitting her mental states into one category or another.

If the above scene depicts someone overcome by various dynamic desires, passions, intentions, and judgments, a scene in one of Haywood's later novels, *The History of Miss Betsy Thoughtless,* shows an action that appears rather more strategically pursued. Here, though, the ambiguity arises as to the question of guilt due to the uncertainty of the third-person narrator. Throughout this novel, Betsy is usually the one who is duped, and so she is in this sense more "unknowing" in the sense described by Spacks than the protagonist of *Fantomina*.[43] "Thoughtless" can thus be understood as an indicator of Betsy's heedless, unknowing, and inadvertent progression. However, in at least one moment early in the novel, the word "thoughtless" can also be seen to describe the narrator's lack of access to Betsy's seemingly self-deceiving thoughts. In the scene in question, Betsy enjoys eliciting the attentions of an admirer, a Mr. Saving. She appears to entice him deliberately:

> It was not till after Miss Betsy had reason to believe she had engaged the heart of her lover too far for him to recall it, that she began to take a pride in tormenting him. While she looked on his addresses as of a piece with those who called themselves her admirers, she had treated him in that manner which she thought would most conduce to make him really so; but no sooner did she perceive, by the tokens aforementioned, and many others, that his passion was of the most serious nature, than she behaved to him in a fashion quite the reverse, especially before company; for as she had not the least affection, or even a liking towards him, his submissive deportment under the most cold, sometimes contemptuous carriage, could afford her no other satisfaction, than, as she fancied it, it shewed the power of her beauty, and piqued those ladies of her acquaintance, who could not boast of such an implicit resignation, and patient suffering from their lovers.[44]

Although the narration is not clear about what Betsy knows she is doing and the extent to her strategizing, we do know enough to recognize that it is deliberate. We know that "she began to take a pride in tormenting him," a pride that implies a satisfaction in a feat accomplished. We are to presume that Betsy knows she is not just "engag[ing] the heart of her lover," but "tormenting"—a word that contains the sense of excessive, even needless, harm to another. Additionally, "no sooner did she perceive . . . that his passion was of the most serious nature, than she behaved to him in a fashion quite the reverse," this shift in behavior is prompted by a perception, which implies awareness of a strategy. We read the word "perceive[s]" not strictly in the visual sense, but in the more capacious sense of "perception" as understanding or recognition.

However, the grammar makes this difficult to see and, instead, easy to interpret as blindly or unknowingly tormenting behavior, for it resists disclosing whether Betsy feels guilt and "views herself" in any distanced or critical way. The ambiguity is accentuated when her guardian, Mr. Goodman, attempts to convince Betsy to not pursue the relationship with Mr. Saving. He communicates to her "the danger to which a private correspondence renders a young woman liable." We are told,

> She seemed convinced of the truth of what he said, and promised to follow, in the strictest manner, his advice.
>
> Whether she thought herself, in reality, so much obliged to the conduct of her guardian in this, I will not take upon me to say; for tho' she was not charmed with the person of Mr. Saving, it is certain she took an infinite pleasure in the assiduities of his passion: it is therefore highly probable, that she might imagine he meddled in this affair more than he had any occasion to have done.[45]

Is she convinced by Mr. Goodman's words of warning about her behavior? So it "seemed." Does she in fact think herself obliged to the conduct of Mr. Goodman in his warnings? The answer: "I will not take [it] upon me to say." The narrator concludes, as we did above, that "it is certain she took an infinite pleasure in the assiduities of [Mr. Saving's] passion," so "it is therefore highly probable" that she believes that Mr. Goodman "meddled in this affair more" than he needed to. However, accessing the degree to which she believes herself to be doing something morally wrong can only be approached probabilistically. The perspective of the narrator has become simply a part of the social setting, guessing at the thoughts of someone in their mix. Perhaps this absence of explication reflects an absence of reflective thinking on Betsy's own part. Or perhaps, as in *Fantomina*, novels can only reflect a social awareness of people and not much more than that; perhaps they are only able to gesture toward (without conclusively showing) the interior world in which people silently deceive themselves.

Across these isolated moments in these four novels, we have seen several tendencies when approaching scenes that appear to convey something like acting against better judgment: first, we have seen the narrator abstaining from description, as in the beginning of *Robinson Crusoe* and in *Betsy Thoughtless*. This strategy appears to foreground the view that the narrator can only know so much about the inner life of a character, even if it be the same character at an earlier point in life, as in Crusoe's case. Second, we have seen the narrative draw upon the terminology of spiritual or supernatural paradigms, as in both of Defoe's novels and briefly in *Fantomina*. In these cases, specifically moral terminology serves to articulate and make sense of the phenomenon in question, which in turn distance the narrative from strictly causal description. Lastly, we have seen the tendency of shifting into narration of purely physical and psychological causes and effects, eliminating the sense of volition or akrasia at all, as in moments in *Moll Flanders* and *Fantomina*.

As we found in the period's contemporaneous philosophy, the novel's commitment to causal explanation dissolves the closer it gets to akrasia, and akrasia dissolves the closer it gets to causal explanation. These moments in Defoe and Haywood reveal a mix of inheritances and some formal inconsistency, but also a sense of the opportunities of fiction writing, specifically when it comes to the ambiguities made possible by the narrator's undetermined perspective. We find more self-conscious experimentation with modes of bringing out the falsity of a character's mind in Laurence Sterne.

STERNE

We normally understand rational intentional action as taking on the structure "If X then Y," in which X stands for "*P* believes doing *A* is for the best," and Y stands for "*P* does *A*." Novels, one might think, are good at showing how X results in Y: how believing doing something would be for the best results in the doing of that thing; or, conversely, how, if -Y then -X, or, if the person did not do that thing, then we can infer that person did not believe doing it was for the best. Consider, then, this moment from Laurence Sterne's *A Sentimental Journey*, narrated by the protagonist Yorick: "I wish'd to let [her hands] go," he tells us, "and all the time I held them, I kept arguing within myself against it—and still I held them on."[46] In this sentence, X results in -Y (i.e., even though *"P* believes doing *A* [letting her hands go] is for the best," the result is *"P* not doing *A"*). As a result, the sentence seems to upend our expectations of one of the chief privileges of the novel form: its capacity for causal explication. We might be tempted to merely laugh at the sentence, understanding it as a part of a parody novel, which mocks the readiness of readers to anticipate clarity and explanation in descriptions of characters and depictions of their actions. But the sentence is doing more than that. Indeed, as the rest of this section will try to spell out, in structuring the sentence as a contradiction, Sterne has sought to express the condition of akrasia—that is, to get at what *it is like* to be a problem to oneself—by itself performing the illogical (disorienting) experience through its grammar. In a manner more explicit and self-conscious than in the examples from Defoe or Haywood, the text here presents the failures of causal or logical narration as a way of capturing or showing the dynamics of akrasia.

A Sentimental Journey indeed stands out as offering a peculiar kind of account. Early in the novella, the protagonist Yorick tells us, "I write not to apologize for the weaknesses of my heart in this tour,—but to give an account of them."[47] What kind of account of weakness is this? A medical textbook might purport to "give an account" of a weak heart; this might provide physiological reasons for deficient anatomical functionality. A spiritual autobiography would seem to give an account of a weak heart in another sense: a narrative account that exhibits in confessional form one's own incontinence or failure. Sterne's narrative is not quite either of these. Rather, as we see in the sentence "I wish'd to let them go . . . and still I held them on," the work tends to put forward unsatisfying, incomplete, or false types of explanatory accounts, illogical formulations that offer up a sense of failure. What results is a narrative account that performs the failures of explanatory accounts. Delivering this kind of incomplete or insufficient explanatory account then becomes a way of conveying the undermotivated experience of akrasia.

Sterne's fiction is full of seemingly irrational people who pose problems to novelistic attempts at representation.[48] In Sterne's nine-volume *Life and Opinions of Tristram Shandy*, published between 1759 and 1767, irrationality largely takes the form of the motif of the "hobby-horse": "When a man gives himself up to the government of a ruling passion," as Tristram tells us in volume 2, "——or, in other words, when his HOBBY-HORSE grows head-strong,——farewell cool reason and fair discretion!"[49] Nearly every character in that novel has his own "hobby-horse" or "ruling passion," to which a person knowingly submits despite the many absurdities it can introduce. The novel itself seems to take on the structural logic of following Tristram's "ruling passions" or various inclinations that subvert a rational structure, moving in seemingly random directions, "cluttering like hey-go-mad," like the various humours or "animal spirits" referenced throughout the work.[50] However, the "hobby-horse" motif of irrationality is less clearly an example of the self-conflicting mode of akrasia than the types of actions we see in *A Sentimental Journey*, which are more strongly and consistently accompanied by a sense of moral guilt. For this reason, it is worth focusing more exclusively on a collection of representative moments in that second shorter work.

A Sentimental Journey centers on Yorick, the benevolent if heedless parson originally introduced in *Tristram Shandy*, through various sentimental and humorous encounters across France. These episodes are structured geographically as well as topically, tracing movements around the country and the movements of the heart. What attracts our interest about this novella is Yorick's attempts to make sense of his actions by recourse to the mysterious laws of his heart. He often tells us that the passions resist understanding, which makes his whole constitution unknowable and ungovernable. Near the end of the novella Yorick says, "I felt such undescribable emotions within me, as I am sure could not be accounted for from any combinations of matter and motion."[51] In another moment he tells us, "There is no regular reasoning upon the ebbs and flows of our humours; they may depend upon the same causes, for ought I know, which influence the tides themselves."[52] What laws his emotions and humours obey he is not sure; perhaps they obey the same gravitational laws as the tides, or perhaps they are not legible on the terms of "matter and motion." As

Markman Ellis notes, "the rhetoric of the body" in this novel "articulates a wide range of non-volitional sanguinary impulses"; this illegibility, Ellis writes, contributes to the way the novel "appears categorically different and inexplicable to the empiricist discourse of science, with its endeavour to restrict ambage and control ambiguity."[53] In this sense, any explanation of action can seemingly be directed back to the unexplainable mysteries of the heart, the "non-volitional sanguinary impulses," or the broader unfathomable network of causes that includes those that move the tides.

We would be amiss, however, to take Yorick completely at his word and to see him as a simply ungovernable combination of forces. It serves his interest, after all, to blame his actions on his nonvolitional impulses. A Humean kind of "account" that makes sense of one's actions, thoughts, and reasons by referring back to the ungovernable passions would seem to benefit Yorick by letting him off the hook. For Yorick, it would be great if reason was the slave of the passions. We can recall that Hume's full line in the *Treatise* was "Reason is, *and ought to be,* the slave of the passions" (italics mine). Yorick, deducing the "is" from the "ought," in a reverse of the naturalistic fallacy, wants his reason to be the slave of his passions, so he holds on to a metaphysics in which it is.

We might then observe that one of the functions of the foregrounding of an ontology of unknowable passions is to occlude the deeper question of guilt and the important thematic issue of the status of the "moral will." As Arthur Cash has argued, Sterne's "keen interest in psychology, expressed so well in both the sermons and novels, did not lead him to adopt that attitude so familiar to us in the twentieth century—psychological determinism. For him self-knowledge, self-judgment, and self-correction were, in the long run, products of the moral will."[54] Even when Sterne uses language that may appear to us to evoke "psychology," or foreground the philosophical or scientific terminology of his day, its broader context and set of concerns are moralistic, indeed spiritual. For instance, we might turn to one of Yorick's sermons in *Tristram Shandy* (read aloud by Corporal Trim in volume 2), which dwells specifically upon weakness of will, and we can note its serious spiritual engagement with the condition in the classic Christian understanding. It describes how "PASSION [gets] into the judgment-seat, and pronounc'd sentence in the stead of reason":

I make no doubt but the knowledge of right and wrong is so truly im-
pressed upon the mind of man,—that did no such thing ever happen, as
that the conscience of man, by long habits of sin, might (as the scripture
assures it may) insensibly become hard;—and, like some tender parts of
his body, by much stress and continual hard usage, lose, by degrees, that
nice sense and perception with which God and nature endow'd it:——Did
this never happen;—or was it certain that self-love could never hang the
least bias upon the judgment;—or that the little interests below, could
rise up and perplex the faculties of our upper regions, and encompass
them about with clouds and thick darkness.[55]

Although Yorick's language here can be seen as drawing upon physiological terminology ("like some tender parts of his body, by much stress
and continual hard usage"), it is delivered in the midst of a discussion
of "knowledge of right and wrong," "the conscience of man," and "long
habits of sin." The language employed indeed picks up on Augustine and
scripture: "clouds and thick darkness" recalls Paul's inscrutable confusion,
Augustine's moments of blankness, and the perversity of turning away
from God's will.[56]

Keeping these concerns in mind, we can see Yorick's employment of
Humean terminology as a way of misdirecting blame, making akrasia (in
which one has oneself to blame) into compulsion (in which various other
forces and entities are to blame). Yorick wants to think of his humors as
the tides and follows up that line by saying, "I'm sure at least for myself,
that in many a case I should be more highly satisfied, to have it said by the
world, 'I had had an affair with the moon, in which there was neither sin
nor shame,' than have it pass altogether as my own act and deed, wherein
there was so much of both."[57] Here we see a willful misdirection away from
attention to "my own act and deed" and toward an idealized view that his
humors, following the laws of the tides, "had an affair with the moon, in
which there was neither sin nor shame." This declaration of a wish for a
reality without sin or shame only underlines the sense in which sin and
shame are deep underlying concerns for the character in question.

In Yorick's narrative, we do get certain kinds of "clouds and thick
darkness"—nonexplanations and nonrepresentations—but these come

through, not in the explicitly spiritual language that had previously grounded the notion of weakness of will, but in the confusing opacity of descriptive language itself. The most vivid example arises in the chapter entitled "THE TEMPTATION./PARIS." The scene begins with mishaps and misunderstandings that can fairly be called out of Yorick's control:

> As the fair *fille de chambre* was so near my door she turned back, and
> went into the room with me for a moment or two whilst I wrote a card.
>   It was a fine still evening in the latter end of the month of May—the
> crimson window curtains (which were of the same colour of those of
> the bed) were drawn close—the sun was setting and reflected through
> them so warm a tint into the fair *fille de chambre*'s face—I thought she
> blush'd—the idea of it made me blush myself—we were quite alone; and
> that super-induced a second blush before the first could get off.
>   There is a sort of pleasing half guilty blush, where the blood is more in
> fault than the man—'tis sent impetuous from the heart, and virtue flies
> after it—not to call it back, but to make the sensation of it more delicious
> to the nerves—'tis associated—[58]

Here indeed the fault is on the lighting—the crimson window curtains caused a warm tint in the face of the *fille de chambre,* and the idea of her blushing caused him to blush himself. Blushes, being the kinds of occurrences that arrive unbidden, are "more in fault than the man." The use of the language "associated" likewise nods toward the associationist philosophies of psychology. However, to stop there is to give in to Yorick's preferred interpretation of the scene, which employs the Humean mode of accounting for himself: the autonomous passions determine him, overtaking his capacity for reason. As the passage continues, however, the text increasingly gestures toward the way that Yorick is doing—purposely, freely, knowingly—what he knows he shouldn't be doing: "——but I'll not describe it.—I felt something at first within me which was not in strict unison with the lesson of virtue I had given her the night before—I sought five minutes for a card—I knew I had not one.—I took up a pen—I laid it down again—my hand trembled—the devil was in me."[59] "The devil's" entry into the scene recalls Moll's thieving scene, changing the tone of the scene by virtue of changing its metaphysics. The Humean passions turn out to be not so benevolent, giving credit instead to a dangerous, if plea- surable, pursuit. It is here that we can observe some differences between the "account" of morally guilty action in a novel like Defoe's *Robinson Crusoe* and the "account" in Sterne. Both make reference to "the devil," which signifies a change in metaphysics, and both appear to take the spir- itual elements of moral guilt seriously. However, what we find in passages like the one above are first-person retrospective characterizations that more self-consciously reproduce a less self-conscious narrator. While in *Robinson Crusoe* we observed a tendency for the narrator to abstain from explanation in moments of akrasia, here that absence is manipulated to produce ironic effects.

What cannot be accounted for in the structure of sin is here evoked through negative uses of language such as, in this instance, the dash. These dashes seem to stand in for spoken hesitation, pauses, or gestures as to what resists articulation. So we are invited to read a sentence like "——but I'll not describe it" as akin to musical notation ("[rest] [rest] [rest] but I'll not describe it"). Visually, it appears as if a word has been crossed out. It could be said to connect one temporal moment (on the left) to another (on the right) without providing any content as to the journey that has taken place (in this sense reminiscent of Sterne's squiggly lines at the end of volume 6 of *Tristram Shandy*).[60] In this context, it accentuates a logical disconnect between intentions and bodily movements: "—I sought five minutes for a card—I knew I had not one.—I took up a pen—I laid it down again—my hand trembled—the devil was in me." The active verbs in "I sought," "I knew," "I took," and "I laid" are not only disconnected from each other, but also from the physical manifestation that follows, presented in passive construction ("my hand trembled"). One would think there must be causal relationships between these actions, but the narrator is unable to provide it, and the dash serves to direct our attention to precisely that fact.[61]

If the dash is one tool produced to self-consciously signify the failures of language, then Yorick's obvious casuistry (or false reasoning) is another. Following the above passage, Yorick begins to give an excuse as to why he cooperates with the devil, resulting in a form of self-excuse produced in evident bad faith: "I know as well as any one, he is an adversary, whom if we resist, he will fly from us—but I seldom resist him at all; from a terror, that though I may conquer, I may still get a hurt in the combat—so I give up the triumph, for security; and instead of thinking to make him fly, I generally fly myself."[62] Yorick explains that he does not resist the devil because he "seldom resist[s] him at all"—a character trait that is meant to serve as a sort of explanation for his continuing the pursuit. However, this is not so much an explanation as a tautology: I follow the devil because I am one to follow the devil. In shifting to a mode of describing his own irrationality, he describes himself as having reliable character traits, again presenting himself as a bundle of habits and passions in order to exculpate himself. A reader might be tempted to take Yorick's words here as operating in the mode of causal explanation. This would be to take Yorick as a narrator concerned with spelling out the nature of his character and the reasons he does what he does, whereas Yorick is taking advantage of his role as narrator of a novel to make it seem as if he is providing a causal explanation, for what he is giving us is less of an explanation and more of an excuse.

As we move forward in this scene, we arrive at the expression of paradox briefly discussed at the beginning of this section. Yorick's narration of his movements, decisions, and actions begins to fall apart, drawing attention to the failures of narration by stipulating causes:

> I took her by the hand, and led her to the door, and begg'd she would not forget the lesson I had given her—She said, Indeed she would not—and as she utter'd it with some earnestness, she turned about, and gave me both her hands, closed together, into mine—it was impossible not to compress them in that situation—I wish'd to let them go; and all the time I held them, I kept arguing within myself against it—and still I held them on.—In two minutes I found I had all the battle to fight over again—and I felt my legs and every limb about me tremble at the idea.[63]

We would be mistaken to read this as a scene of inevitable compulsion. Yorick claims that "it was impossible not to compress them in that situation": Is that the case? After all, Yorick is able to "wish" to let them go and "argue" within himself against it. The paradox is articulated in the sentence "I wish'd to let them go; and all the time I held them, I kept arguing within myself against it—and still I held them on." This can be read as a version of Paul's "For what I want to do I do not do, but what I hate I do." Both phrases preserve the sense of paradox and in so doing evoke the confusion of being that person. After all, Sterne might have chosen to write this sentence differently. He might have written it, like the philosophers, more "completely": "I wish'd to let them go, *but deeper down I had a stronger wish to hold them on,* and so I held them on." In this version, the novelist delves into the subconscious to provide the deeper reasons for the eventual action. There is no more contradiction, because the mental states have been modified to match the action. Alternatively, the novelist might have written the sentence like this: "I wish'd to let them go, *but my passions made it impossible,* and so my hands continued to hold them on." In this version, there is no freedom in the action, because the passions had ultimate power over what occurred. Sterne writes his sentence to avoid these options, stressing the "wish" on the one hand and the freedom of the (conflicting) action on the other. What results is an unresolved expression that portrays an unresolved person.

Another way of putting it is that, in narrating X ("*P* believes doing *A* is for the best") not resulting in Y ("*P* does *A*"), the novel is not merely pointing us to the fact of -Y ("*P* doesn't do *A*") as a plot point. More radically, it is asking us to shift attention to the premise with which we began—"If X then Y"—by asking us if that premise is even correct at all. The experience is not only felt as negative through the negativity of the outcome, but in the confusion produced by the premise not connecting to the outcome. This is in a sense the confusion described by Aristotle as the failure to match the knowledge of the minor premise with the knowledge of the universal premise in the "practical syllogism" of action.[64] What is regretted in the case of Aristotle's akratic man, as in the case of Yorick, is not just what the action brought about, but the confusion of not syncing the universal and the particular—that is, of not being coherent to oneself. The effect is a disorienting one. The novella's interest here is on that experience of disorientation.

The dash, the casuistry, the grammatical contradiction: these are tools that stand out as distinctly formal and uniquely literary in the manner in which they draw attention to the deceptive potential of a piece of writing. As negative manipulations of language, they perform and express the phenomenon of betraying oneself in a way that a linear narration of causes and effects cannot. As the scene ends, we are told, "I had still hold of her hands—and how it happened I can give no account, but I neither ask'd her—nor drew her—nor did I think of the bed—but so it did happen, we both sat down."[65] Here we have again the expressive but empty gesture of the dash as well as the logical contradiction of going through with an undermotivated action. Additionally, here we find one more encounter in which a character struggles to "give an account" of himself. However, this one begs to be read as a performance of a failed narrator. Yorick, after all, can give an account: he privately and silently allowed himself to sit down. But this may be difficult to explain in the Humean sense of "giving an account," insofar as the Humean epistemology is ill equipped to convey the sense of "neglecting" or "ignoring"—the way that Yorick knew the stronger reason but ignored it and went forward with the weaker. Yorick can give an account of his action, but it is the narrative type of account: an account that dramatizes the failure of an explanatory account.

In this sentence and throughout the novel, Sterne then uses an effect that would be instrumental in Romantic-era novels and beyond: he expresses human irrationality not by seeking to successfully stipulate the causal mechanisms of mind and body, but rather by *unsuccessfully* stipulating the causal mechanisms of mind and body. For Sterne, as for the authors considered in the following chapter, it is only through the failure of the sentence that the novel can represent the failure of the person.

The novel form's ability to ironically portray the experience of knowingly conflicting and guilty action will be explored more thoroughly through versions of free indirect discourse in the Romantic-era novels of William Godwin and Jane Austen in chapter 3.

3

AKRASIA AND FREE INDIRECT DISCOURSE IN ROMANTIC-ERA NOVELS

Godwin and Austen

IN THE MIDST OF a memorable discussion of Jane Austen's *Emma* (1815) in his book *Jane Austen, or The Secret of Style*, D. A. Miller elucidates a special quality of free indirect discourse by centering on a single sentence repeated before and after the chapter break of chapters 2 and 3, in volume 2: "Emma could not forgive her."[1] Miller observes that the repetition of this sentence allows us to see the two ways in which it may be read: first, as "the indirect and impersonal *performance* of Emma's consciousness" and, second, as "the mere matter-of-fact *notation* of that thought."[2] It is able to "perform" what Emma would think about Jane Fairfax, in the sense that she might say, "I cannot forgive her," and it is also able to denote a fact about Emma's state of mind as a third-person omniscient narrator. This is possible because the sentence emulates the character's "direct speech" without leaving the perspective of the narrator; also, because it does not leave the narrator's perspective, it can be read as the narrator's simple description of the character's mind or plain "indirect speech."

I think we can say even more about this sentence's two possible perspectives. We might notice that the two readings of the sentence take on two quite different meanings when we focus on the status of Emma's supposed volition. This becomes clearer when we look more carefully at the words "could not" and the difference in meaning they convey when considered from an inside and from an outside perspective: when we read them either as vocalized by Emma herself or as matter-of-fact third-person notation, we register two very different views of the will.

We can better grasp this duality in perspective if we shift to another, similar example from *Emma*. In this scene, just before Emma utters an unkind joke about Miss Bates in the company of Miss Bates, Frank Churchill, Mr. Knightley, Harriet Smith, Jane Fairfax, Mr. and Mrs. Weston, and Mr. and Mrs. Elton, we are given a paragraph break comprised of a single sentence: "Emma could not resist."[3] Unlike the example considered by Miller, this sentence is delivered only once, and not in the midst of a narrator's discussion of Emma's train of thought, but instead in an extended quoted conversation. For these reasons, we are more likely to speed past it, for it seems to point our attention to the action that follows. If we pause over it, however, we can recognize that the sentence can also be read in two different ways: as a "performance of Emma's consciousness", and as a "matter-of-fact notation of the thought," and the difference is significant. If we read the sentence as a mere notation, we understand Emma as being sincerely unable to act any differently than she did, taking the words "could not" literally: it was not within the range of available possibilities for her mental capacity at that point and time. Alternatively, when we read the sentence as a performance of her consciousness, we discover quite the opposite: if "I cannot resist" were a sentence Emma speaks privately in her mind, we understand instantly that Emma *can* resist. Just as I might say in passing, "I cannot resist having one more chocolate," I mean something more like "It is very hard for me to resist," which implies exactly that "I can resist," with the added qualifier that I say, "I cannot resist," in order to justify my going ahead with it.

After all, Emma would not have said aloud, "I cannot resist," precisely because those words would have been recognized as false to those around her: "Yes, you *can* resist, Emma. You must resist," a friend might say. This is exactly the basis on which Mr. Knightley chastises her afterwards. Emma attempts to defend herself: "Nay, how could I help saying what I did?— Nobody could have helped it."[4] Mr. Knightley is not convinced, because he recognizes (as do we) that her words "how could I" are strategically put forward to make it sound like she was literally incapable in order to mask that the opposite was the case. "Emma could not resist" plays both meanings at once, asking us to recognize the difference between saying a person cannot in actuality "resist" an action, and saying that the person tells herself she cannot resist in order to have an excuse for proceeding with that action. In this way, free indirect discourse can take advantage of some of the tricky slippages that arise when we talk about the will. It can evoke the way we may choose to talk about it as causally compelled or not, depending on when it serves our interests to do so.

This chapter focuses on early versions of free indirect discourse (hereafter referred to as FID) in expressions of akrasia in Romantic-era novels— specifically, *Fleetwood* (1805) by William Godwin, and Austen's *Emma*. Like the ironic formulations we saw in Sterne's *A Sentimental Journey*, FID appears particularly well suited to convey, without remarking upon or explaining, the falsities and insufficiencies of a character's mind: for these cases, as in Sterne, the failure of the person is offered up in the form of the failure of the sentence. More specifically, the doubleness of FID observed by Miller, as I've begun to suggest above, can evoke the mindset of the akratic who foregrounds the weaker reason, pretending (and knowing that she or he is pretending) it is a strong reason. Because, as we have seen in chapter 2, the nascent novel form was motivated to convey such a condition without lapsing into purely explicit causal description, which would negate akrasia's reality, or falling back upon moral or spiritual terminology, thus sacrificing the aim of causal explication, this kind of ironic formulation stands out for its unique representational capacities.

Godwin is an especially illuminating figure in this context because of his close relationship to philosophy proper. Over the course of the 1790s and early 1800s, Godwin grew increasingly skeptical toward philosophy's explicating and totalizing aspirations, seeking in novels new and different ways to write about people. This is especially apparent when we focus on Godwin's treatments of will and action in his philosophical treatise *Political Justice* (1793) in comparison with his considerations of intemperate individuals in his second and third novels, *St. Leon* (1799) and *Fleetwood*. While *St. Leon* tends to recuperate the mechanistic mode of characterizing the mind in what Miller would call "matter-of-fact notation," *Fleetwood* more experimentally puts forward modes of subtly "performing" a character's consciousness while remaining in the narrator's voice. This strategy allows him to falsely perform a person's contradictions and self-deceptions in ways that neither his philosophy nor his earlier straightforward causal modes of narration allowed. Strictly speaking, it is unclear whether the nomenclature "free indirect" can be correctly ascribed to first-person narratives like Godwin's, but, because the effect of narration subtly shifting into vocalizations of the character's consciousness is largely similar, I refer to the technique as a version of FID.[5] While Godwin's novels are not often discussed for his uses of versions of FID, Austen's novels (and *Emma* in particular) arguably occupy more critical attention to the formal device than those of any other English-language novelist. By emphasizing the importance of an akratic motif in *Emma*—that is, the knowing wrongness of some of Emma's stances and decisions—we can gain new perspective on FID's special importance and the novel's epistemologically privileged mode of exhibiting the ways people often foreground their weaker reasons.

FID has long been identified with its capacity for irony. "The classic case of the sentence said to represent two points of view is the ironic sentence," linguist Ann Banfield tells us in the midst of a discussion of FID, "and one can arguably claim that the central place accorded to this notion in modern criticism is a consequence of the preoccupation with narrative texts containing representations of consciousness."[6] One can identify in such sentences a particular importance in the purposeful concealment of one stance and the purposeful foregrounding of another, thus making it an especially important tool for "narrative texts containing representations of consciousness." This can allow FID the special ability to offer up a critical view of the character in question; as Monika Fludernik has written, FID can "condense and exaggerate a character's utterance or attitudes with the intention of implicitly criticizing those speech acts and beliefs."[7] This is clearly the case in an example like that already considered in *Emma*. However, we can add that FID plays not just a critical function but also an expressive function, not unlike what we have seen in Sterne: in simultaneously representing two conflicting levels of consciousness, it presents or exhibits this kind of state of mind—what it is like to be a problem to oneself. The linguist V. N. Vološinov has observed that FID is "congenial to irony" because it partakes in a "'silencing' of prose": because this sentence can be mistaken for plain "matter-of-fact notation," it "silences" the true statement (that "Emma *could* resist"), and, as a result, it mirrors Emma's own mind, which also seeks to "silence" what she, on some level, knows to be true.[8] The classic conception of the akratic mind considered in chapter 1—in the accounts of the philosophers who argue that the akratic acts upon a "weaker reason"—is indeed one that "silences" itself. So, while some moments of akrasia in Defoe and Haywood represent internal conflicts as a series of mental or bodily states unfolding in time, in which differing sensations or thoughts arise dialectically or dialogically, in Austen's ironic sentence the contradiction is brought forth in a single unresolved formulation.

Most critics and linguists understand FID as distinctive to the novel form and as appearing first in the eighteenth- and nineteenth-century European novel.[9] For Banfield, the technique can only arise within "written narrative," and it appears in the novel form in this period simply because of the widespread and extended use of written narrative in the period: it is a result, she says, "of the transformation of western culture into a literate culture."[10] In his analysis of the technique in *The Dual Voice* (1977), Roy Pascal argues that it offers advantages for novelists who encountered limitations with writing as narrators in strictly third-person or first-person modes. The enclosed social settings of Austen's novels, Pascal writes, allowed an opportunity for the narrator "to evoke thought-processes as the characters themselves know them."[11] These accounts can be supplemented by the observation that FID also allows a "silencing" effect, which exhibits a person's failure without explaining it away, and that such a condition makes up an important part of "narrative texts containing representations of consciousness," particularly in an age in which spiritual paradigms no longer provide the authoritative vocabulary for making sense of such experiences. Among its other benefits, FID also allows writers to express the divided, self-deceiving, self-silencing, akratic state of mind—a condition that is increasingly relevant for narratives of this period concerned with autonomy and self-possession—in ways that linear causal narration itself cannot.[12]

In Godwin and Austen, we find still more variations of what we have been calling akrasia to add to those we have seen in Defoe, Haywood, and Sterne: avarice (*St. Leon*), rage (*Fleetwood*), and the minor cruelties committed by someone handsome, clever, and rich (*Emma*). These novels stand out for their interest in preserving knowingness with the freedom of guilty action, and, in this respect, they consider moral failing on the level of something like practical reason more than on knowledge, belief, or theoretical reason. We first turn to Godwin.

GODWIN

In the early pages of *St. Leon: A Tale of the Sixteenth Century*, the narrator, an older St. Leon in a repentant retrospective tone, tells us how he arrived in Paris and succumbed to his old gambling addiction. "All the demon seemed to make his descent upon my soul," he writes. "This was the first time that I had ever felt the struggle of conscious guilt and dishonour.... I did not take into the account the ungovernableness of my own passions."[13] *St. Leon* tells the story of a sixteenth-century aristocrat who, after recklessly gambling away his money, encounters a stranger who imparts on him the philosopher's stone, endowing St. Leon with the capacity for endless riches and immortality. Most of the novel depicts his fall from happiness with the acquisition of the elixir—the effects of his secrecy on the stability of his family, his persecution on account of his mysterious wealth, the death of his wife, and more. At the center of the novel is St. Leon's battles with himself: his struggles with greed and his gambling addiction. As Gary Kelly has written, *St. Leon* is "about the adventures of a man wholly unable to govern his life by reason."[14]

However, as in the quote provided above, Godwin's novel also places great trust in the narrator's retrospective capacity for reason—that is, rationalization, explication, and causal connections between events. In proclamations like "I did not take into the account the ungovernableness of my own passions," the narrator exemplifies the tendency of describing temperamental fluctuations with clarity or, put another way, the ability to rationally reconstruct irrationality. This tendency comes through in a sentence that usefully contrasts with the sentences considered earlier from *Emma*. St. Leon narrates that, as he approached the gambling tables, "I resisted—I yielded."[15] Whereas in *Emma* we are told that she "could not resist," which we understood as an ironic performance of Emma's mind, here Godwin's narrator uses the verbs "resisting" and "yielding" as simple events. They are presented as two separate actions, divided grammatically by a dash that indicates temporal division. The sentence can also be contrasted with two other expressions of akrasia we have already considered, both in first person, like Godwin's sentence: the formulation of Paul "For what I want to do I do not do, but what I hate I do" and Yorick's sentence "I wish'd to let [her hands] go ... and still I held them on." Those sentences in different ways depend upon the effect of paradox, the surprise of contradiction, the performance of logical failure. The sentence in *St. Leon,* however, does not convey contradiction in simultaneity, but rather two clashing operations that occur at two different moments in time—first resisting, then yielding.

Throughout the novel, St. Leon describes his actions by explicating the psychological and physiological causes behind them. After winning "a considerable sum" while gambling, the narrator tells us, "this incident produced a strong impression upon me, and filled my mind with tumult and agitation."[16] He continues, "The very tumult of my thoughts operated strongly to lead me once more to the gaming-table," and "this frame of mind led me on insensibly to the most extravagant of adventures. It threw me in the first place into the hands of notorious gamblers."[17] In each of these phrases, "me" is the passive object that has been the recipient of a "strong impression," which has "led" it to one or another location. His "failures to resist" are in this sense automatic and perfectly explicable consequences or entailments of mental and bodily states.

In one respect, the difference from Austen resides in the use of first-person retrospective narration rather than third-person omniscient narration. In its retrospective stance, Godwin's novel more clearly borrows from the epistolary tradition, in which thoughts and actions are reported directly to a reader. But these moments also speak to the tensions inherent in Godwin's philosophy of action—tensions we find spelled out in the *Enquiry Concerning Political Justice* (1793). In the first edition of that text, Godwin argues that the "theory of the human mind is properly, like the theory of every other series of events with which we are acquainted, a system of mechanism; understanding by mechanism nothing more than a regular connexion of phenomena without any uncertainty of event, so that every incident requires a specific cause, and could be no otherwise in any respect than as the cause determined it to be."[18] It follows, then, that all actions obey a "doctrine of necessity"—not merely "involuntary actions," or physiological compulsions not caused by the mind, but also "voluntary actions," or actions that proceed from the mind's understanding of truths. Indeed, when it comes to voluntary action, Godwin follows the line of argument from Jonathan Edwards, David Hartley, and Joseph Priestley that sees man as perfectible because of this doctrine of necessity: as Mark Philp has put it, "The connection between ideas, and our preference for one idea over another . . . are governed by a rational necessity that is fully causal."[19] This view, rooted in theories of predestination, becomes adapted in Godwin's atheist paradigm so that psychologically understanding something to be true results automatically in action: "The perception of something true, joined with the consciousness of my capacity to act upon this truth," Godwin writes, "[is] of itself sufficient to produce motion in the animal system."[20]

Notably, if the human frame is a "system of mechanism," then it also does not make sense to say that someone struggles with one's will:

> According to [necessitarian] doctrine it will be absurd for a man to say, "I will exert myself," "I will take care to remember," or even "I will do this." All these expressions imply as if man was or could be something else than what motives make him. Man is in reality a passive, and not an active being. In another sense however he is sufficiently capable of exertion. The operations of his mind may be laborious, like those of the wheel of a heavy machine in ascending a hill, may even tend to wear out the substance of the shell in which it acts, without in the smallest degree impeaching its passive character.[21]

To the extent that man is "capable of exertion" and not purely a "passive being," it is merely in the sense that a wheel exerts pressure in carrying a machine up a hill. As Godwin explains, in a turn of phrase remarkably similar to Hume's nonexplanation of akrasia considered in chapter 1, if a person's motives are divided, "it is equivalent to the putting equal weights into the opposite scales of a balance. If one of them have a greater tendency to preference than the other, that which has the greatest tendency must ultimately prevail."[22]

In the late 1790s, however, Godwin grew increasingly dissatisfied with this characterization of volition. His 1797 essay collection, *The Enquirer*, touts a new essayistic style of philosophical interrogation based in epistemological humility, departing from the highly rationalist model of systematization that he refers to as "a method of investigation incommensurate to our powers."[23] "The intellectual eye of man," he continues, "perhaps, is formed rather for the inspection of minute and near, than of immense and distant objects."[24] This new preference for the up-close manifests in a preference for the particular over the abstract. Better to consider a phenomenon like human action by looking at people's experiences rather than working one's way down from a necessitarian philosophical worldview. This new intellectual orientation is also connected to a new concern over "intemperance"—specifically, the "impatient" and "impetuous" attitude that had accompanied the French Revolution. Taking up a less totalizing and more modest philosophy is a way of being more even-keeled: he "is desirous of assisting others, if possible, in perfecting the melioration of their temper."[25] As we will see, it also allows Godwin new ways to think about intemperance, for human action, he comes to recognize, is not best understood through top-down systematic philosophy, but through a more "minute" form of "inspection" into people's lives. We can see this new orientation to thinking about action in the revisions to *Political Justice* and then, more fully, in his novels after 1797.

In its second edition, published in 1796, Godwin returns to the subject of human agency and includes a new chapter solely devoted to giving more nuanced accounts of volition.[26] In this chapter, entitled "The Voluntary Actions of Men Originate in their Opinions," Godwin moves beyond the two categories of action ("voluntary" and "involuntary") he had established in the 1793 version. He adds a third category, "imperfectly voluntary action," which describes cases in which people act in voluntary ways even though they do not readily or easily access the reasons behind those voluntary actions, as when someone follows a course of action by habit. Godwin crucially notes that in order to grasp such a case, we need to draw from "experience and history" rather than from an a priori rationalist system. He writes, if *all* actions were under the designation of purely "voluntary action,"

> the human mind would then be a very simple machine, always aware
> of the grounds upon which it proceeded, and self-deception would be
> impossible. But this statement is completely in opposition to experience
> and history. Ask a man the reason why he puts on his clothes, why he
> eats his dinner, or performs any other ordinary action of his life. He
> immediately hesitates, endeavours to recollect himself, and often assigns
> a reason the most remote from what the true philosophy of motive would
> have led us to expect. Nothing is more clear, than that the moving cause
> of this action was not expressly present to his apprehension at the time
> he performed it. Self-deception is so far from impossible, that it is one of
> the most ordinary phenomena with which we are acquainted. . . . Here
> then we are presented . . . with a striking instance of men's acting from
> motives diametrically opposite to those which they suppose to be the
> guides of their conduct. . . . Are not these facts in express contradiction
> to the doctrine, that the voluntary actions of men in all cases originate in
> the judgements of the understanding?[27]

Here "experience and history" teach us something new: man can acquire habits from social circumstances that go unquestioned and forgotten, and, as a result, men can act "from motives diametrically opposite to those which they suppose to be the guides of their conduct." This philosophical category gives shape to an experience that maintains the lived experience of contradiction not through any dramatic moment of akrasia, but through the necessary practice of abridgement so that "the understanding fixes for itself resting places" and does not need "continually to go back and revise the original reasons which determined it to a course of action." This is a philosophy of habit, which man can observe and recognize as wrong but still choose to ignore or neglect while proceeding against his better judgment. In this sense, Godwin's revised conception recalls Aristotle's conception of akrasia as "having knowledge in a sense and yet not having it, as in the instance of a man asleep, mad, or drunk" or acting upon "perceptual knowledge" rather than "knowledge proper," a conception that likewise involves a degree of inconsistency or contradiction at the level of the person.[28] Godwin's revised philosophy of action then begins to make room for something like akrasia. Taking these revisions seriously, we can read his second and third novels as expressly interested in "imperfectly voluntary action." Indeed, it is in his novels that we see Godwin taking particular interest in the subject of distempered action and with an up-close view on the "experience" of the intemperate, impatient, and impetuous. It is there that we find not just sustained and experimental explorations of the ethics and dynamics of this sort of action, but also the challenges of representing it in language.

St. Leon's attention to forms of self-deception and irrational action reflects Godwin's evolving interest in the less rational or predictable predilections of human mind and behavior. Still, in scenes like those discussed above, the notational form conveys the character at a distance with causes that can be explicated, thus removing any felt sense of divided agency in the character at the time of the action. In what is perhaps a growing realization that the human mind is a site that thwarts all pretensions for linguistic representational capacities, the novel occasionally proclaims that characterizing St. Leon's state is "impossible." "No reading of my story, no mere power of language and words," the narrator tells us at one point, "can enable a by-stander to imagine" his condition.[29] In one passage, the narrator's excessive descriptions appear to serve as compensation for what causal physical language ultimately can never do—convey how a person can be diametrically at odds with himself:

> No man who has not felt, can possibly image to himself the tortures of a
> gamester, of a gamester like me, who played for the improvement of his
> fortune, who played with the recollection of a wife and children dearer
> to him than the blood that bubbled through the arteries of his heart,
> who might be said, like the savages of ancient Germany, to make these
> relations the stake for which he threw, who saw all my own happiness
> and all theirs through the long vista of life, depending on the turn of a

card! . . . Never shall I cease to recollect the sensation I have repeatedly felt, in the instantaneous sinking of the spirits, the conscious fire that spread over my visage, the anger in my eye, the burning dryness of my throat, the sentiment that in a moment was ready to overwhelm with curses the cards, the stake, my own existence, and all mankind. How every malignant and insufferable passion seemed to rush upon my soul! . . . My mind was wrapped in a gloom that could not be pierced! My heart was oppressed with a weight that no power human or divine was equal to remove! My eyelids seemed to press downward with an invincible burden! My eyeballs were ready to start and crack their sockets! I lay motionless, the victim of ineffable horror![30]

Godwin paints an evocative scene of interior violence with striking physical and physiological descriptions ("conscious fire," the "anger in my eye, the burning dryness of my throat," "sentiment," "passion," "blood," "mind," "heart," "eyelids," "eyeballs"). The sentences notably depict St. Leon as the passive recipient of physical onslaughts ("seemed to rush upon my soul," "my mind was wrapped in gloom," "my heart was oppressed," "my eyelids seemed to press downward," "I lay motionless, the victim of ineffable horror!"). However, at the same time, the passage begins by noting that "no man who has not felt [the tortures of a gamester] can possibly image [them] to himself." It appears that Godwin's version of the scene of temptation and weakness of will indicates the limits of mere indirect speech. It is in his next novel that Godwin experiments with fusing indirect and direct speech in order to evoke the sense of a subject's failure.

Like *St. Leon, Fleetwood, or, the New Man of Feeling* centers on someone who holds beliefs and judgments that he regularly betrays in action. The first half of the novel (volume 1 and the first half of volume 2) describes Fleetwood's Rousseauvian education, his childhood years communing with nature, his education at Oxford, his life as a libertine in Paris, followed by sincere declarations of repentance at the errors of his ways, promising to live a more virtuous life. However, in volume 3, Fleetwood proves to be a suspicious and irritable husband to the young Mary Macneil, despite his awareness that his outbursts are wrong and unnecessary, almost ruining his marriage and nearly killing his spouse. As has been observed by other critics, the novel presents itself as an inversion of the novel of development and the sentimental novel genre (as indicated in the novel's subtitle, "The New Man of Feeling," a reference to Henry Mackenzie's 1771 *Man of Feeling*). Fleetwood's "upbringing," or *bildung*, results in a maladjusted adult, which, as Gary Handwerk has written, "marks the way in which its author seeks to map misogyny, tracing its origins to the whole framework of natural education" modeled by *Emile*.[31] One might observe it is a novel that begins by resembling Rousseau's *Emile* and ends by resembling Rousseau's *Confessions*.[32]

Indeed, more than *St. Leon* and more like Rousseau's *Confessions*, this novel leans into what philosopher Peter Goldie has called the "the ineluctable ironic gap" that arises in autobiographical memory, a gap "between internal and external perspective," making possible a "memory equivalent . . . of free indirect style."[33] The autobiographical style, like that we have already seen in Defoe, Sterne, and Godwin's *St. Leon*, necessarily involves a conflation of narrator's external (bird's-eye) view of the character and narrator's memory from the internal perspective of the character. With this novel, we can see how it is possible to augment the ironic capacities of this gap by foregrounding the internal perspective of the past-tense character by remaining in the narrational (external) mode, thereby displaying the "false" qualities of such a character without commenting on them from the perspective of the narrator.

Fleetwood's formal experimentations appear most notably in volume 3 after Fleetwood has married and is presented with the task of living amicably with his wife. At times, the novel veers closely to the techniques of *St. Leon* in which the narrator (present-tense Fleetwood) attributes distinct causes to past-tense Fleetwood's actions. "The reader must recollect my character, as an old bachelor, as a man endowed with the most irritable structure of nerves," he tells us at one point.[34] In this way, past-tense Fleetwood is intermittently presented as an object of knowledge whose tendency to act and react in given ways can be predicted by a set of physical conditions. However, more frequently, the novel presents Fleetwood's thoughts without supplemental explanation of the mental or bodily states that preceded them. In some cases, the novel depicts Fleetwood's erratic and anxious mind by presenting his thoughts as direct speech indicated by quotation marks. In one scene, Fleetwood discovers that the young Mr. Matthews has visited his house, which briefly sends Fleetwood into a spin of paranoia regarding Mary's fidelity. He then periodically tempers his suspicions with his certainty that Mary is innocent:

> At first I felt in the higher degree irritated against her behaviour. "What chance," said I, "have we for happiness, if, supposing me to be in the wrong,—it is impossible I should be wrong!—she, instead of soothing my weakness, thus answers me with taunting and retort?"
>
> Soon, however, I came to see the subject in a different light. "Fleetwood! Fleetwood!" said I, striking my forehead with my hand, "what is it you are doing? I have entered upon a serious and weighty task, the guardianship of the felicity of a young woman, who, without reserve, or defence, or refuge against me, has thrown herself into my power. What engagements did I form to her father! with how solemn protestations did I undertake to remove all uncertainty from his mind! . . . Look upon this young creature! Soft, and tender, and winning as she is, shall I be her destroyer? Do I doubt her innocence? Truth and honour are written in her front, in characters which folly itself cannot mistake. . . . What a brute am I, to misuse, and give uneasiness to so much excellence! I will throw myself at her feet, and with tears of anguish confess to her my fault."
>
> Full of these sentiments of remorse, I hastened back by the way I came, and entered the house.[35]

In this passage, Fleetwood's inner disputes are vocalized and can thus be portrayed as reportable actions. This strategy allows Godwin to evoke the scene of internal conflict while borrowing from the tools of theater, insofar as the mode of soliloquy proves particularly fruitful for expressing the dilemma of a self-loathing state. Godwin here is likely inspired by Shakespeare, whose weak-willed protagonists offer rich models as they reflect through soliloquy on their own failures. Fleetwood's "What a brute am I" echoes Hamlet's "O, what a rogue and peasant slave am I": Godwin recognizes the dramatic irony of characters who muse aloud on matters of the self that ought to be fully under one's control.

However, *Fleetwood* is a novel and not a stage drama: Godwin's internal dialogue through quotation marks indeed reads not as a conflict before our eyes, but as a past-tense series of events bracketed with the words "said I." Elsewhere in volume 3, the novel presents past-tense Fleetwood's thoughts, but does so without the use of quotation marks, instead moving seamlessly between the voice of present-tense Fleetwood-the-narrator into the mind of past-tense Fleetwood-the-character. In one of many such instances, Fleetwood grows angry with Mary for requesting the chance to attend social gatherings and make acquaintances of her age: "Our discussion terminated in the formal churching, and the commencement of a tremendous series of wedding visits. Artful hussy! In the way she put it to me, could I refuse? Could I refuse a thing upon which, in this mild and specious temper of mind, her heart appeared to be set?—I wrong her. There was no art in what she did; it was all the most adorable ingenuousness and sincerity."[36] The transition between the first sentence, simply the narrator's description of events, to the second sentence ("Artful hussy!") proceeds, to quote Monika Fludernik, "without any noticeable shifting of gears."[37] We have moved to what appears to be the interior direct speech of past-tense Fleetwood without quotation marks. As we continue, however, the absence of quotation marks or the accompanying phrases "I said" or "I thought" allows the possibility that we are reading the exclamations of the narrator. The following sentences ("In the way she put it to me, could I refuse? Could I refuse a thing upon which, in this mild and specious temper of mind, her heart appeared to be set?—I wrong her") can be read as either the unquoted direct speech of the past-tense character, the exclamations of the present-tense narrator, or as shifting back and forth between the two. The ambiguity becomes particularly pronounced with the dash and the sentence "I wrong her." Have we shifted from a depiction of past-tense character's effusions to the present-tense narrator expressing regret at his narrative choices? Are we remaining with the erratic voice of the intemperate past-tense character throughout? Or are we with the voice of the present-tense narrator, who is himself adopting the erratic qualities of the character he is seeking to depict?

This convergence of the narrator's and character's voices allows a new sense of the narrator's sympathy for the character, as if the narrator is prepared to relive and reembody the state of mind of his former self. However, with this sympathy then comes a new sense of irony, "throw[ing] into ironic relief all false notes struck by a figural mind," as Dorrit Cohn writes.[38] Throughout volume 3, Godwin employs further strategies for conflating the perspectives of narrator and character in order to convey Fleetwood's "false notes," which come through often when we are told that past-tense Fleetwood was "incapable" of doing or thinking otherwise. Volume 3 begins with one such scene, in which Fleetwood grows furious with Mary while simultaneously acknowledging the overdetermined and ultimately unjustified nature of his anger. Fleetwood has introduced Mary to his mansion for the first time, and in touring the house, she selects a closet that she would like to have for herself. However, Fleetwood had privately cherished the closet, hoping it would remain his own. In what he recognizes is overcompensating frustration, he takes a walk in his garden and mulls over his situation:

> I will go, and tell Mary what she has done. I will confess to her all my weakness. Nothing could be further from her thought than to occasion me this disturbance, and it will afford her the purest pleasure to repair it.
>
> May I perish, if ever I breathe a syllable on the subject! What, shall I paint me thus pitiful and despicable in her eyes? Shall I tell her, that I love nobody but myself, and regard her gratifications with indifference? I will not tell her so! . . .
>
> I was incapable, however, of passing a just judgment in the case, and the transaction had an unfavourable effect upon my mind."[39]

The final sentence ("I was incapable, however, of passing a just judgment in the case") might look at first like a plainly indirect instance of speech—a notation of the thought—from the voice of the narrator. However, the claim appears particularly dubious in the light of the internal monologue we have just read. For one thing, because we have just read the conscious deliberations of the character's mind, we see that Fleetwood was indeed quite "capable" of "passing a just judgment in the case," even though he did not. Further, because we have just immersed ourselves (without quotation marks) in past-tense Fleetwood's consciousness, the narrator appears sufficiently capable of embodying and performing the character's language. Thus, as we saw in the four-word sentence from *Emma,* "I was incapable . . . of passing a just judgment" presents itself in something like a first-person retrospective FID: it appears to be a sentence that performs what past-tense Fleetwood would say to himself ("I am incapable of passing a just judgment"). As in the case of Emma, we then read this latter phrase as a way of saying, "I will not pass a just judgment, but I say I am incapable of it so I feel less guilty about not passing a just judgment."

Over the course of volume 3, it becomes increasingly unclear whether Fleetwood means to present his self-deceptions repentantly (as in *St. Leon*) or to reproduce them performatively. In a moment of calm after several of Fleetwood's vicious outbursts, he reflects upon the character of his wife, Mary:

> Deeply in love as I was, I could not help speculating, with no agreeable reflections, from the new lights I had derived on the character of my wife. Fickle and capricious I judged her; and, thus judging, I could not avoid sometimes viewing her under the notion of a beautiful toy, a plume of costly feathers, or a copious train of thinnest gauze, which nods gracefully, or floats in a thousand pleasing folds, but which is destitute of substance, firmness, or utility. There must be something, I thought, radically defective in so fluctuating a character. She acted (thus I construed her demeanour) inconsiderately and idly; she could be induced to no fixed spirit of attention; she was at one moment sunk in the lowest depths of misery, and at another wild with extravagant gaiety, with no interval to qualify the transition, with no self-government to give propriety or moderation to either. A being acting thus, was it entitled to be ranked in the scale of moral existences? What dependence could be placed upon the consistency of any thing so versatile? What principles could dwell in the bosom of so mere a woman?[40]

We may begin to read this passage as a distanced retrospective notation of a character's thoughts. However, as it proceeds, the narrator increasingly inhabits past-tense Fleetwood's consciousness. The first three sentences tell us how Fleetwood "speculat[ed]," "judged," and "view[ed]" her. Then it continues, "There must be something, I thought, radically defective in so fluctuating a character. She acted (thus I construed her demeanour) inconsiderately and idly; she could be induced to no fixed spirit of attention." Here the modifier "I thought" moves from being a part of the core grammatical sentence toward being embedded within parentheses as "(thus I construed her demeanour)." Eventually, the notations of past-tense Fleetwood's thoughts disappear entirely, as the clauses following semicolons are no longer given a speaker. This produces new ambiguities regarding the levels of awareness available to both the character and the narrator. The sentence that ends the paragraph—"What principles could dwell in the bosom of so mere a woman?"—leaves open the question whether the narrator, out of sympathy, continues to voice such questions himself, or if it is the unquoted direct speech of the past-tense character. Given this ambiguity, some earlier sentences in the paragraph also present new questions: "Fickle and capricious I judged her; and, thus judging, I could not avoid sometimes viewing her under the notion of a beautiful toy." We may ask, Which Fleetwood here is doing the judging? Who is doing the viewing? As we do as the narrator does and "judge" and "view" the character and the narrator together, we recognize not only that his observations of his wife are divorced from reality, but also that they accurately describe himself. "Fickle," "capricious," "radically defective," "fluctuating," "inconsiderate," "idle," "no fixed spirit of attention," "no self-government to give propriety or moderation": Fleetwood is building a fictional picture of Mary as a way of justifying his inattention to himself.

In wavering between perspectives and allowing various moral interpretations, Godwin's third novel opens itself up to the sorts of troubles discussed at the start of chapter 2—namely, the worry that, in maintaining the sense of a character's akrasia, the character is troublingly underexplained and thus implausible. Indeed, this was the view of a number of readers and critics upon the novel's publication who complained that the character of Casimir Fleetwood was "insufficiently motivated" and "implausible."[41] Walter Scott wrote in the *Edinburgh Review* in 1805 that Fleetwood is quite simply a "selfish madman" to whom we cannot relate.[42] The *Anti-Jacobin Review and Magazine* wrote that "some of these adventures are such, we are persuaded, as never occurred to a human being . . . while the sentiments and actions ascribed to the principal character, are, in many cases, not only extravagant, but ridiculous."[43] We might say that, for these readers, Fleetwood had betrayed Fielding's principle of "conservation of character"; the character's actions did not cohere. Godwin had sought to write an "under-motivated" character in the mold of an akratic, truer to the kinds of "imperfectly voluntary action" he articulated in the second edition to *Political Justice*, but "under-motivated" can also be considered a failure on the part of the novelist. How to write an "under-motivated" character in the sense that the illogical, broken, unaccountable features of a person feel plausible or true—this was one of Godwin's tasks, and evidently it would endure as a formal challenge.

Indeed, like Godwin's critics, we may be unsure what to make of the scene in which Fleetwood is full of unreasonable jealousy after a public dance and lashes out at Mary: "I felt irresistibly prompted to avenge my sorrows by inveighing against the neighbourhood, the evening."[44] The words "I felt irresistibly prompted" again offer several interpretations. We may read this imprecision as a mark of Godwin's shortcomings as a novelist. Alternatively, we could observe the ambiguity as essential to the novel's effects: it is phrased just so that it may be interpreted either as an irresistible compulsion or as a free and intentional act operating on the false excuse that it is based in an irresistible compulsion. The words "I felt" can be read in the indirect mode of past-tense "matter-of-fact notation" that indicates that a "feeling" arrived to him (he as the passive recipient) by "irresistible prompts." At the same time, "I felt" not only allows this passive meaning, but also the phenomenological meaning of "I felt as if." We may then read the sentence as a free indirect performance of past-tense Fleetwood's mind, as he might say to himself, "I feel *as if* I am irresistibly prompted," implying then that he is not actually irresistibly prompted.

In such instances, Godwin experiments with a technique that would prove increasingly fundamental for Austen and the nineteenth-century novel form: a technique that seeks to capture the sense of internal personal conflict by momentarily inhabiting the perspective of the character in order to present without explicitly explaining or commenting upon the insufficient or unjustifiable qualities of the character's thoughts. If Godwin can help us see the emergence of FID as a representational response to a formal and epistemological problem, then Austen can help us think more about the grammatical logic by which this device gives shape to open-eyed irrationality.

AUSTEN

Unlike Godwin's novels, *Emma* has long been at the center of critical discussions on FID. Insofar as Austen's novels are told in third-person omniscient narration rather than first-person retrospective narration, their usage of FID fits the more traditional definition of the formal device. Further, Austen's dips into FID register as considerably more controlled and decisive. This has allowed it to be interpreted in a range of ways, including as a tool for the novel's control over its moral arc (Wayne C. Booth), as a stand-in for the social discourse of "gossip" (Casey Finch and Peter Bowen), as a representation of the mediation between character and social consciousness (Frances Ferguson), or as the flaunting of a certain kind of authorial "Style" (D. A. Miller).[45] Interpreting FID as a tool for representing a divided and self-conflicting consciousness does not minimize its significance in any of these other senses, but it does suggest one important ability and role for this technique in this novel and in novels after Austen: the ability to depict people who tell themselves they cannot help but do something.

All of Austen's novels are centrally concerned with the themes of forbearance and restraint, but among her protagonists, Emma Woodhouse stands out in the sense that she does not always successfully refrain from doing what she (at some level) knows she shouldn't do. Another way of saying this is that Emma knows better. This "knowingness," which we can distinguish from the "unknowingness" we have seen attributed by Patricia Meyer Spacks to Eliza Haywood's heroines, means that Emma is more clearly a figure that invites us to think about guilt and, relatedly, forgiveness. Emma is not just "handsome" and "rich," as the first sentence tells us, but also "clever." Besides being socially intelligent and perceptive, Emma is in many aspects of her life wise, caring, and genuinely kind, and it is precisely these qualities that make Emma's minor crimes so hurtful. To quote Ferguson, "The novel is hard on Emma to exactly the same extent

that it is committed to her. Moreover, it is hard on her *because of* this at-
tachment. . . . The novelist makes Emma's blameworthiness inseparable
from her privileged position."[46]

We also know that Emma *can* forbear, because we have seen her do
it. We see this when Mr. John Knightley arrives to Highbury and offers
brusque and unpleasant remarks, often breaking the peace with Mr.
Woodhouse and others. In one scene he offers some offhandedly down-
putting remarks about Mr. Weston, which prompts the following characterization of Emma: "Emma could not like what bordered on a reflection
on Mr. Weston, and had half a mind to take it up; but she struggled, and let
it pass. She would keep the peace if possible."[47] The phrase "she struggled,
and let it pass" reads as plain indirect matter-of-fact notation rather than
free indirect discourse. However, there would be no different reading of
Emma either way, because there is no failure, and thus no cause for deception. For this reason, a performance of Emma's consciousness falls in
line with an external description. Emma would say the truth to herself in
this moment: she could, and does, resist. We also know from early on that
Emma is able to recognize the goods of forbearance, patience, and self-
control. This recognition is especially brought out in Emma's relationships
to Miss and Mrs. Bates, through her various visits to their home. Emma
"knew she was considered by the very few who presumed ever to see im-
perfection in her, as rather negligent in that respect [in paying the Bates's
due attention], and as not contributing what she ought to the stock of their
scanty comforts."[48] The story of Emma's ability—or choice—to forbear is
told over the course of the novel through her visits to the Bates household
and culminates, as we have seen, in the line delivered during the scene at
Box Hill, "Emma could not resist."

At the same time, if the story of Emma is the story of increasing though
inconsistent forbearance, we can see forbearance as the defining trait of
her foil, the unfailingly consistent Jane Fairfax. "Her sensibilities, I suspect, are strong," Mr. Knightley remarks about Fairfax, "and her temper
excellent in its power of forbearance, patience, self-control."[49] Fairfax is
the anti-Emma if only in the sense that she endures the entirety of the
novel's agonizing developments without saying or doing what she knows
she should not.

Indeed, *Emma* is not a novel that is as interested in the difference between what Emma "knows" and "does not know" as it is interested in the slippage between what Emma "allows herself to see," and what she "declines to see." The novel knows there is a difference between seeing and allowing oneself to see: one cannot fault someone for not seeing, but one can fault someone for having been able to see something, yet, at some level, choosing not to. Emma's akrasia is unlike St. Leon's or Fleetwood's in this sense, because it arises on this more minute scale of perception and acknowledgement, or what Amélie Rorty has characterized as "akrasia of belief."[50] Indeed, Emma's errors based on outright ignorance carry far less moral weight than those in which we feel that she could have and ought to have seen things differently. The pain felt by the reader when Emma urges Harriet Smith to turn down Mr. Martin's marriage proposal can be attributed to the fact that Emma ought to have seen that Harriet and Mr. Martin were right for each other, and, further, that she was *capable* of seeing that. She would have allowed herself to see it had she not been so consumed with taking up a project that was so "highly becoming her own [Emma's] situation in life, her leisure, and powers."[51] On the other hand, the pain that Emma causes Jane Fairfax by mindlessly flirting with Frank Churchill is not felt to be quite as cruel, and that is at least partly because Emma does not know she is causing Fairfax pain. To be sure, there are reasons to be annoyed by her and Frank's careless behavior in these scenes, but it is not clear that Emma *ought* to have seen that Jane and Frank are secretly engaged in the same way or to the same degree that she ought to have seen that Mr. Martin was the right match for Harriet.

In several moments of sustained FID, we indeed can see the "knowing" qualities of Emma's consciousness due to the strategically crafted nature of her internal utterances. In one of the first sustained dips into FID in the novel, we shift into Emma's rationale for why she should attend to Harriet Smith. What we find here are a series of sentences that demonstrate a self-justifying psychology, assertions that imply degrees of self-deception:

> Encouragement should be given. Those soft blue eyes and all those
> natural graces should not be wasted on the inferior society of Highbury
> and its connections. The acquaintance she had already formed were

unworthy of her. The friends from whom she had just parted, though very good sort of people, must be doing her harm. . . . *She* would notice her; she would improve her; she would detach her from her bad acquaintance, and introduce her into good society; she would form her opinions and her manners. It would be an interesting, and certainly a very kind undertaking; highly becoming her own situation in life, her leisure, and powers.[52]

It would be easy to read this passage as reflecting the ways in which Emma is simply wrong—wrong in her judgments about Harriet and the Martins. But the sentences' overdetermined emphases reveal that on some level Emma is trying to convince herself so she can proceed with what she wants to do: take Harriet on as a project. This involves boosting the reasons for doing so and neglecting the reasons for not doing so. The sentences register as crafted and strategic by words such as "should" and "must." The task is "highly becoming," the words chosen not to express Emma's wish that she looks good to the outer world, but that she looks good to herself. The final sentence emphasizes the nature of the self-utterance as excuse: "It would be an interesting, and certainly a very kind undertaking." Here the word presented first, "interesting," as if it were temporally first in her own internal utterance, appears the more accurate one, but it is promptly modified with the word she would prefer to attach to herself—"kind." These sorts of phrasings show us a calculating mind who is putting words together to convince herself.

In a sentence like "Encouragement should be given," then, we see how the two possible readings of this sentence—first as performance and then as narration—map onto Emma's consciousness as deceiver and deceived. In this sense, it presents what Ann Banfield has called the tendency of FID to evoke the flip sides of consciousness—"reflective consciousness," or the "active faculty capable of forming and producing [the ideas of sensible things]" and "non-reflective consciousness," or the "passive faculty of perception, that is, of receiving and recognizing [those ideas]."[53] It performs how Emma might think to herself, "Encouragement should be given," a rationale devised on the level of reflective consciousness and meant to deceive herself, and it represents the thought "Encouragement should be given," which deceives her on the level of her nonreflective consciousness, because it is presented as a fact (and is grammatically confusable for the narrator's authoritative voice). Likewise, the final sentence, "It would be an interesting, and certainly a very kind undertaking; highly becoming her own situation in life, her leisure, and powers," risks appearing like a narrator's description and can possibly convince the reader: this suits Emma's purposes, because this is how she would like to be read. Here too FID works to put forward the red herring reading of plain indirect speech in order to give cover for proceeding. FID thus performs the mode of self-deception and highlights the distinctively conscious and crafted nature of the character's thought process. In this sense, a passage like the one above "throw[s] into ironic relief all false notes struck by a figural mind," but not merely because the notes are "false" by nature of being incorrect, but by nature of being purposely false, or falsified.[54]

If Emma's fault of willful blindness can be seen in the FID formulation of "Encouragement should be given" (with respect to Harriet), and her fault of willful negligence can be seen in the FID formulation of "Emma could not resist" (with respect to Miss Bates), then her fault of willful resentment can be seen in the phrase "Emma could not forgive her" (with respect to Jane Fairfax). As already discussed, D. A. Miller understands the sentence, which repeats on either side of the chapter break of volume 2's chapters 2 and 3, as able to be read in its first instantiation as a FID performance of the character's consciousness and then in the second as a plain indirect speech "matter-of-fact notation of the thought." Frances Ferguson rightly describes Miller's reading as quasi-musical: "We realize that we are no longer in a world of examples that can be explained in purely grammatical terms. Position—on one side or the other of the chapter break—has become tone."[55] However, it is worth pausing over the necessary grammatical implications of such a sentence. Banfield writes about FID, "In language is already contained—as part of what language knows—the very distinction that philosophy seeks to make explicit between reflection, Descartes' *cogito,* the 'I am thinking' whereby the subject knows that he knows, and the other conscious states which underlie it and may never be reflected upon."[56] To read this line's repetition less musically and more grammatically would prompt us to acknowledge that there is a semantically necessary ironic doubling effect in *each* instantiation of the sentence, regardless of the context. After all, there is no reading of "Emma could not forgive her" that logically makes sense as plain indirect speech. Put another way, there is no way to understand Emma as *actually* incapable of forgiveness. One of the important things this novel knows is that forgiveness is a capacity of the will. (Emma may not know many things about Jane Fairfax at this point and time in the novel, which may be frustrating for her, but she certainly knows enough to release her resentment.) Miller suggests that the second iteration of the sentence pops up as "a little bit of information for the plot," but that cannot be exactly right, for this sentence cannot be correct: it must also be voiced and, in some sense, ironic. It must be seen, then, as delivered tongue-in-cheek to some degree, holding on to the irony of the previous chapter before letting it go with the turn to focus on Mr. Knightley. In other words, Emma could forgive her before the chapter break, and she could forgive her after the chapter break.

This ironic capacity of this sentence only comes through once we credit the essential role of forgiveness as correlated with choice in this novel.[57] It is important to know that Emma could forgive her. As we have seen, Emma is a character who is perceptive and clever; she is also a character who is open to changing. The novel narrates a character's development into someone who no longer occludes from herself the sorts of realities that would impair her ego, and with respect to Jane Fairfax, into someone who no longer carries resentment. In these ways, she bears similarities to the character M from Iris Murdoch's narrative example in "The Idea of Perfection" (1964) discussed in chapter 1. M, we might recall, dislikes her daughter-in-law D, but undergoes a shift prompted by a shift in attention: "M tells herself: 'I am old-fashioned and conventional. I may be prejudiced and narrow-minded. I may be snobbish. I am certainly jealous. Let me look again.'"[58] Looking again is a minor act. It is on some quiet level a choice. Both Murdoch and Austen recognize the difficulty of explicating such a phenomenon in notational causal language. For Murdoch, this type of interior shift in attitude is unobservable by her philosophical contemporaries (particularly, empiricism and behaviorism). For Austen, it is conveyed in her novel through the slow disappearance of FID until its ironic functions are no longer necessary, and reflective consciousness and nonreflective consciousness are joined. In this way, too, both writers take on these themes of hardness of heart and weakness of will but not within the Christian paradigm that had previously provided their conceptual scaffolding. If, in an earlier moment, that weakness was conveyed as "spiritual sickness" through the language of "clouds and thick darkness," for Austen, and later for Murdoch, these phenomena are conveyed by the privileges of narrative's formal equipment.

In chapter 4, we shift our focus from prose fiction to various forms of "life writing"—specifically, the periodical essays of Samuel Johnson and the autobiography of Jean-Jacques Rousseau. Johnson and Rousseau are two writers who documented their own difficulties doing what they know they should do. In doing so, they offer up a historically distinct mode of writing about a self, one that refuses causal explanation as the suitable mode of giving an account of oneself and instead prioritizes the value of ongoing and never-foreclosed *interpretation*. This approach produces a distinctly literary kind of writing that is also an improvement upon the contemporaneous philosophy at least in the sense that it allows these writers to credit and investigate what they take to be an important feature of human experience—namely, open-eyed irrationality.

4

AKRASIA, LIFE WRITING, AND INTERPRETATION

Johnson and Rousseau

WHAT COUNTS AS AN explanation for laziness? Why even seek an explanation—would it help? In the comic strip below, Nancy asks the same question twice, once aloud to herself, not expecting an answer, and the second time into a search engine, as if hoping to find an explanation.[1] Her text is likely met with autofill options and a prepared set of suggestions for articles like "The Procrastination Gene" from the *New Yorker* (2014) or "The Science Behind Our Urge to Procrastinate" from the Huffington Post (2017).[2] The comedy of the strip comes from the fact that the search for

Nancy © 2019, reprinted by permission of Andrews Mcmeel Syndication for UFS; all rights reserved

explanation occurs with an already formed understanding that no useful explanation can be given, and, doubly, that the search itself exemplifies the attitude she is bemoaning. No such explanation is possible here, as she well knows, because no "explainer" piece could get to the fact that it is *she,* not a gene or a neuron or a reflex, that does the staring, the typing, the staring, the typing. The condition is hers, and she knows it. Nonetheless, while she may not find an explanation, she does something by articulating the condition to herself. The speech bubble in the left frame—the question spoken aloud—is itself, if not an explanation, an account, a testament, and so, in its own way, a gesture toward understanding.

This sort of representation of one who knowingly partakes in what one knows one should not appears 1,600 years before *Nancy* in the *Confessions* of Augustine who writes, "Grant me chastity and continence . . . but please, not yet!"[3] The appeal here to a transcendent God as the source of strength comes with the suppressed understanding that the strength of the will must partly come from himself and, further, with the acknowledgement that he does not want on one level what he is asking for on another. The utterance then can appear to us as taking the shape of a joke, in which the "wish" statement is immediately revealed as ironic, negating itself in the sentence's formulation. Yet the activity of writing in both cases—Nancy typing her question, and Augustine as author writing the *Confessions*—seems to offer, not just knowing defeat, but also possibility for deliverance through expressing that defeat. One can indeed imagine Nancy "writing through" her condition by taking to Facebook. "What are you thinking?" the status box prompts. For the procrastinator, this is a trap and an opportunity. It may be that writing about oneself is to continue to fall prey to the uroboros of procrastination. Or it may be that it offers a way out, and that the only way out is in.

In the eighteenth century, we can identify a historically distinctive approach to writing about one's own akratic condition. In the work of two well-known figures in European literature and philosophy in particular, Samuel Johnson and Jean-Jacques Rousseau, we can see the beginnings of a new attitude toward what it would mean to "understand" akrasia. The understanding here is not through an explicit appeal to a spiritually weak will—although Christian morality is important for both figures—nor is it through the kind of causal analysis of minds and bodies that defined the epistemology of the Enlightenment philosophers discussed in chapter 1. For both Johnson and Rousseau, to write about the ways one knowingly and intentionally and freely betrays oneself in action means to adopt a different idea of "explanation" altogether—one that is intrinsically narrative, with an investment in character, and that invites an active, open-ended, and ongoing engagement from the reader. This is not a retreat from the wish for understanding. As in the case of Nancy above, the practice of writing may not allow irrationality to be solved or resolved, but it does allow it to become visible and, in an important way, legible. In this respect, Johnson and Rousseau both can be (and have been) seen as conceptual predecessors to Freudian analysis, which calls for continual reexamination of conflicts. This mode of approaching a person is aligned with a mode of approaching a written text: both contain conflicts that call for attention, not solution, and this itself brings a kind of knowledge, one that, as I hope to show, gets Johnson and Rousseau to preserve and interrogate akrasia in ways their contemporaraneous metaphysicians do not.

The name of the mode of knowing that best fits what I have described above is "interpretation." Although, classically, the idea of interpretive practice meant something like exegesis—decoding or translating an authoritative text through the disclosure of a hidden meaning—what Johnson and Rousseau are doing resembles something closer to the more modern use of the word that began to take shape with the work of Friedrich Schleiermacher in the early 1800s: a discursive and dialogic process with any text that can illuminate and disclose but never finish the work of understanding.[4] Later writers who would take up the science of interpretation known as "hermeneutics," like Wilhelm Dilthey, Martin Heidegger, and Hans-Georg Gadamer in the late nineteenth through the mid-twentieth centuries, would expound upon the circular conversational practice of understanding as it applies not merely to texts but also to questions around ontology, epistemology, and aesthetics. In different ways, for these later philosophers, hermeneutics allows one to attend to the limitations of a methodology that aims for conclusive knowledge about the factic or ontic realm (as that of the modern natural sciences) by instead attending to the necessarily situated, practical, and dialogic conditions of the knowledge encounter.[5] Staying attuned to the conversational quality of understanding a text means staying attuned to both what is "given" and what one "gives," as well as the fact that the relation between the two is ongoing. Although it is not my aim to propose a concrete genealogical line from Johnson and Rousseau to these later philosophers, the hermeneutic tradition can help us articulate what it might mean to engage in an open-ended way with a written work in a historical context in which a different methodological approach to understanding is seen as privileged. In the eighteenth century, instances of something like akrasia, of acting intentionally against reason, highlight the need for an inconclusive mode of inquiry in writing.

In Johnson's periodical essays from the *Rambler* (1750–52) and the *Idler* (1758–60), and in Rousseau's *The Confessions* (completed in 1770, published between 1782 and 1789), we see examinations of akrasia as motivating the need for an *interpretive* as opposed to mathematical, decompositional, or causally explicable modes of approaching a person and a text. It is a practice significantly inspired by Augustine's *Confessions*, but in a different key and for a different moment. Both Johnson and Rousseau have been described by twentieth-century theorists in somewhat sweeping ways as modern inventors of interiority that have inherited qualities of Augustine's interiority and set the stage for a figure like Freud. Walter Jackson Bate, for instance, has described Johnson as an example of someone who "concretely and dramatically exemplifies the Augustinian tradition of individualism and 'interiority'—that 'it is within the soul itself that man must search for truth and certitude' (*in interiore homine habitat veritas*)."[6] He also emphasizes Johnson's connections to Freudian "depths of interiority": "as in no other classical moralist," Bate writes, "we have a profound anticipation of what was to be the wide-scale nineteenth- and twentieth-century discovery about the mind that went on from the major Romantics down through the clinical exploration of the unconscious that follows Freud."[7] It is an attitude taken toward the mind that comes through particularly vividly in Johnson's portrayals of self-betrayal and self-deception: "His clairvoyant sense of the complex 'treachery of the human heart,' and its capacity to destroy both its own peace and its own perception of reality, provides an anticipation of Freud. . . . The part of Johnson that really anticipates psychoanalysis . . . is to be found in Johnson's studied and sympathetic sense of both inner 'resistance' and what in psychoanalysis are called 'defense mechanisms,' or, in Johnson's phrase, 'the stratagems of self-defence.'"[8] We see these sorts of characterizations about Rousseau as well; his indebtedness to Augustine is even more obvious, given the title of his autobiography, and claims as to his status as inventor of modern interiority even more common.[9] Peter Brooks has explicitly connected Rousseau's writing and rewriting about his guilty acts to Freud's concepts of "denial" and "denegation";[10] he writes about the episodes of Rousseau's confusing actions recounted in his work,

> No analytic moral logic will give the answer to the question, why did I behave that way? . . . Questions such as these cannot be addressed—as they might have been earlier in Rousseau's century—by a *portrait moral,* a kind of analytic topography of a person. The question of identity, claims Rousseau—and this is what makes him at least symbolically the *incipit* of modern narrative—can be thought only in narrative terms, in the effort to tell a whole life, to plot its meaning by going back over it to record its perpetual flight forward, its slippage from the fixity of definition.[11]

Rousseau's reflections on his behaviors require an understanding in narrative terms that opens itself up to "the effort" to convey meaning "by going back over it" and recording "its slippage from the fixity of definition."

Rather than seeking to make a broad claim about these figures as inheritors of Augustine's interiority or progenitors of Freudian analysis, my aim here is to focus on the particular structure of akrasia as a figure that calls for a distinctive approach to understanding a person through writing. Hence my focus will be restricted to the episodes of something like "intentional irrationality" in both of these writers, contrasting these cases with engagements in Augustine as well as in and Enlightenment philosophy. In Johnson's case, these meditations are mostly on the condition of akratic *in*action—indolence, procrastination, torpor, lassitude. In this respect, they will set us up for the poetry of indolence and procrastination to be considered in chapter 5. In Rousseau's case, we will focus on some of his most famous "crimes," widely discussed scenes that raise questions about authorial intention while also demanding to be seen as exemplifications of undermotivated or underjustified intentional actions.

Rousseau requires special mention as this book's only non-English author. His sustained engagements with the philosophers in question and, even more significantly, his profound influence through *The Confessions* in particular on English novelists and poets—for instance, Godwin's novels considered in chapter 3 and Wordsworth's autobiographical poetry considered in chapter 5—necessarily puts him at the center of our story about akrasia and English literature in the long eighteenth century. Indeed, there is probably no other major eighteenth-century work that is so explicitly concerned with akrasia as Rousseau's *Confessions*. Insofar as it is a first-person retrospective narrative focused on guilty actions, Rousseau's autobiography also picks up on some of the observations we have made thus far in chapters 2 and 3 with regard to Defoe's *Robinson Crusoe* and *Moll Flanders*, Sterne's *A Sentimental Journey*, and Godwin's *St. Leon* and *Fleetwood* (the latter two, written after *The Confessions*, were in ways inspired by it).[12] While we find some similar ambiguities and ironies in *The Confessions* as we found in *A Sentimental Journey* and *Fleetwood*, Rousseau's text allows us to perceive the particular problems that arise for an author who seeks to write truthfully about himself.

JOHNSON

In *The Life of Samuel Johnson*, James Boswell writes about his subject, "For though indolence and procrastination were inherent in his constitution, whenever he made an exertion he did more than any one else."[13] This comment seems to get at the surprising clash between the extraordinary scope and quantity of Johnson's achievements and his reputation as one of English literature's most famous procrastinators. As Sarah Jordan has put it, Johnson's tendencies toward indolence and procrastination are inherently connected to boredom and insomnia, creating a "vicious circle": "One reason idleness is so hard to escape is that it leads to boredom (for which Johnson had a great capacity), which causes an indolence that prevents occupation, which leads to even greater boredom and indolence"; these are connected too to "Johnson's late rising . . . : his insomnia led to late sleeping, which made him accomplish little during the day and therefore feel guilty; this guilt then kept him from sleeping at night."[14]

Johnson's tendencies appear idiosyncratic, but when we consider the particularities of his condition, we can also understand him as a product of his time. This is a period in English history that witnessed the growth of a new middle class, which meant a new widespread experience of leisure and its sister condition, idleness. J. H. Plumb has described these changes in the terms of the new availability of a "leisure industry" (beach resorts, sporting events, musical entertainment) brought about by "growing affluence in eighteenth-century British society."[15] Necessarily, with increasing affluence for this class comes the anxiety that, as Benjamin Franklin put it, "time is money," which means that to "spend" one's time in a state of leisure is to be wasting it, or at least not spending it profitably.[16] Thus we see a historically specific version of indolence, one that is not quite the same as older sloth or acedia. Traditionally, sloth had been understood as a monastic vice, pertaining to neglect of spiritual duties, and in a Stoic tradition appears as the opposite of "fortitude." In Aquinas's thirteenth-century definition, sloth—as one of the seven deadly sins—is "sorrow for spiritual good" (or "an aversion from man's *spiritual* good") and "negligence" with respect to good works.[17] What we are beginning to see in the eighteenth century is a shift in inaction away from the spiritual connotations of sloth as "falling away" from the world toward notions of laziness as "falling behind" in time. This mode of inaction is more specifically about a body physically still but in a state of regret with regard to time's linear flow. "Indolence," which had originally meant "indifference to pain," increasingly comes to mean "state of rest" and then, as epitomized in James Thomson's *Castle of Indolence,* a sense of "laziness."[18] The word "procrastination" too sees a sharp uptick at around 1750 as well; the word, deriving from the Latin "pro-" (putting off) and "crastinus" (to tomorrow), begins to appear in English writing in the seventeenth century, but it is in the stretch between approximately 1750 to 1820 that it begins to be used with more regularity.[19] "Idleness" takes on different connotations as well; as Willard Spiegelman has shown, it begins to be medicalized, as in Robert Burton's *Anatomy of Melancholy (1621),* where it is described as "the *malus genius* of our nation."[20] Together, "indolence," "procrastination," and "idleness" can all be distinguished from the older conceptions of sloth or acedia, both of which are more overtly moralistic and pertaining to sin, but also more isolated and not quite as banal, ordinary, and everyday as these newer notions. What these changing definitions reveal is that in this period the mind and body are increasingly conceived in linear-temporal terms, and the akratic version of indolence is now a causal "blip," a puzzle, that a logical rearrangement of parts could help explain and solve.

For a writer like Johnson, this condition demands something different than the confessional form inherited from the Augustinian model that conceives of laziness as sloth or spiritual lack. It also demands something different from the naturalistic philosophical approach inherited from Locke or the medical sciences that can solve disorganization by either explaining it systematically or offering a diagnosis and prescription. A different knowledge practice is required, which means a different relationship between the writer and the subject.

The periodical essays of the 1750s are continually obsessed with themes like weakness of will and self-deception. As Paul Alkon has noted, these themes appear earlier in his career with the *Life of Mr. Richard Savage* (1744), where Johnson "observes that Savage 'was always able to live at peace with himself' by refusing to admit the part played by his own faults in bringing about many of the misfortunes that overwhelmed him. . . . After describing some of the ways in which Savage managed to avoid admitting—even to himself—what he was really like, Johnson observes that 'arts like these' are in fact 'arts which every man practises in some degree, and to which too much of the little tranquillity of life is to be ascribed.'"[21] If Johnson's sentiments as a moralist come through in the biography, it is in the periodical essays that we can see the condition most consistently and interestingly investigated. Indeed, as Bate has observed, these essays could themselves be understood as "arts" of self-distraction, for they provided Johnson "the opportunity . . . to defer other and more demanding work"; as Bate continues, "Johnson himself said that the *Rambler* had been written 'by way of relief' from his work on the *Dictionary;* and Sir John Hawkins was probably justified in saying that, when Johnson began the *Idler* 'his motive . . . was aversion to a labour he had undertaken'—the great edition of Shakespeare."[22] Many of the essays give the sense that they are the products of anxious hours—anxious insofar as they are pursued at the expense of something else. As enterprises pursued to make money (we know that Johnson was quite serious about "want[ing] the work to sell"), they also distract from his more demanding tasks.[23] Time is often phrased in monetary terms, as something that should be used wisely, and, when one has a lot of it, something one should not waste. In the *Idler* no. 31 (November 1758), Johnson describes how idleness can cause a man to "fill the day with petty business," so that "life may be passed unprofitably away without the tediousness of many vacant hours."[24] Idleness is often described as being "rich with time," allowing one to thoughtlessly devalue what one currently has. In the *Idler* no. 59 (June 1759), too, he describes the difficulty of enjoying the present moment by thinking instead about how it might have been used at another time: "Whatever advantage we snatch beyond the certain portion allotted us by nature, is like money spent before it is due, which at the time of regular payment will be missed and regretted."[25]

If Johnson's essays construe indolence as bound up in anxiety of a financial understanding of time, they also dwell on the condition as a causal explanatory puzzle brought about by the difficulties of understanding it in terms of a naturalistic philosophy of psychology. Profoundly influenced by and engaged with the work of Locke, Johnson writes about weakness of will in ways that can at times seem close to the approach of that philosopher and the others discussed in chapter 1.[26] In the *Rambler* no. 28 (June 1750), he describes the man who allows himself to continue in a self-destructive lifestyle by telling himself excuses: "He that spends his days and nights in riot and debauchery, owns that his passions oftentimes overpower his resolution. But each comforts himself that his faults are not without precedent, for the best and the wisest men have given way to the violence of sudden temptations."[27] Here we have an examination of self-deception with a sort of accompanying explanation: in such a case, he explains, the man tells himself that others ("the best and wisest men") have themselves given in to temptations, which grants him the license to proceed. This example is perhaps reminiscent of Locke's example of the drunkard in chapter 1.

Another example pairs with Locke's discussion even more vividly: in the *Rambler* no. 8 (April 1750), Johnson describes the man who begins to allow himself to think and imagine the advantages of going through with a wicked act: "The happiness of success glittering before him, withdraws his attention from the atrociousness of the guilt, and acts are at last confidently perpetrated, of which the first conception only crept into the mind, disguised in pleasing complications, and permitted rather than invited."[28] Locke's account of the man who acts against better judgment contains some similar phrases ("though he has in his view the loss of health and plenty, and perhaps the joys of another life: the least of which is no inconsiderable good, but such as he confesses, is far greater, than the tickling of his palate with a glass of Wine, or the idle chat of a soaking Club"). However, we can recall that in the example of Locke, the example shifts between *narrative* that preserves the sense of contradiction in akrasia and *fixed solution* that eliminates the sense of akrasia by instead reducing the action to compulsion by states of "uneasiness." This "uneasiness," Locke says, ultimately "determines the *will* to the accustomed action." In this way, the drama ends and akrasia disappears, for the man is now explained in terms of causal necessity. In Johnson too the akratic man is a confusing puzzle of contradicting thoughts, beliefs, intentions, and actions. But if these are confusing psychological qualities that demand some sort of solution, the sorts of "explanations" Johnson provides are also notably different sorts of explanations than those found in Locke. When he says in the *Rambler* no. 28, "He that spends his days and nights in riot and debauchery . . . comforts himself that his faults are not without precedent, for the best and the wisest men have given way to the violence of sudden temptations," this explanation preserves the sense of voluntary self-deception rather than explaining the conflict away.[29] In the passage above, the writing preserves the sense of a conflict persisting for and by the person: the man "withdraws his attention from the atrociousness of the guilt, and acts are at last confidently perpetrated, of which the first conception only crept into the mind, disguised in pleasing complications, and permitted rather than invited." The phrases "withdrawing attention," "disguised in pleasing complications," and "permitted rather than invited" all describe the self-deceiving mind that knowingly follows through with the weaker reason. Johnson thus does not allow the characterization to slip into the language of compulsions, forces, or entities—doing so would eliminate the sense that these confusions are a person's confusions and that the failures are the person's failures. Johnson's accounts are not like Locke's in the important sense that description is itself a mode of explanation. The explanation of "how" the action arises comes through the identifications of the conflicts, but it is not a "how" that goes all the way down to removing contradiction.[30]

One way to distinguish between Johnson and Locke is to observe that Johnson's genre of life writing maintains the moral, or the normative, component that had been divorced from the metaphysical descriptions of "the will" in Locke. If it is no longer primarily construed as sin, it is still always *felt* as a problem for a person—not just a confusion, but a failure—and preserves the phenomenological reality of failure that Locke had mostly pushed out of the picture. Alkon articulates this difference between Johnson and Locke: "One of the distinctive qualities of [Johnson's] moral essays is their harmonious acceptance of Lockean descriptive psychology within a broader framework of ethical concern. Far from rigidly opposing his prescriptive morality to the scientific aims of Locke, Johnson was able to remain, as he asserted we all are, perpetually a moralist, while at the same time enlisting the naturalistic theories of Locke in the service of an endeavor to teach the moral discipline of the mind."[31] This genre of the periodical essay, insistently personal and insistently moral, can be understood as standing out for its ability to take seriously what philosophical frameworks, which have divorced the metaphysical from the ethical, do not—namely, a condition like akrasia, in which the causal is intertwined with the moral and a metaphysical problem is an ethical problem.

Insofar as Johnson's characterizations of akrasia remain moral, they also contain elements that can be compared to the philosophical reflections on akrasia by Aristotle, which, as discussed in chapter 1, did not "explain away" akrasia, but rather characterized it as a problem that arose on the level of the soul or the agent. In his characterizations of the akratic man in the *Rambler* no. 8, as we saw, Johnson uses phrases like "withdrawing attention," "disguised in pleasing complications," and "permitted rather than invited." These might be said to recall Aristotle's conceptions of akrasia as involving "forgetting," "neglecting," or "ignoring" the stronger premise in the syllogism of practical reason. These verbs admit contradiction, reflect the person's failure—still, for Aristotle and Johnson alike, they serve as kinds of explanations. In the *Idler* no. 27 (October 1758) Johnson writes, "Some, however, there are, whom the intrusion of scruples, the recollection of better notions, or the latent reprehension of good examples, will not suffer to live entirely contented with their own conduct; these are forced to pacify the mutiny of reason with fair promises, and quiet their thoughts with designs of calling all their actions to review, and planning a new scheme for the time to come."[32] In this somewhat confusing passage, Johnson suggests that the intrusion of well-meaning thoughts and memories of what is good and best to do will not successfully stand alone; instead the person needs to quell the "mutiny of reason" by creating promises to himself. However, he continues, resolutions do not suffice on their own. The person needs to somehow assent to, rather than neglect or ignore, such a resolution. This is the degree to which akrasia involves a slight silencing of one or another reason.

However, here as well we need to draw a distinction between Johnson's essays and philosophy proper. Unlike Aristotle's writing, Johnson's writing has a communal spirit, meant to reach outward and elicit the sympathy of readers who might feel Johnson's pain and who likewise might find in Johnson's writing the glimmers of suggestion, help, assistance. *Idler* no. 27 continues:

> There is nothing which we estimate so fallaciously as the force of our own resolutions, nor any fallacy which we so unwillingly and tardily detect. He that has resolved a thousand times, and a thousand times deserted his own purpose, yet suffers no abatement of his confidence, but still believes himself his own master, and able, by innate vigour of soul, to press forward to his end, through all the obstructions that inconveniences or delights can put in his way.
>
> That this mistake should prevail for a time is very natural. When conviction is present, and temptation out of sight, we do not easily conceive how any reasonable being can deviate from his true interest.[33]

Uses of the first-person plural ("we") and the assurance that "this mistake" is "very natural" remind us that this piece of writing functions as a public reflection aimed at a community of readers. It is indeed a form of help not because observations on weakness of will can directly assist the condition, but because it can encourage self-examination, modeled by the author's own self-examination, inviting a reciprocal dynamic with a reader. To this degree, Johnson's essays do not merely explain, but also narrate, describe, and perform, weakness of will. In this way, they do not end in clarity; they recuperate confusion. And this, it turns out, is itself a kind of clarity.

These qualities of Johnson's essays are all brought forward with particular vividness in two essays in particular: the *Rambler* no. 134 (June 1751) and the *Idler* no. 31 (November 1758). Quoting the relevant passages at length, including the prolonged sentences, repetitions, and confusions, is essential to conveying their full effect. The first of these two begins with the author reflecting upon his inability to focus and write the essay due for that day. What it turns into is at once a narrative, an explanation, and a performance of procrastination. The combination of the three is essential to the essay's form and function, explanatory and meliorative, personal and communal:

> I sat yesterday morning employed in deliberating on which, among the various subjects that occurred to my imagination, I should bestow the paper of to-day. After a short effort of meditation by which nothing was determined, I grew every moment more irresolute, my ideas wandered from the first intention, and I rather wished to think, than thought upon any settled subject; till at last I was awakened from this dream of study by a summons from the press: the time was come for which I had been thus negligently purposing to provide, and, however dubious or sluggish, I was now necessitated to write.
>
> I could not forbear to reproach myself for having so long neglected what was unavoidably to be done, and of which every moment's idleness increased the difficulty....
>
> The folly of allowing ourselves to delay what we know cannot be finally escaped, is one of the general weaknesses, which, in spite of the instruction of moralists, and the remonstrances of reason, prevail to a greater or

less degree in every mind: even they who most steadily withstand it, find it, if not the most violent, the most pertinacious of their passions, always renewing its attacks, and though often vanquished, never destroyed.

It is indeed natural to have particular regard to the time present, and to be most solicitous for that which is by its nearness enabled to make the strongest impressions. When therefore any sharp pain is to be suffered, or any formidable danger to be incurred, we can scarcely exempt ourselves wholly from the seducements of imagination; we readily believe that another day will bring some support or advantage which we now want; and are easily persuaded, that the moment of necessity which we desire never to arrive, is at a great distance from us.

Thus life is languished away in the gloom of anxiety, and consumed in collecting resolution which the next morning dissipates; in forming purposes which we scarcely hope to keep, and reconciling ourselves to our own cowardice by excuses which, while we admit them, we know to be absurd. Our firmness is by the continual contemplation of misery hourly impaired; every submission to our fear enlarges its dominion; we not only waste that time in which the evil we dread might have been suffered and surmounted, but even where procrastination produces no absolute encrease of our difficulties, make them less superable to ourselves by habitual terrors. When evils cannot be avoided, it is wise to contract the interval of expectation; to meet the mischiefs which will overtake us if we fly; and suffer only their real malignity without the conflicts of doubt and anguish of anticipation.

To act is far easier than to suffer; yet we every day see the progress of life retarded by the *vis inertiae,* the mere repugnance to motion, and find multitudes repining at the want of that which nothing but idleness hinders them from enjoying.[34]

The immediate takeaway is the sense of how much there is to say about not being able to say anything. Here, perhaps, we can say is an example, not of an undermotivated character, but an overmotivated character, whose abundance of desires, wishes, and intentions produce no corresponding action. This piece of writing is an investigation of this condition, which is to say it is partly explanation and partly treatment.

This is a condition not to be treated in purely moral or purely explanatory terms. Johnson's fluid writing style, which shifts between observation and suggestion, opens itself up for the purpose of prompting recognition and self-reflection. The final effect is not an answer or a diagnosis, but rather a text that makes visible what is to be worked through. The shifts between narrative, explanation, and suggestion are vital to this effect. The first two paragraphs begin in the mode of personal anecdote: a specificity that invites the reader in. The third paragraph switches to generalized observation ("It is indeed natural"), again using the first-person plural "we"; now more general claims can be tentatively made. This mode continues into the fourth paragraph, but at the very end of that paragraph, it switches into suggestion, with "it is wise to contract the interval of expectation; to meet the mischiefs which will overtake us if we fly; and suffer only their real malignity without the conflicts of doubt and anguish of anticipation." This is not an exhortation but a mild consideration ("it is wise") that is meant to strike one as common sense after arriving to this point, for the writer's journey is the reader's journey.

As we saw earlier, Johnson does provide explanations of a sort as to how this indolence persists. It is a matter of having "particular regard to the time present, and [being] most solicitous for that which is by its nearness enabled to make the strongest impressions"—favoring the short term over the long term. The narrative also helps us see how and why regard to the time present prevails, with "submission to our fear" as one reason, and "forming purposes which we scarcely hope to keep" is another. However, notably, these "reasons" are also themselves expressions of weakness, neglect, or irrationality. Submission to fear and forming self-deceiving purposes: these are both answers and nonanswers. Why does one have "particular regard to the time present" when one knows one shouldn't? It is an explanation on one level, as an account of someone in a narrative sense, but it is not an explanation on another level, for it does not provide a causal solution. After all, the person has neglected or ignored the stronger reason.

We can also observe that Johnson "gives an account" of indolence not just in the narrative sense of delivering an anecdote and in an explanatory sense of presenting reasons for how/why it occurs, but also through the very performative presentation of the essay itself. The length of the sentences and the repetition of ideas both serve to give the sense of someone trying to grasp what is occurring. Phrases have a contorted logic, which nicely convey what it is like to procrastinate and knowingly put off what one knows one ought to do. "I rather wished to think, than thought": the sense is familiar, but it is also presented in such a way as to invite recognition of the seeming paradox of the condition. Can one wish one's way into thinking? The formulation seems phenomenologically right but logically wrong. Likewise, "forming purposes which we scarcely hope to keep, and reconciling ourselves to our own cowardice by excuses which, while we admit them, we know to be absurd": Is not the idea of forming purposes precisely that you would keep them? How does one excuse oneself with rationales "we know to be absurd"? What, then, is the point of such excuses? It seems that they serve to deceive on one level, but not on another. Johnson does not proceed to parse how this is so. To get that far down would clear things up, but to clear things up is to give up on your community of readers and no longer speak the language of the procrastinator. It would not be a solution but an abandonment of the problem.

As narrative, explanation, suggestion, and performance, this passage also functions to help move past procrastination insofar as it offers the opportunity for self-interpretation. It returns to the symptoms to describe them and, by putting them into words, further understand them. As such, it does not seek to transcend or eliminate these problems, but to become familiar with them and to live with them. And the practice of interpretation is not only the author's own: the reader is invited to take part in these confusions and, crucially, to associate with them. The text that requires interpretation mirrors the person that requires interpretation: both demand forms of understanding that are not to be foreclosed by clear solutions that render the causal logic linear and coherent, but are rather left open. A clarity is achieved in the recognition.

The *Idler* no. 31 more explicitly discusses the strategies procrastinatory people take to distract from their anxieties of inactivity:

> As pride sometimes is hid under humility, idleness is often covered by turbulence and hurry. He that neglects his known duty and real employment, naturally endeavours to croud his mind with something that may

bar out the remembrance of his own folly, and does any thing but what he ought to do with eager diligence, that he may keep himself in his own favour.

Some are always in a state of preparation, occupied in previous measures, forming plans, accumulating materials, and providing for the main affair. These are certainly under the secret power of idleness....

The art is, to fill the day with petty business, to have always something in hand which may raise curiosity, but not solicitude, and keep the mind in a state of action, but not of labour.[35]

This is a personal admission, ironically presented in a periodical called the *Idler*. But it is more explicitly a combination of generalized observation, explanation, and suggestion. One way that idleness functions in the world is by being "covered by turbulence and hurry." Idleness takes the subject of the sentence rather than the person who experiences it, which helps to convey the passive sense in which people allow their idleness to the upper hand. In the next sentence, however, the idle man becomes the subject, and so the ironies are made explicit: he "endeavours to croud his mind with something that may bar out the remembrance of his folly, and does any thing but what he ought to do with eager diligence, that he may keep himself in his own favour." Here the self-deceptions are portrayed not without a sense of humor, but, as we saw in Sterne, the humor only works because the phrase means to get at what it is actually like: there is more than a grain of truth in it. The "art," or technique, for procrastination is something he can readily identify: to "fill the day with petty business," to take on an easier task, but that is a task nonetheless, an occupation that resembles the real harder work. Still, diagnosis does not itself immediately yield improvement. This is exactly the conundrum of a weak-willed condition: procrastination exists not in spite of recognition of what is to be done, but because of that recognition. Writing thus does not offer a way out of the uroboros of procrastination, but it does make that experience visible—available on another plane, making it real to oneself and to the (real or imagined) community of readers.

As the essay continues, it turns to a fictional character, "my old friend Sober," who, the diaries of Hester Thrale tell us, is intended "as [Johnson's] own portrait."[36] Sober takes up manual activities so as to distract himself from what is to be done. In this sense, we can understand the construction of this fictional character not just as a way to clearly represent this condition, but as a performance of the author's desires to outsource and project his problems onto someone else. The externalization of Johnson's procrastination allows a new kind of conceptualization, for this person can himself be a subject for interpretation. Johnson's essay ends mourning Sober's state: "Poor Sober! I have often teaz'd him with reproof, and he has often promised reformation; for no man is so much open to conviction as the idler, but there is none on whom it operates so little. What will be the effect of this paper I know not; perhaps he will read it and laugh, and light the fire in his furnace; but my hope is that he will quit his trifles, and betake himself to rational and useful diligence."[37] This humorous ending turns the tables explicitly on Johnson, who has been fictionalized, but it is Johnson just as it is all other procrastinators. The expression is not a moral exhortation but a "hope." Procrastination is not something that can be quickly cured, but, in inviting association, an essay can help a reader and a writer diagnose through reliving and through this transparency, find a way to move on. Taking oneself as a person to be interpreted rather than solved or re-solved may or may not help the person "get to work," but it captures the person's self-defeats in a way that can be acknowledged, and acknowledgement is the beginning of understanding.

ROUSSEAU

In the *Idler* no. 84 (November 1759), Johnson wrote, "He that writes an apology for a single action, to confute an accusation, or recommend himself to a favour, is indeed always to be suspected of favouring his own cause; but he that sits down calmly and voluntarily to review his life for the admonition of posterity, or to amuse himself, and leaves this account unpublished, may be commonly presumed to tell truth, since falshood cannot appease his own mind, and fame will not be heard beneath the tomb."[38] It is a nice thought, but it does not seem to apply to the author of *The Confessions of Jean-Jacques Rousseau*. Although the confessor presents himself as setting down to "review his life for the admonition of posterity," it is not clear that his "review" of "his life" was done "calmly" and without the interest in "apology" or "confut[ing] accusation[s]." It can be said, however, to "tell truth" of a certain sort. But of what sort? At the very start, he tells us that it is his goal to "display to my kind a portrait in every way true to nature"; likewise, somewhat later, he declares it is aim to "make my soul transparent to the reader's eye."[39] But what kind of transparency is this?

The question of the nature of "transparency" has been at the center of many critical engagements with this text in reflections by Jean Starobinski, Paul de Man, Steven Knapp and Walter Benn Michaels, among others. One way we can begin to ask the question as it pertains to akrasia is to ask how transparency differs from what we found in Augustine. What does it mean to exhibit personal failures in a context removed from the appeal to the spiritual and potentially perverse ontology of the will and God's free grace? What kind of writing is then made possible by the removal of such paradigms while preserving interest in weakness of the will?

Essential to starting any discussion of Rousseau in this text is to note his idiosyncrasies when it comes to social interactions. "My passions are extremely strong," he writes in book 1, "and while I am under their sway nothing can equal my impetuosity. I am amenable to no restraint, respect, fear, or decorum. I am cynical, bold, violent, and daring."[40] Although amenable to no restraint, later on he can reconstruct everything in painstaking detail: "I can only see clearly in retrospect," he writes. "It is only in my memory that my mind can work. I have neither feeling nor understanding for anything that is said or done or that happens before my eyes. . . . But afterwards it all comes back to me, I remember the place and the time, the tone of voice and look, the gesture and situation; nothing escapes me."[41] The dilemma for Rousseau, Starobinski has written, is that "his is a transparency without spectators. Worse, other people mistake him for someone he is not."[42] In other words, "error lies in other people's perception. . . . Although he thinks he has laid his soul bare, the truth about him remains hidden, as though he were wearing a disguise or a mask. He seems, through no fault of his own, to be hiding dreadful secrets, even though he has stripped himself naked in public."[43] He seems to be unable to express himself truthfully to others even when he wants to.

However, there is a broader issue at play in interrogating Rousseau's actions, one that speaks to the time in which he lived. Rousseau's difficulties to make himself "understood" appear to be a function of the fact that, for him, feelings and thoughts that are undisclosed in the moment provide the causes and reasons for his actions. To make himself visible in this text, then, is not just to "confess" or own up to his failures, but to explain them with a thoroughness such that guilt is explained away. Consequently, transparency wavers between two meanings. There is the Augustinian meaning of transparency, in which confession offers up the self-inflicted, knowing, and backward acts so that they may be truthfully told and the writer may truthfully confront them. This sense is what Paul de Man means when he writes about Rousseau, "To confess is to overcome guilt and shame in the name of truth: it is an epistemological use of language in which ethical values of good and evil are superseded by values of truth and falsehood. . . . By stating things as they are, the economy of ethical balance is restored and redemption can start in the clarified atmosphere of a truth that does not hesitate to reveal the crime in all its horror."[44] The morality of the condition is a matter of fact and is brought out by truth-telling; moral failing and truth go together. There is, though, another meaning of transparency Rousseau employs, and this is the meaning espoused by Locke when he writes at the beginning of the *Essay Concerning Human Understanding* that it is his goal to shed "all the light we can let in upon our own minds."[45] When it comes to a person's actions, Lockean transparency means identifying, explicating, and, as MacIntyre has put it, "laying bare" the "mechanisms which underlie action."[46] This mode of transparency is not moral, just notational, about "what happened," especially if its level of transparency is at the level of subpersonal causes that are no longer intentional.

Indeed, Rousseau's confessions often seem to begin as moral confessions but shift into causal description that lets himself off the hook. As Starobinski writes, Rousseau "occasionally begins with an admission of ignorance about himself, but he never *ends* with one. . . . In this respect he is unflaggingly optimistic, sure of his firm grasp on the inner truth."[47] It is a tendency that, as de Man also writes, "will indeed exculpate the confessor, thus making the confession (and the confessional text) redundant as it originates."[48] Another way to understand this dynamic is as between a conception of truth-telling about action as inherently moral or not: Does a telling of an akratic action need to take on a moral structure (as in Aristotle, Augustine, Murdoch, and Johnson), or can it be told in the mode of morally neutral description (as was the goal of Locke and, to some extent, Davidson)? Rousseau's seeming ambivalence on this idea of truth—his movement between understanding actions as morally implicating on the one hand but as consequences of events that do not involve his moral subjectivity on the other—results in puzzling and inconclusive interrogations of akrasia. In their uncertainty, these interrogations, as we will see, themselves bolster the importance of an unforeclosed interpretive stance when approaching the text and the person it represents.

In his very first confession, Rousseau exhibits this tension between two modes of transparency in his approach to describing his baffling actions. He tells how as a younger man he stole money from a friend despite having no need or even desire for the money itself. "The incident is worth the telling," he says, "for it involves such an absurd mixture of boldness and stupidity that I should find it most difficult to believe if it concerned anyone but myself":

> It was in Paris. I was walking, at about five o'clock, with M. de Francueil in the Palais-Royal when he took out his watch, looked at it, and said, "Let us go to the Opera." I agreed, and we went. He bought two tickets for the amphitheatre, gave me one and went on ahead with the other. I followed him in, but on reaching the doorway found it congested. When I looked in, I saw that everyone was standing. So, thinking I might easily be lost in the crowd, or at least make M. de Francueil think so, I went out again, presented my ticket, asked for my money back, and walked away. But what I had not suspected was that the moment I got to the door everyone sat down and M. de Francueil clearly perceived that I was no longer there.
>
> Nothing could have been so far from my natural disposition as this act. But I note it as a proof that there are moments of a kind of delirium, in which men cannot be judged by what they do. I did not exactly steal that money. What I stole was the use of it. But it was a theft and, what is more, it was a disgraceful one.[49]

On the surface, the episode recalls Augustine's famous confession of stealing the pears from his neighbor's tree. "But it was not poverty that drove me to conceive the desire to steal, and to act upon that desire," Augustine writes. "I lacked only righteousness, and my stomach turned at it; I had grown fat on wickedness. What I stole, I already had in abundance, and of much better quality too. I did not steal so as to enjoy the fruits of my crime, but rather to enjoy the theft itself, and the sin."[50] As in that scene, Rousseau here emphasizes that it is not the object of the theft that he wanted. It is wholly unclear whether Rousseau sought to avoid the crowded setting or if he had privately decided he did not want to see the opera but was too embarrassed to convey this to M. de Francueil. Like so many of Rousseau's actions in *The Confessions,* it strikes one not merely as antisocial or self-serving, but pointlessly contrary and pursued for the sake of contrariness itself.

At the same time, while Rousseau stresses that he acted "disgracefully," he also declares that "there are moments . . . in which men cannot be judged by what they do." He is guilty, but, also, not really. The implication is that he cannot be purely judged by the action alone, because his underlying intentions are not what we might assume them to be from a mere narrative like the one just given. Rousseau wants the reader to comprehend some deeper qualities of his character that must be supplemented separately. Thus, in framing this incident, Rousseau writes, "As the reader learns more of my life, he will get to know my disposition and feel all this for himself without my needing to tell him. Once this is clear, he will have no difficulty in understanding one of the apparent contradictions in my character: the combination of an almost sordid avarice with the greatest contempt for money."[51] Rousseau lays out dispositional character traits, which we may be able to know and understand "as the reader learns more of [his] life." The reason he acts in such a way is due to a "sordid avarice," perhaps a kleptomaniac's instinct, despite an apathy toward the stolen good itself. This manner of explanation seems to rewrite a morally infused narrative (of a "disgraceful" act) into one to be understood by recourse to a static character trait. However, this "cause" is clearly itself in need of an explanation and is indeed framed as a vice. Does he enjoy the thrill of theft? Does he find satisfaction in the spectacle of his being found out?

In the unsuccessful half-attempt at a causal explanation, questions like these inevitably arise. Crucially, to the reader and to the writer, they are unsolved, and the represented person is left as something of an open book.

Intermittently throughout the text, Rousseau acknowledges the difficulties in accounting for his dysfunctional actions with value-neutral explanatory language. In book 4, he claims he wants to portray his behaviors "from all points of view," showed "from all lights," suggesting that an unbiased perspective toward himself is possible, but in book 8 he notes that actions are sometimes not separable from ethical language.[52] He writes, "Here I am once more at one of those critical moments in my life in which it is difficult to confine myself to a narrative because it is almost impossible that even the narrative will not carry some hint of censure or apology. I will try, however, to convey how and with what motives I acted, without adding praise or blame."[53] Here he stresses the aim of "convey[ing]" the "motives" for acting as if doing so eliminates the possibility of moral or normative evaluation. Notably, he uses the words "motives [*motifs*]" rather than "reasons [*raisons*]" for acting, recalling Hume's vocabulary for brute causation rather than personal expression of action. Still, as we saw in the narrative at the opera, at some point the language of motives will need to come up against the realm of the moral. In this sense, he is seeking (in vain) to avoid what Johnson embraced: writing about failed action in ways that are inherently moral.

It is indeed in the failure of Rousseau's attempts to provide coherent causal explanations of his actions that these episodes gain their distinctive interpretive richness. This is clearest in the episode that has received the most attention in this text—the scene in which the young Rousseau describes stealing a ribbon from the home of Mme de Vercellis and then adamantly blames the disappearance on the innocent young cook Marion.[54] He writes, "I boldly accused her. She was confused, did not utter a word, and threw me a glance that would have disarmed the devil, but my cruel heart resisted. In the end she firmly denied the theft. But she did not get indignant. She merely turned to me, and begged me to remember myself and not disgrace an innocent girl who had never done me any harm. But, with infernal impudence, I repeated my accusation, and declared to her face that she had given me the ribbon."[55] Here again the scene conveys the Augustinian sense of a weak-willed wrongdoer. He adopts Augustine's rhetoric of sin by characterizing his "infernal impudence," leaving out any further psychological motivation or anguish. The actions are described plainly: "I repeated my accusation, and declared to her face that she had given me the ribbon." He is the author who "can only see clearly in retrospect" and thus portrays the wickedness of his past self from a distance. In continuing, however, Rousseau begins to attribute a series of mental causes to his vindictive action of accusing Marion: "I was not much afraid of punishment, I was only afraid of disgrace. But that I feared more than death, more than crime, more than anything in the world. I should have rejoiced if the earth had swallowed me up and stifled me in the abyss. But my invincible sense of shame prevailed over everything. It was my shame that made me impudent, and the more wickedly I behaved the bolder my fear of confession made me.... Utter confusion robbed me of all other feeling."[56] Like his qualifying statement regarding his theft at the opera, here he intimates that we might better understand his action if we attribute it to some identifiable elements of his character—namely, fear of "disgrace," "sense of shame," and "utter confusion." Although these traits are found in Augustinian rhetoric as well, importantly, Rousseau's causal attribution tidily omits any sense of volition. Past-tense Rousseau committed this deed because a series of traits and mental states "made [him]" impudent, and his sense of shame "prevailed over everything" and "robbed [him] of all other feeling." This is reminiscent of Moll Flanders when she tells us she committed her first theft while "Distracted and Raving" and with "no manner of design in my Head."[57]

The passage becomes particularly puzzling, however, when Rousseau's account changes, and he asserts that his "inner feelings" at the time of the accusation can not only explain but also excuse his action: "But I should not fulfil [sic] the aim of this book if I did not at the same time reveal my inner feelings and hesitated to put up such excuses for myself as I honestly could. Never was deliberate wickedness further from my intention than at that cruel moment. When I accused that poor girl, it is strange but true that my friendship for her was the cause. She was present in my thoughts, and I threw the blame on the first person who occurred to me."[58] Under this reading of the action, Rousseau was not merely brought to an inexcusable act out of a confused sense of shame and fear of disgrace; he went through with an action that turned out to be wicked, but can be excused because the action was not originally rooted in wicked intentions. In this way, Rousseau is redescribing his akrasia as if it were an accident, implying that his intentions can be uncoupled from the consequences of an action. Indeed, he emphasizes not the guilty action itself, but instead the good and defensible intentions that, regrettably, the action did not follow. However, this explanation, though intended to clear things up, further muddles the picture. Firstly, it is unclear whether we can even believe that the accusation was uttered in a "delirium" in whch she was simply "present in [his] thoughts." This is difficult to square with his earlier admission that the accusation came from a sense of shame and fear of guilt, motivating a strategically malicious accusation ("I repeated my accusation, and declared to her face that she had given me the ribbon"). Further, there is the question as to whether an utterance like "Marion" can be plausibly understood as detached from the intentional structure of language.[59] How can such an utterance be produced and understood unintentionally without the underlying meanings (and necessary moral implications) the utterance carries? This doubling-down on self-excuse seems not to absolve but further implicate the teller of the narrative who, in providing a transparent explication of the causes of his action, has in some ways fused with the past-tense character. But it is not that the narrator is simply lying; what his contorted accounts reveal are the limits of the mode of seeking to explain an akratic action through identifying the reasons for it—or, alternatively, the meaningless causes of it. Against his better judgment, he conveys akrasia through his failures to explain it.

Indeed, like with Sterne's Yorick, the vividness of the condition is made possible through a blocked or unsuccessful causal analysis. If it was with a self-consciously ironic sentence for Sterne, for Rousseau it is with a truthful mode of conveying something about himself: the writing expresses human irrationality not by successfully stipulating the causal mechanisms of mind and body but by unsuccessfully stipulating the causal mechanisms of mind and body. This is the same transparency and opacity we might find in Nancy's next blog post, which would likely be a medium better suited to examining procrastination than a study identifying a corresponding gene or neural network. Rousseau's text and Johnson's essays stand out in literary history as offering models of "writing a self" that foreground the difficulty of getting it right and, more pointedly, the insufficiencies of logical, causal, or systematic analyses of irrational acts. It suggests what the dominant philosophy of their time refuses—how a work of writing's incompleteness might not be a flaw but rather a virtue. In these accounts, the gaps open up the text to being read, and, upon being read, it turns back and reads you.

With chapter 5, we move to lyric poetry. Dwelling on the importance of akratic indolence and procrastination for William Wordsworth and John Keats, we also see how these conditions produce the need to prioritize the value of *maintaining contradiction* as a constitutive principle of poetry itself. This allows poetry to stand out as an exemplary mode of writing for not just examining but also enacting the mode of intentional irrationality, or the writing of the weaker reason.

5

AKRASIA AND THE POETRY OF ANTINOMIES

Wordsworth and Keats

SAVING THE BEST FOR LAST, William Empson describes the seventh of the "seven types of ambiguity" found in poetry as that of "full contradiction, marking a division in the author's mind."[1] For Empson, with the presentation of such a contradiction, the speaker "satisfies two opposite impulses and, as a sort of apology, admits that they contradict, but claims that they are like the soluble contradictions, and can safely be indulged; by admitting the weakness of his thought he seems to have sterilised it, to know better already than any one who might have pointed the contradiction out; he claims the sympathy of his audience in that 'we can none of us say more than this,' and gains dignity in that even from the poor material of human ignorance he can distil grace of style."[2] The appearance of such a poetic contradiction gives way, not to the reconciliation of these "two opposite impulses" (they do not follow each other in time such that the one corrects or replaces the other), but rather to a kind of "apology," an admission of weakness that seeks some half-dignity ("grace of style") in acknowledging or recognizing that weakness. After all, "we can none of us say more than this." This characterization of knowing defeat or acknowledged illogic in poetry replicates the condition discussed in the previous chapters of this

132

book—that of Yorick in *A Sentimental Journey*, for example, who performs the failure of causal narration in his first-person recounting of himself, or that of Samuel Johnson, whose failures of articulation in his periodical essays appeal to a sympathetic reader who can partake in Johnson's own attempts at self-interpretation. The focus for Empson, though, is poetry, and his characterization can perhaps help us recognize a special importance of akrasia to poetry—a mode of linguistic expression with a long history of being equated with the antirational or irrational, from Plato onward, a sense brought out too in Cleanth Brooks's suggestion that "the language of poetry is the language of paradox."[3] For some, poetry could be called the mode of writing the weaker reason: a way of examining, if not performing, the condition of intentional irrationality.

In this final chapter, we turn to poetry from the Romantic era in order to examine its distinctive response to the puzzling formulation of akrasia. Although Empson does not privilege the Romantic era in his discussion, we can see this period as especially significant for the development of the idea of poetry as a site for thinking with contradiction—whether Kantian antinomy, the generative irony described by Friedrich Schlegel, or the Keatsian mode of being in a state of "uncertainties, Mysteries, doubts, without any irritable reaching after fact & reason."[4] Through the work of William Wordsworth and John Keats, we find that the akratic condition motivates the need for a poetry that stands in a mode of abeyance, able to foster conflicts or antinomies without resolving them. It requires the "language of paradox," the lyric mode of "surmise," or the stance of what Keats famously called "negative capability."

In the work of both Wordsworth and Keats we can identify committed engagement with a particular kind of akrasia—namely, akratic inaction, presented in modes of indolence or procrastination, as already considered with Samuel Johnson. As we will see, these engagements with akratic indolence can be understood in relation to a broader intellectual crisis regarding the nature of action and the will. Indeed, both Wordsworth's and Keats's treatments of this trope can be understood in relationship to the thought of distinct interlocutors who wrote about the confusions of human agency in philosophical prose—specifically, Samuel Taylor Coleridge and William Hazlitt. Distraught by what he understood to be a miserably unproductive state, Coleridge inquired repeatedly into the metaphysics of the will. Wordsworth, though sympathetic to the frustrations of indolence, examines this condition in *The Prelude* (1805, revised version 1850) through a different kind of writing, one that performs the condition of procrastination and embodies the multidirectional logic of a self-beguiling akratic. Keats, meanwhile, was greatly influenced by the writings on human agency and aesthetics by Hazlitt. Connecting the non-mechanistic and disinterested stance of human agency to the disinterested ontology of art, Hazlitt provided Keats with a vocabulary for thinking about disinterestedness and the ways that both a person and a poem can maintain opposite impulses on a single occasion.

Coleridge and Hazlitt then stand out as important bridges between Romantic poetry and the Enlightenment philosophy around human agency. In order to see their significance more clearly, it will be necessary to anchor these figures to the thought of Immanuel Kant. The relevance of Kant to Wordsworth's and Keats's poetic experiments with indolence lies in his identification of what he called an antinomy, or unresolved contradiction—specifically, the "Third Antinomy" in the *Critique of Pure Reason*—between how the will is construed through a philosophy of nature (or theoretical philosophy) and through a philosophy of freedom (or practical philosophy).[5] As Coleridge and Hazlitt each recognized, the mode of understanding the will as following efficient causation (as discussed in chapter 1) was necessary but insufficient: the trouble was how to understand the idea of the will's freedom in the context of a natural philosophy. Wordsworth and Keats, as we will see, avoid this mode of thinking in the terms of a philosophical system, but in their own ways, they take this conflict as an opportunity for poetic expression. Interestingly, it is in Kant's turn to aesthetics in the *Critique of the Power of Judgment* (the third critique) that he establishes an intermediary domain, a philosophy concerned with purposiveness grounded in the faculty of judgment, that can connect theoretical philosophy (grounded in the faculty of understanding) and practical philosophy (grounded in the faculty of self-legislating reason).[6] It would be wrong to suggest that Wordsworth and Keats replicate Kant's move toward aesthetics in their own poetic treatments of human agency, but for Kant, Wordsworth, and Keats alike, the path to taking the

conflicting logics of the will seriously lies in taking antinomy seriously—
that is, in refusing to collapse human agency into a matter of either mere
causation or spontaneously free self-legislation.

To say that Wordsworth and Keats take antinomy—*this* antinomy, or
the antinomy of the will—as an opportunity for poetry is also to notice
that they are doing a certain kind of thinking in their poetry, but that it
is a thinking different from the kind we find in philosophy proper. In *The
Prelude*, like elsewhere in his poetry, Wordsworth explicitly urges against
"false thought / And false philosophy" (12:75–76), preferring to think
"through the turnings intricate of verse" (5:627). "Hard task to analyse a
soul," he tells us in book 2 of *The Prelude*, in which

> Not only general habits and desires,
> But each most obvious and particular thought—
> Not in a mystical and idle sense,
> But in the words of reason deeply weighed—
> Hath no beginning. (2:227–36)

As his *Prelude* narrates (particularly in book 10), Wordsworth found
stifling and limited the philosophy that so occupied Coleridge, including
the sorts of systematic thinking in Godwinian philosophy (as discussed in
chapter 3).[7] For Wordsworth, poetry offers an opportunity for a thinking
through that does not arrive at resolution. As Adam Potkay has put it,
Wordsworth "ponders the *antinomies* he sees in moral thought. . . . For
example, we feel ourselves to be free (capable of undetermined moral
thought or action), but yet we know ourselves, at least insofar as we are
material beings, to be causally determined."[8] In this way, Wordsworth
"incites attempts 'to weigh things and their opposites.'"[9] Likewise, Simon
Jarvis has suggested that Wordsworth, contra Coleridge, who sought to
"reconcil[e] all the anomalies" in a sort of "system," wanted a different
sort of philosophical approach—one that took the form of a "philosophic
song": "Not that philosophy gets fitted into a song—where all the thinking is done by philosophy and only the handiwork by verse—but that the
song itself, *as song*, is philosophic. It might mean that a different kind of
thinking happens in verse—that instead of being a sort of thoughtless

ornament or reliquary for thinking, verse is itself a kind of cognition, with its own resistances and difficulties."[10] Wordsworth's mode of philosophic song suggests that a musical (rather than mathematical) mode of thinking, one that privileges "pondering" and "weighing," may be better suited to addressing some areas of human inquiry.

In Keats as well, thinking is less like doing philosophy systematically than like listening—or, even more so, looking—carefully. Thus, when we read Keats, to follow the famous interpretations of Cleanth Brooks, we do not look for resolved ideas that the poems contain—to do so would be to miss their music or their shading.[11] To read Keats is to attend to to the relations between tones and to pictorial juxtapositions, relationships that themselves bring forward ideas in combination, often contradictions (like "the feel of not to feel it"), by evoking what cannot be "said" in rhyme or prose.[12] As Brooks has written, the structure of poetry "unites the like with the unlike. It does not unite them, however, by the simple process of allowing one connotation to cancel out another nor does it reduce the contradictory attitudes to harmony by a process of subtraction. The unity is not a unity of the sort to be achieved by the reduction and simplification appropriate to an algebraic formula. It is a positive unity, not a negative; it represents not a residue but an achieved harmony."[13] In Keats as with Wordsworth, the mode of regretful akratic inaction, conveyed through the operations of paradox, achieves a harmony or unity through dissonance, which is not to be reduced or simplified. A doubling effect is maintained, and poetry's insistence to maintain it is what distinguishes it from the ethos of philosophy.

This knowing weakness in the irreducible doubling in engagements with the akratic condition for these Romantic poets can also be understood through Friedrich Schlegel's "romantic irony." As Anne K. Mellor has written, for Schlegel, the philosophical impulse of staying with antinomy (refusing "resolution or synthesis," for "the thesis and antithesis remain always in contradiction") allows a philosophical irony, and this connects to an artistic irony that privileges a mode of "hovering."[14] The ironic artist, Mellor continues, "must constantly balance or 'hover' between self-creation (*Selbstschöpfung*) and self-destruction (*Selbstvernichtung*)" and one of the places we can find this mode is in the "unresolved debates" of Keats's odes.[15] This "ironic" stance may recall the ironic formulations we found in Sterne, Godwin, and Austen. In those authors, a statement's falsity projects its own self-conflicting dynamics, unjustifiably foregrounding the weaker reason ahead of the stronger. In both types of irony, the literary unit (the sentence, the poem) is presented without resolution, foregrounding falsity or self-negation. For the prose considered earlier, this form of presentation allows a suitable depiction of someone false to him or herself; for Keats's poetry, as we will see, it holds up a self-conflicting dynamic that joins what is frustrating to what is generative about being two things at once.

This generative artistic stance of regretted (in)action is only possible within the context of a historically specific figuration of indolence in culture, philosophy, and aesthetics. Indolence has long been noted as an important theme for English Romantic poetry, explored in especially wide-ranging fashion in Willard Spiegelman's *Majestic Indolence* (1995). In his study, Spiegelman discusses the trope of indolence's historical journey, from thirteenth-century sloth and acedia through Robert Burton's melancholy and eighteenth-century idleness, and this trajectory helps prepare him for readings of the Romantic poets as concerned with connotations of indolence as freedom, work, and play. For Spiegelman, the positive and negative connotations of indolence and their connections to the freedom associated with artistic experience (in Kant) together help contribute to a focus on "the aesthetic (i.e., formal, mimetic, and expressive) achievements" of these poets—specifically, Wordsworth, Coleridge, Keats, and Percy Bysshe Shelley.[16] The focus in this chapter is more specifically on the negative—frustrated, conflicted, akratic—dimensions of indolence, which come through in explorations of paradox more than freedom or leisure. To this end, the intellectual history backdrop, which informs our understanding of the philosophical writings of Coleridge and Hazlitt, is vital to the reading of the poetry in question. As already discussed with respect to Johnson in chapter 4, the historical change most relevant to the puzzle of akratic inaction in this period is the sense in which sloth or acedia as sin is replaced with a more banal, linear sense of indolence as a blip in the causal mechanism of the mind, one that can be understood less as "falling away" from the world than "falling behind" the time clock.

Attending to the negative connotations of indolence also means emphasizing the flip side of the forms of willed inaction, "idleness," and "wise passiveness"—related genealogically to pastoral *otium* (leisurely excess)—associated with the Romantic era.[17] As Anne-Lise François has shown, the period's interest in withdrawal, "recessive action," "declined experience," "minimal realization," and "nonappropriative contentment" contributes to a particular valuation of aesthetics as a resting point, specifically a conception of "aesthetic experience as a respite from the rushed action of a modernity so bent on bringing about the future that it leaves no time for the taking—deferral or postponement—of time."[18] But we can also see the poetry of Wordsworth and Keats as carrying the sense of guilt, heaviness, or knowing uneasiness in that mode of withdrawal or apparent "ease." In Wordsworth in particular, we can also discern in "wise passiveness" a concealment of worry that he is not only *taking* his time but also wasting it—or, put otherwise, not spending it profitably. The financial sense of time hangs over this poetry even while the poetry purports to elude it.

This also means that for Wordsworth and Keats the best mode of representing indolence is not through a personification of conflict, but through producing conflict through poetic construction itself. This makes their constructions altogether different from Spenser's Acrasia from book 2 of *The Faerie Queen* (1590) or the figure of Indolence in James Thomson's *Castle of Indolence* (1748). Both of those poetic treatments of inaction depend upon classical personifications in which the conflict is summed up in a single figure. In his efforts to write "in a language near to the language of men," Wordsworth famously sought modes of expression more immediate and less inherited from English poetic tradition; for Keats, as we will see, personifications breed as much unfamiliarity as familiarity and accentuate the poet's distanced relationship to literary meaning and literary history.[19] The spiritual, moral, and didactic elements of Spenser and Thomson are not quite present in Wordsworth or Keats either; as Spiegelman has written, Wordsworth and Keats were both uncomfortable with the way Thomson's poem "attempts to be both psychological and moral or didactic, and these two aims are not mutually compatible."[20] These poets, then, as with some of the novelists and as with the essayist Johnson, seek to convey something like akrasia without fully rooting it in the spiritual or moral terms that had been essential to the trope in earlier instantiations in English literary history.

First we will consider poetic treatments of types of akrasia in *The Prelude*, which we can read as a procrastinatory poem—one offered as a sort of response to Coleridge and his philosophical puzzles. By embodying the mode of willful distraction with the heaviness of guilt, the poet of *The Prelude* produces poetic dynamics of contradiction that do not propose a single metaphysics of human agency, but instead foregrounds the mysteries of agency, which are conveyed through the mysteries of verse. Keats holds a more distanced relationship to indolence, for he approaches it through tropes that are familiar to him from Sydney, Shakespeare, Thomson, Wordsworth, and others. Keats's "secondhand" status as a poet allows him a more distanced relationship to the craft of poetry, which gives indolence more pictorial qualities. Keats is influenced by Hazlitt's characterizations of human agency and art as both in the mode of "disinterestedness," and this conception works its way into Keats's poetry of indolence. For Keats, indolence is the beginning of art: it is the stance of negative capability, which is not *in*capability, but rather the capability of being negative— being capable of being incapable. With both of these poets, we get not just literature about akrasia, but also literature as akrasia. In their works, akrasia is not just a subject for literature; it is its basis and starting point.

WORDSWORTH AND THE POETICS OF PROCRASTINATION

The Wordsworth who wanders lonely as a cloud and floats on high o'er vales and hills gazes without thinking and in that gazing receives all that the natural world can offer him: the fluttering, dancing, and twinkling daffodils. Action is not required to receive their gifts; indeed one is most likely to enjoy them without any overt effort, but rather "in vacant or in pensive mood" on one's couch. This is Wordsworth's familiar "idleness" from "To My Sister": "And bring no book: for this one day / We'll give to idleness." One "gives" to idleness in the mildest of senses, more of a "giving in" than a "giving." This is also the "wise passiveness" of "Expostulation and Reply." In that poem, the question arises to the speaker:

Why, William, on that old grey stone,
Thus for the length of half a day,
Why, William, sit you thus alone,
And dream your time away? (1–4)

The reply arrives several stanzas later:

The eye it cannot chuse but see,
We cannot bid the ear be still;
Our bodies feel, where'er they be,
Against, or with our will. (17–20)[21]

The phrase "cannot chuse but" (which shows up at various points through-out *The Prelude* as well) conveys a sense of the "will" as playing no role in the receiving of the world's pleasures.[22] It is indeed a view of the will (or lack thereof) that might seem consistent with a vitalist metaphysics—that of Spinoza's or Schelling's—in which bodily states predetermine willed choice.[23] Also like Hume, William here appears to not only propose this ontological structure of mind but also get behind it: reason not only *is* but also *ought to be* the slave of the passions, impressions, and sensations.

However, other moments in Wordsworth's corpus might call on us to view the sentiment here with some suspicion: Is there not a concealment of angst in the kind of holiday taken? Do not these withdrawals from the work-clock come at a price? Inaction might be understood not just as the positively inflected idleness but also in the more negatively inflected indolence, which carries a half-muted sense of frustration—an indolence described in the preface to the *Lyrical Ballads* as "the most dishonorable accusation which can be brought against an Author," for it "prevents him from endeavouring to ascertain what is his duty, or, when his duty is as-certained prevents him from performing it."[24]

This is the confusing and frustrating condition that prompts the be-ginning of *The Prelude*. Wordsworth's thirteen-book autobiographical epic traces the growth of a poet and ends in a triumphant celebration of the imagination and the agencies of man, mind, and nature. However, it starts out with a conundrum: the poet had marked out for himself an enormous artistic task—the writing of *The Recluse*—but could not get himself to start it. So the poet turns to an easier task, a preparatory enterprise, to be conceived of as a "prelude," which can serve as an excuse of preparing the ground for what would follow, but is for the moment more simply a more achievable undertaking. Understood in this way, *The Prelude* stands out as an exemplary procrastinatory poem. Like all procrastinatory activities, it is pursued intentionally, but in a state of guilt. It is crafted strategically so as to distract by somehow simulating the "real thing" and so involves a kind of work that bears resemblance to the work that needs to be done. His writing endeavor in this sense recalls Johnson's words: "Almost every man has some art by which he steals his thoughts away from his present state."[25]

The self-deception is evident from the early pages of book 1, in which he describes his yearnings "towards some philosophic song / Of truth" (1:230–31, 1805 version)—namely, *The Recluse*.[26] He continues:

But from this awful burthen I full soon
Take refuge, and beguile myself with trust
That mellower years will bring a riper mind
And clearer insight. (1:235–38)

If the inactive mode is a kind of "refuge" in much of Wordsworth's poetry, here it is one taken self-consciously so as to avoid a burden he has created for himself. It is hardly a restful refuge, for it is built in self-beguilement. The "trust" he hopes to maintain is hardly solid, given that it follows the words "beguile myself with." Further, it is a trust in nothing but time: "mellower years" will bring a "riper" mind, as if he only needed light and water. One gets the sense that the best thing to do is to "put off" (*pro*) until "tomorrow" (*crastinus*) or to heed the words of the Gospel of Matthew (6:34): "Take therefore no thought for the morrow: for the morrow shall take thought for the things of itself."[27]

The self-beguiling start to *The Prelude* must be understood not only in the context of Wordsworth's own writing enterprise but also in the context of his relationship to his friend Coleridge, to whom *The Prelude* was dedicated, and whose bouts of indolence, depression, and addiction led him to try and grapple with questions of the ontology of the will in his philosophical prose. "Constitutional indolence, aggravated into languor by ill-health; the accumulating embarrassments of procrastination; the mental cowardice, which is the inseparable companion of procrastination": these are some of the characteristics Coleridge ascribes to himself in the *Biographia Literaria*.[28] In his notebooks in particular, Coleridge describes the conundrum of indolence as a conundrum in a double sense, not just as a practical problem but also as an intellectual problem, the former deepened by the latter. It is a "deep and wide disease in my moral nature," he writes. "Love of Liberty, Pleasure of Spontaneity, these all express, not explain, the fact."[29] What would it mean to "explain the fact" of akratic inaction? This was the question we asked about the *Nancy* comic at the start of chapter 4. Coleridge can't Google it, but that wouldn't help anyway. He can take to philosophy to help him think through the ontology of the will, but that strategy too will prove to be limited in its offerings.

An early enticing philosophical option for Coleridge was to be found in David Hartley's associationism, which he had thought successful in accounting for the active powers in man through the universe law of passive association. However, as he would recount in the *Biographia Literaria*, this model, like those that held to other materialist or mechanistic conceptions of the will from Hobbes and Spinoza onward, is based upon absurd premises: if this "theory of the will" were accurate, then "our whole life would be divided between the despotism of outward impressions, and that of senseless and passive memory."[30] Hobbes's model was absurdly "purely physiological," and Hume's reductionism "degraded the notion of cause and effect into a blind product of delusion and habit."[31] Indeed, these philosophies were not merely mistaken on intellectual grounds, but themselves contributed to indolence, were themselves philosophies *of* indolence. As he writes in the *Dejection* ode from 1805, "I may not hope from outward forms to win / The passion and the life, whose fountains are within." There must be an active wellspring in the will; as the couplet that follows reads, "O Lady! we receive but what we give, / And in our life alone does nature live."[32] Quite in contrast to the giving to idleness, here we see that active giving makes receiving possible. Otherwise, too dependent upon outer forms, we settle into a state of inaction that results in misery.

Coleridge's philosophical journey takes him from an embrace of the Kantian primacy of the will to an embrace of its inherently spiritual authority, but it is the Hartleian/Godwinian model of philosophy to which *The Prelude* most explicitly responds.[33] Indeed, the poem presents itself as a response not only to Coleridge's condition but also to the cul-de-sacs of philosophy more generally.[34] It performs a revitalization of the will (the poet's imaginative spirit is "revived" as early as the end of book 1) and even appears to offer a sort of suggestion as to how to understand agency—agency as not self-legislating but rather dependent upon custom and habit.[35] In books 8 and 13 in particular, Wordsworth offers different ideas as to the nature of agency in the imagination and fancy.[36] However, Wordsworth's "response" to Coleridge is best understood neither in the mode of offering an alternative metaphysics nor in the mode of a direct call to action. *The Prelude* is best understood not as explanatory or normative in its aims, but as expressive, and this expression is itself a form of recognition (mild explanation) and of encouragement (mild assistance).

"Thus from day to day," Wordsworth tells us when describing his anxiously unproductive state in book 1,

> I live a mockery of the brotherhood
> Of vice and virtue, with no skill to part
> Vague longing that is bred by want of power,
> From paramount impulse not to be withstood;
> A timorous capacity, from prudence;
> From circumspection, infinite delay. (1:235–44)

Wordsworth's articulation of his weak state is not aimed at resolution, explanation, or the elimination of contradiction, but operates through the presentation of those contradictions, much like we found in Johnson. Less mathematical than musical, we have a repetition of parallelisms, from "day to day" to "vice and virtue," and Wordsworth presents the imbalance of the weaker impulses that succeed and the stronger impulses through the disharmony of juxtaposed musical notes rather than through the clarity of a common conceptual denominator. The effect on the reader is not meant to be satisfaction through explanation, but the recognition of a familiar state of disorientation. Like some music, the effect is to somehow, through formal effects, be expressive of a felt condition without creating that feeling in you. To borrow a memorable insight about Wordsworth's poetry by Adam Potkay, "Even when 'sad' it does not sadden": "As music, it does not even *express* sadness but, to use the philosopher Peter Kivy's distinction, is *expressive of* sadness, in the way that a St. Bernard's face may be said, quite apart from any inference about its emotional state, to 'look sad.'"[37]

The procrastinatory attitude kicks off the poem and also sustains it through the syntax of Wordsworth's seemingly leisurely mode of walking throughout. This "wise passive" mode of walking is, however, given the impulse of the poem as a work of self-beguiling delay, best seen as containing a contradiction between putting forward the outer picture of a self who is "willed" and an inner picture of a self who is strategically ("willfully") conceiving of himself as such. We can indeed discern anxiety in Wordsworth's famous walks. In book 1, it is described as "stray[ing] about":

Ah, better far than this to stray about
Voluptuously through fields and rural walks
And ask no record of the hours given up
To vacant musing, unreproved neglect
Of all things, and deliberate holiday. (1:252–56)

The walking, we must recognize, is done in the context of getting his mind off of the "awful burthen" of a writing task. The "voluptuousness" then reads as excessive in its eagerness for calm. The desire to "ask no record of the hours" stands out as particularly self-deceiving, for to mention "the hours" is to be aware of them. This phrase contains the contradiction inherent in "deliberate holiday"—indeed, in the mode of leisure newly available to the middle class in England in the eighteenth century—that if you can afford to waste time, you must also be aware that this time comes at a price. If "time is money," as Benjamin Franklin put it, then it is never free. (There ain't no such thing as a free walk.) The voluptuous walker must know this, even as he pretends to escape the time frame in which he is permanently fixed. These lines then contain two speakers, a deceiver and a deceived, in a sense that is similar to the double voice identified in free indirect discourse in chapter 3—a voice that allows oneself to go through with what one at the same time recognizes is not for the best.

Upon recognizing the concealed sense of guilt in these articulations of supposed restful walking, we can also attend to Wordsworth's grammar of ease and find concealed anxiety there as well. Before characterizing the "awful burthen" that prompted the writing of this work, the poet describes himself as "occupied in mind" and in the mode of "lingering":

> Thus occupied in mind I lingered here
> Contented, nor rose up until the sun
> Had almost touched the horizon; bidding then
> A farewell to the city left behind,
> Even with the chance equipment of that hour
> I journeyed towards the vale which I had chosen. (1:95–100)

Here it is both the subject and the syntax that linger. While there are several direct actions in this sentence ("I lingered" and "I journeyed"), the clauses do not begin with these actions but with the subordinate clauses "Thus occupied in mind" and "bidding then / A farewell to the city left behind, / Even with the chance equipment of that hour." We register that the self is always already in a flow when the action comes: actions always follow from preexisting states rather than from a discrete sense of the subject. The subject does not "rise" up of his own accord. Instead, the verb is delivered in the negative ("nor rose up until"). In waiting for objects of the natural world to provide the means for movement, the poem reproduces grammatically the speaker's procrastinatory mode.

Cluing in to the ambivalences of agency also helps us recognize the singular importance of a grammar of ambiguity in Wordsworth's poem more generally. This produces a lyric mode of "surmise," which, Geoffrey Hartman has written, "approves ... of such fluidity.... it likes 'whether ... or' formulations, alternatives rather than exclusions, echoing conjecture ... rather than blunt determinateness."[38] The mode of surmise attains particular importance in these moments in which the nature of agency or the will is uncertain—not just passive but at odds with itself, not just active but also hanging back and self-beguiling. This ambiguity produces a poetics of multiple options that reads not just as deception but as genuine ambivalence that mirrors the ambivalence as to how to understood one's own will. In one of the first lines of the poem, the poet declares that he is set "free" from the confines of the city and tells us, "Now I am free, enfranchised and at large, / May fix my habitation where I will" (1:9–10). If paused over, we can see the sentence as maintaining two opposite meanings, depending on how we understand the word "will." Given the context, we are led to believe that, by the words "where I will," the poet means "wherever it may be that I will be," using "will" as a future-tense modifier. But, read more literally, the phrase could also be interpreted as using the word "will" as a direct verb, conveying the meaning "where I will myself to go." The first reading conveys the strategic sense of being without agency as a mere voyeur to the necessitarian movements, whereas the second conveys the Kantian sense of freedom in choice. The ambivalence is possible because of the vagueness of the grammar, a vagueness essential for delivering a sense of the person as maintaining different impulses at one and the same time.

This ambiguity also comes through in Wordsworth's frequent use of double negatives that conceals agency. Slightly later in book 1, the poet tells us,

> Whereat, being not unwilling now to give
> A respite to this passion, I paced on
> Gently, with careless steps, and came erelong
> To a green shady place where down I sate. (1:68–71)

Instead of declaring himself "willing . . . to give / A respite to this passion," the poet tells us he declines to "not will": "I never said I was *willing,* I just said I was *not un*willing." The double negative allows both a poetics of calm and serenity and a strategic abdication of agency, an allowing oneself to waste time in the acknowledgement of guilt. It's a good way of talking if you don't want to be blamed for anything.

If the effects of ambiguity and surmise pervade these moments in which the question of the will is held off as uncertain and unsteady, akrasia plays other roles in Wordsworth's poem as well. Indeed, akrasia also appears as a central motif in characterizations of the poet's childhood in book 1, and these instances can help bring out the poem's investment in the darkness or mystery of articulation. In its movements through various "spots of time" in which the poet as a child engaged in guilty acts, book 1 contains moments reminiscent of Augustine's *Confessions*. Early on he describes his childhood adventures as a "plunderer" (1:336):

> Sometimes it befel
> In these night-wanderings, that a strong desire
> O'erpowered my better reason, and the bird
> Which was the captive of another's toils
> Became my pre. (1:324–28)

Against his "better reason," he steals "the captive of another's toils," here replicating the scene of Augustine stealing the pears in the *Confessions*, and attributes to it an explanation that is not really an explanation: "I did not steal so as to enjoy the fruits of my crime, but rather to enjoy the theft itself, and the sin."[39] The lack of a clear motive or motivation to Augustine's act was brought out through the language of darkness: "Wherever my inclinations took me," Augustine writes in book 2 of the *Confessions*, "a dark cloud came between me and the clear skies of your truth" [*et in omnibus erat caligo intercludens mihi, deus meus, serenitatem veritatis tuae*].[40] In Augustine, the "dark cloud [*caligo*]" was a product of the will's perversions and its inexplicable embrace of evil. In Wordsworth's passages of akrasia, the mysterious self-perversions of action are also represented through darkness, but it is a different kind of darkness. The scene above is set amid his "night-wanderings," which evokes the aimless and guilty nature of the pursuit. It also evokes Wordsworth's related poem "Nutting," in which, after ravaging the peaceful natural setting, he feels "a sense of pain when I beheld / The silent trees, and saw the intruding sky" (lines 52–53). In another "spot of time" slightly later in book 1, the poet describes how he "lustily" stole a shepherd's boat and, afterward, how

> for many days my brain
> Worked with a dim and undetermined sense

Of unknown modes of being. In my thoughts
There was a darkness—call it solitude
Or blank desertion. (1:417–22)

These lines evoke Augustine's *caligo,* but in Wordsworth's *Prelude* there is no freely given grace and no true sense of sin. The "blank desertion" plays differently.[41]

This "blank desertion" at times appears to be a part of an alternative metaphysics proposed by Wordsworth, one in which there is

a dark
Invisible workmanship that reconciles
Discordant elements, and makes them move
In one society. (1:352–55)

But, more consistently, the darkness of *The Prelude* speaks to the darkness of the mind and the darkness of words. Considered this way, darkness is not necessarily negative; it speaks not just to the gap between knowledge and action, between the deceiving mind and the deceived, but also to the mysterious spaces held in words. "Visionary power," he tells us in book 5,

Attends upon the motions of the winds
Embodied in the mystery of words;
There darkness makes abode, and all the host
Of shadowy things do work their changes there
As in a mansion like their proper home.
Even forms and substances are circumfused
By that transparent veil with light divine,
And through the turnings intricate of verse
Present themselves as objects recognised
In flashes, and with a glory scarce their own. (5:619–29)

Here the natural processes of the winds are encapsulated within the domiciles of words, which are the houses of darkness. They offer glimpses of light, which, in the darkness, help to give shape to that which we cannot fully see. Through the "turnings intricate of verse," we can see "flashes" of that which we hope to represent. As in Sterne or Rousseau, the blankness is that of being without words, without the tools of explication that bring causal chains of connections to light; however, even in the blankness of words there are ways to bring truths to light "in flashes," through modes of expression more elliptical and peripheral.

The realization of the negative powers of the mind climaxes in the young poet's journey to the Alps in book 6, in which he encounters the mind's anticipatory strength of "Imagination!" We can reflect upon this moment and understand it as also made possible by Wordsworth's procrastination. One condition of a self-recognized internal darkness leads to another. When we consider the impetus for this journey, we can recognize that it proceeds according to the very same logic (or illogic) as that which motivated the writing process in book 1: it too is conceived as a way of distracting from more pressing work by taking to a more achievable enterprise. He tells us, "An open slight / Of college cares and study was the scheme" (6:342–43). He walks in order to get away from his school work. As in book 1, he finds himself surrounded by an oppressive condition that he had built for himself:

> I was detached
> Internally from academic cares,
> From every hope of prowess and reward,
> And wished to be a lodger in that house
> Of letters, and no more—and should have been
> Even such, but for some personal concerns
> That hung about me in my own despite
> Perpetually, no heavy weight, but still
> A baffling and a hindrance, a controul
> Which made the thought of planning for myself
> A course of independent study seem
> An act of disobedience towards them
> Who loved me, proud rebellion, and unkind.
> This bastard virtue—rather let it have

A name it more deserves, this cowardise—
Gave treacherous sanction to that over-love
Of freedom planted in me from the very first,
And indolence, by force of which I turned
From regulations even of my own
As from restraints and bonds. (6:20–48)

As in Johnson, we see here a prolonged explicit narration of the contrary dynamics, the length of which mimics the difficulty of conceptualization. It is indeed a rather lengthier meditation upon the frustrated dereliction of duty and filial disobedience than we saw in *Robinson Crusoe*. The voice makes frequent amendments and revisions in order try to articulate the condition in its subtlety ("and should have been / Even such, but for . . . ," "no heavy weight, but still," "rather let it have / A name it more deserves"). Additionally, it does not allow the comfort of explanation by reducing the intentional dynamics to merely passive dynamics. Personifications stand in to stage the internal battle—"cowardise" gives sanction to an "over-love / Of freedom" and "indolence"—but they do not displace the action, for they are all ultimately "his": "I turned / From regulations even of my own."

This sets us up for a characterization of seeming calm that we can understand instead as concealing the speaker's anxieties. In order to justify his continuing with his procrastinatory walk, he needs to construe the activity as guilt-free and, further, needs to construe his will in a purely passive mode rather than as a free and active entity. He construes his walking through the Alps as though it were a motion akin to the ongoing movement of rivers, breezes, streams, gales, birds, and fish:

Upon the bosom of the gentle Soane
We glided forward with the flowing stream:
Swift Rhone, thou wert the wings on which we cut
Between thy lofty rocks. (6:385–88)

Like a breeze
Or sunbeam over your domain I passed
In motion without pause. (6:605–7)

> Finally, whate'er
> I saw, or heard, or felt, was but a stream
> That flowed into a kindred stream, a gale
> That helped me forwards, did administer
> To grandeur and to tenderness. . . . (6:672–76)

> I seemed to move among them as a bird
> Moves through the air, or as a fish pursues
> Its business in its proper element. (6:697–99)

These expressions may be understood as exhibiting the wisely passive mode, but in context, they also deserve to be seen as strategies of concealment: after all, to think of oneself as a stream, a breeze, a bird, a fish, or a cloud is to avoid thinking of oneself as a person. Clouds don't procrastinate, and this makes the desire to be a cloud all the more appealing. It is a familiar wish by now—to be something that simply obeys nature's causal laws—that we have encountered in figures from Hobbes to Yorick. In Wordsworth's case, it is a wish to forget one's work, a wish as temporary as a holiday and just as deliberate.

Still, this mode of self-deception that covers anxiety leads to positive ends. Wordsworth's procrastination has produced *The Prelude,* and his escape from school led to an encounter with his unexpected imaginative powers. The indulgence in the weaker reason may yield unexpected goods. The representation of it allows one to, if not understand oneself, then see oneself, and, as we have seen in Johnson, seeing is a step to understanding. The vision, in this case, is one of blankness, which is a vision Coleridge's favorite philosophies could not see.

KEATS'S DISTANCED INDOLENCE AND DISINTERESTED AESTHETICS

In a collection of letters dated May 1817 to his friend Benjamin Robert Haydon, John Keats describes his unproductive condition:

> I cannot write while my spirit is fe[a]vered [*sic*] in a contrary direction
> and I am now sure of having plenty of it this Summer—At this moment I

am in no enviable Situation—I feel that I am not in a Mood to write any to day; and it appears that the lo[o]ss [sic] of it is the beginning of all sorts of irregularities ... truth is I have a horrid Morbidity of Temperament which has shown itself at intervals—it is I have no doubt the greatest Enemy and stumbling block I have to fear.[42]

In descriptions we may find all too familiar by now, Keats characterizes his "mood" and "temperament" as at odds with his intent to write, and a deficiency of unified attention with which to accomplish his stated purpose. In a letter a few days later to his publishers John Taylor and James Augustus Hessey, he continues: "I went day by day at my Poem for a Month at the end of which time the other day I found my Brain so overwrought that I had neither Rhyme nor reason in it ... instead of Poetry I have a swimming in my head—And feel all the effects of a Mental Debauch—lowness of Spirits—anxiety to go on without the Power to do so which does not at all tend to my ultimate Progression."[43] Keats's formulations here sound like those of Johnson, Wordsworth, and Coleridge, and perhaps even like those of Hamlet, whose "native hue of resolution / Is sicklied o'er" until he "lose[s] the name of action." Indeed, Keats's phrases here and elsewhere in his writing read as particularly "borrowed"—a quality even more explicit in a later letter about indolence sometime between February and May 1819 addressed to his brother George Keats and sister-in-law Georgiana, which prepares some of the thoughts that would be included in his *Ode on Indolence* composed later that year:

This morning I am in a sort of temper indolent and supremely careless: I long after a stanza or two of Thompson's [sic] Castle of indolence—My passions are all alseep [sic] from my having slumbered till nearly eleven and weakened the animal fibre all over me to a delightful sensation about three degrees on this side of faintness—if I had teeth of pearl and the breath of lillies I should call it langour—but as I am ... I must call it Laziness.... Neither Poetry, nor Ambition, nor Love have any alertness of countenance as they pass by me: they seem rather like three figures on a greek vase—a Man and two women—whom no one but myself could distinguish in their disguisement.[44]

This passage reveals a self-consciousness about the way his articulations on indolence borrow from earlier works of literature. Instead of writing, he "long[s] after" reading an older work that depicts indolence: Thomson's *Castle of Indolence*. Further, as he considers the poetic subjects he wishes to engage—poetry, ambition, love—they appear to him not from his own memory or reflections of himself, but rather as "figures on a greek vase," already given representational form.

In this sense, Keats's indolence can be distinguished from Wordsworth's or Coleridge's or Johnson's in the sense that it appears especially—to borrow Lord Byron's pejorative description of Keats's poetry—"secondhand." Much Keats scholarship, from John Bayley to Christopher Ricks to Marjorie Levinson, has understood his poetry through its appropriative style. As Levinson puts it, "His Homer was Chapman, his Dante was Cary, his Provençal ballads translations in an edition of Chaucer, his Boccaccio Englished."[45] We see this effect in the letter to George and Georgiana Keats: not only is indolence featured as a state of feeling disembodied—will detached from purpose—but also the poet is featured as detached from the figure of indolence itself. "Poetry," "Ambition," "Love" pass by as two-dimensional images: even "Ambition" here is not something that Keats experiences as his, but something he recognizes as from afar. They are hesitantly given names, as if he is struggling to identify them: "I should call it langour . . . I must call it Laziness." As these poetic subjects appear for him, flat and already articulated by literary tradition, they uphold the familiar effects of indolence (they fail to rouse inspiration), but they also put the contrary effects of the condition onto an external object such that they can be examined from a contemplative distance.

This distancing quality makes Keats a unique figure for interrogating akrasia in poetry. Indeed, even more than with Wordsworth, with Keats we discover that akrasia is expressed through the dynamics of writing itself, such that we can say that the representations of akrasia shift from the site of the person to the site of the poem. It has often been observed that Keats's removed and belated relationship to literature produces an especially fascinating indulgence in formal experimentation. When it comes to the condition of akratic inaction (indolence) in particular, this position means interrogating the condition, not from his own personal "experience" drawn from the depths of "interiority," but through a formal interest in juxtaposition and contrasts and through something like what Schlegel called the "hovering" mode of irresolution. In Keats we find poetry itself as multidirectional, bending toward opposite inclinations, exhibiting a split between belief and practice, knowing and doing. What is left is the sense of the generative possibilities of keeping akrasia non-disaggregated, keeping the contrary dynamics together.

Keats's relationship to his indolence shifts over the course of his short career as a poet. In his poems from 1816 he seems to write about indolence as if poetry itself can reinvigorate it. In poems like "To My Brother George" (composed in August 1816) and "Sleep and Poetry" (composed around November or December 1816), the problem of languor or listlessness seems curable by writing itself. "To My Brother George" begins, "Full many a dreary hour have I past, / My brain bewilder'd, and my mind o'ercast / With heaviness" (1–3), then continues to appeal to the power of poesy:

> But there are times, when those that love the bay,
> Fly from all sorrowing far, far away;
> A sudden glow comes on them, nought they see
> In water, earth, or air, but poesy. (19–22)[46]

In "Sleep and Poetry," Keats dwells on the various qualities of deadening sleep, and sets his agenda to embark on the project of writing: "O for ten years, that I may overwhelm / Myself in poesy; so I may do the deed / That my own soul has to itself decreed" (96–98). This line reflects a confidence that "decreeing" can lead so efficiently to "doing." We find a separate example of Keats's aspirational notion that poetry can be rehabilitative in his feat of composing his long poem *Endymion* over the course of 1817. He describes in his letters how he conceives of writing *Endymion* as a way of pushing himself into action: it will be, he writes, "a test, a trial of my Powers of Imagination and chiefly of my invention which is a rare thing indeed—by which I must make 4000 Lines of one bare circumstance and fill them with Poetry."[47] The task of making "4000 Lines of one bare circumstance and fill[ing] them with Poetry" indeed determines from the outset that status of poetic lines as "filler." Although reminiscent in some sense of Wordsworth, who wrote that he was determined to "brace [him]self to some determined aim" (1:124) by writing *The Prelude,* hoping to overcome his creative lassitude by "shap[ing] out / Some tale from [his] own heart, more near akin / To [his] own passions and habitual thoughts," Keats does not find that he possesses the authority or personal experiences to write "from his own heart."[48] The poem begins "where old Chaucer used to sing" (134), indicating from the outset that he is residing in the worlds of other poets. Throughout, Endymion is analogized to familiar figures. The character's indolence is described at first not through his own experience but through the eyes of others: "A smile was on his countenance; he seem'd / To common lookers on, like one who dream'd / Of idleness in groves Elysian" (175–77), and he is recurrently described by citing recognizable "types" or "kinds":

> In the self-same fixed trance he kept,
> Like one who on the earth had never stept—
> Aye, even as dead-still as a marble man,
> Frozen in that old tale Arabian. (403–6)[49]

As Keats himself observed, *Endymion* reads as a product of a strained and anxious will. In the preface to the poem that he would later write in 1818, he admits, "The reader . . . must soon perceive great inexperience, immaturity, and every error denoting a feverish attempt, rather than a deed accomplished."[50]

At around the same time, however, Keats also puts forward other ways of understanding a poet's relation to indolence in which the fitting response is not to strive to work past it, but rather to dwell in it and to find this mode of abeyance as valuable in and of itself. In poems like "On Seeing the Elgin Marbles," "Ode to a Nightingale," and the "Ode on Indolence," we see the poet using indolence in line with the idea of "disinterestedness" as theorized by his friend William Hazlitt and as a specific mode of what he would describe as negative capability. The notion of "disinterestedness" is typically understood in relation to aesthetics, but, for Hazlitt, it is crucially connected to an understanding of human agency as well.

The familiar sense of "disinterestedness" in relation to art can be found in Hazlitt's 1818 lectures on the English poets when he describes Shakespeare as "nothing in himself":

> He was nothing in himself; but he was all that others were, or that they
> could become. He had not only in himself the germs of every faculty
> and feeling, but he could follow them by anticipation . . . He had 'a mind
> reflecting ages past,' and present:—all the people that ever lived are
> there. . . . He turned the globe round for his amusement, and surveyed
> the generations of men, and the individuals as they passed . . . He had
> only to think of any thing in order to become that thing, with all the
> circumstances belonging to it.[51]

To be disinterested does not mean to be removed, exactly, but to be able to be engaged in multiple, perhaps incompatible, ways.[52] As David Bromwich has written, "A disinterested investigator, a disinterested judge, a disinterested historian, need not be detached. He may be immersed in a question and, having started on one side, conclude his engagement on the opposite one—or even on the same. What is unimaginable is that he should remain strictly neutral."[53] This definition, however, takes on added dimensions when we understand it in relation to Hazlitt's discussion of the word in his *Essay on the Principles of Human Action,* published in 1805. In this essay, Hazlitt does not use this expression to talk about an exceptional type of artist like Shakespeare, but to talk about human agency in general.

At the very beginning, the essay declares that its aim is to demonstrate that "the human mind is naturally disinterested."[54] It indeed can be understood as a response to the tradition of Enlightenment philosophers from Hobbes, Spinoza, Locke, and Hume to Hartley and Godwin. In this respect, it is inspired by Kant and parallels many of Coleridge's concerns. Philosophers like Hobbes, the French materialists, and the British associationists understood action as operating by physical causal laws, and this outlook, Hazlitt tells us, entails that all human action is necessary selfish. As discussed in chapter 1, for Hobbes, action is determined by desire, and desire is grounded in self-preservation. Hazlitt stresses, somewhat like Coleridge, that philosophy cannot merely accept that the human frame is reducible to mechanistic laws; it will be impossible to "ever arriv[e] at [truth]," he writes, "if at the outset we completely cover our own feelings with maps of the brain, dry skulls, musical chords, pendulums, and compasses."[55] Following this, Hazlitt tells us, individuals do not merely instinctively *re*-act to stimuli; rather, in order to be directed to a future action, they must have the capacity for imaginative abstraction. A future good, he writes, "can only affect me as an imaginary idea, or an idea of truth."[56] Because we imaginatively form abstractions about the future, we are not only capable of acting for the good of ourselves, but also capable of acting for the good of others, in whose minds we can take an interest: "I can only abstract myself from my present being and take an interest in my future being in the same sense and manner, in which I can go out of myself entirely and enter into the minds and feelings of others."[57] For Hazlitt, this capacity for imaginative abstraction crucially allows the ability to compare and contrast—a capacity that would not be possible if the mind were sheer mechanism reacting to strictly linear motives and a solely efficient mode of causation. "To perceive the relation of one thing to another," he writes, "it is not only necessary that the ideas of the things themselves should co-exist . . . but that they should be perceived to co-exist by the same conscious understanding, or that their different actions should be felt at the same instant by the same being in the strictest sense."[58] Human beings are inherently capable of holding different and indeed contrasting ideas at one and the same time. "I am not the same thing," he writes, "but many different things."[59] It is not that Shakespeare is an exemplary person, but that Shakespeare exemplifies this capacity of all people: the capacity of imaginative abstraction, which distinguishes the metaphysics of human agency.

If the word "disinterestedness" takes on an additional connotation when seen in this context, then so does the phrase "negative capability." In his well-known letter to his brothers, Keats uses the phrase to describe the artist's condition ("especially in Literature") of being "in uncertainties, Mysteries, doubts, without any irritable reaching after fact & reason." The formulation speaks to aesthetics but is rooted in the vocabulary of human agency—more specifically, it suggests the human capacity to negate capacity. This can be freeing and aesthetically promising, which means it is a capacity that is as positive as it is negative. In fact, it gives us a twisted version of "weakness of will," something more like a willingness to be weak. It is not simply a neutral declaration of negativity ("it is the case that x is negative"), but a positive making of negativity ("x makes itself negative"). As Anahid Nersessian has emphasized, "It can't be said enough that Keats's Capability is *active,* or even that it is *an action.* The word implies a state of latency, and yet to be negatively capable is already to be undertaking the semideliberate self-compression and self-dissolution that deletes character, crosses it out" (emphasis mine).[60] One needs to put some effort into being negatively capable. The "semi" part of "semideliberate" is key: it is willing in a way, or half-willing. It is the allowing of oneself to be in a state of partial incapacity.

We can see this as a kind of parallel response to the linear model of the causation of action we saw in Hazlitt. For both, it is important to maintain the reality of an existence that is not synthesized or resolved into a singular "output." For the akratically indolent, this means not being *finally* comprehensible in the terms of a physical incapacity to move or the deeper (stronger) desire to stay put. In this sense, there are connections to be made between Keats's indolence and Augustine's weakness of will: as with Augustine, for Keats it would be crucially incorrect to say that there are *two* wills, ontologically distinct, in Manichean fashion, able to be parsed, that clash and compete against each other. Rather, there is *one* will, and it is a will divided. The idea is theological for Augustine and poetic for Keats, but the impulse is the same: it is a refusal to disaggregate, a commitment to the possibility of doubleness in unity, not two things in succession, but two things at once. Keats's indolence is negative and positive, "delicious" and "diligent."[61]

The motif of the poet's weakness of will or willing weakness indeed structures many of Keats's poems from late 1817 onward and makes possible a range of ways of experimenting with poetic contradictions. We can see it in the treatment of indolence in "Ode to a Nightingale" (written in the spring of 1819). In this ode, the speaker gives us two inclinations that are opposites but reside together. First there is the downward inclination associated with numbness and death:

> My heart aches, and a drowsy numbness pains
>   My sense, as though of hemlock I had drunk,

Or emptied some dull opiate to the drains
    One minute past, and Lethe-wards had sunk. (1–4)

The sensation is aching and painful, associated with sinking and opiates, and the pain is combined with nonfeeling. However, indolence is not just a matter of staying lifeless, but also of looking upward, having an eye on what might be:

'Tis not through envy of thy happy lot,
    But being too happy in thine happiness,—
        That thou, light-winged Dryad of the trees,
            In some melodious plot
    Of beechen green, and shadows numberless,
        Singest of summer in full-throated ease. (5–10)

There is the reality and the aspiration; the sinking pain coexists with being "too happy in thine happiness." If akratic action tends to be conveyed as a forward motion with a backward pull, here akratic indolence is a downward motion with an upward pull. It is also, notably, a condition known only to humans, and not to the bird who "hast never known, / The weariness, the fever, and the fret" (22–23). To be a living person means to know this doubling of aspiration and reality—that "to think is to be full of sorrow" (27).

In "Ode to a Nightingale," this doubling also signifies a condition of "fullness," a ripeness that indicates maximum capacity, the apex of life, as well as the verge of complete annihilation. The speaker yearns for

    a beaker full of the warm South,
  Full of the true, the blushful Hippocrene,
    With beaded bubbles winking at the brim,
      And purple-stained mouth. (15–18)

The words "full," repeated in lines 15 and 16 and echoed again in "blushful," emphasize the state of containing too much. Yet there is no release. Indolence is like summer, as in "To Autumn," where summer is a state of fullness—it has "o'er-brimm'd [the bees'] clammy cells" (11). Here too it has gone beyond max capacity: the vintage tastes of "sunburnt mirth," which is a mirth or pleasure that is also overdone.

This is the "too much-ness" of Keats, brought out in a state of being in agential contradictions, but also making possible a luscious, rich, and over-done aesthetic sensibility.[62] The contained contradictions of indolence are brought out as more explicitly connected to the status of the artwork and the privileges of the disinterested mode in "On Seeing the Elgin Marbles" and the "Ode on Indolence." In both of these we see a movement from the condition of the poet (or the person) to the structure of the poem, with the first more negative dimensions of a personal akrasia giving way to a second more positive construal of akrasia as generative dynamics for aes-thetic experience and creation. "Elgin Marbles," composed in February or March 1817, begins with a portrayal of the poet's weak spirit reminiscent of Keats's other poems on indolence to date, including "To My Brother George" and "Sleep and Poetry," but, unlike them, it shifts directions away from the self and so stages an analogy between indolence and the dizzying splendor of encountering objects. The poem's first two lines ("My spirit is too weak—mortality/Weighs heavily on me like unwilling sleep") recall the opening to "To My Brother George" ("Full many a dreary hour have I past,/My brain bewilder'd, and my mind o'ercast/With heaviness"). In both we have the "brain" or "spirit" that is "weigh[ed]" down "heavily" or "with heaviness," made heavier by the awareness of the passage of time, indicated by the prospect of "mortality" or "many a dreary hour." What we have described earlier as the "heaviness" of akratic action, which proceeds with a trace of regret, is here emphasized through the heavy weight of something like unwilling sleep, which presses against the desire to rise and act. As the poem continues through line 10, it reflects on the unresolvable contraries of this mode of existence:

> And each imagined pinnacle and steep
> Of godlike hardship tells me I must die
> Like a sick eagle looking at the sky.
>> Yet 'tis a gentle luxury to weep
>> That I have not the cloudy winds to keep
> Fresh for the opening of the morning's eye.

> Such dim-conceived glories of the brain
> > Bring round the heart an undescribable feud. (3–10)

There are multiple contradictions associated with this state. The speaker is capable of imagining his lofty heights of "pinnacle[s] and steep[s]," but they in turn tell him he "must die." His heaviness is a burden, but it is also a "gentle luxury." His "glories of the brain" are able to energize him, but they are "dim-conceived." Together these contraries bring about "an undescribable feud," a clash that he cannot articulate. As he writes in a follow-up poem to Haydon, "Forgive me, Haydon, that I cannot speak / Definitively on these mighty things" (1–2)—or, as Robinson Crusoe might put it, "I know not what to call this."

From lines 11 on, however, it no longer appears to be the case that the "undescribable feud" primarily or most significantly reflects the indolent state of the speaker. The poem shifts so it is no longer centered on the speaker; there is no more mention of "my spirit" or "I." The feud appears to stand for a broader principle, one exemplified in the Elgin marbles themselves or, one might say, in the construction of the poem:

> So do these wonders a most dizzy pain,
> > That mingles Grecian grandeur with the rude
> Wasting of old time—with a billowy main—
> > A sun—a shadow of a magnitude. (11–15)

This late introduction of the titular subject of the poem—the marbles ("these wonders")—serves to displace the attention on the weak spirit itself and instead focus it outward to objects in the world. They likewise "bring round the heart" a "most dizzy pain," for they also contain contradictory qualities that place the viewer in a disoriented and unresolved stance. The marbles "mingl[e]" the "Grecian grandeur with the rude / Wasting of old time"—a sense of timeless greatness with the inexorable fact of passing time. The dichotomy between heaviness and time recalls the same dichotomy staged earlier in the poem, but now it carries different connotations, turning our attention elsewhere than to external juxtapositions. At the same time, while it shifts from a personal indolence to a set of objects, it also turns from a poem that appears to be concerned with reinvigorating the will to a poem that is content to leave unresolved contraries on the page. With the final lines, a set of images are placed side by side: "a billowy main" and a "sun," on which a formless shadow is cast.

In the 1819 "Ode on Indolence" we see a different kind of shift from the realm of the personal to the realm of the external, and, in the process, we also see a shift from a negative inflection of logical contradictions to a more positive one, one that holds up the value of not-saying or silence. This ode centers on three two-dimensional figures—Love, Ambition, and Poesy—who do not speak. As we have briefly seen already in Keats's letter to his brother and sister-in-law, "Neither Poetry, nor Ambition, nor Love have any alertness of countenance as they pass by me: they seem rather like three figures on a greek vase." These figures are personifications, but, steeped as they are in literary history, they are not able to rouse him:

> One morn before me were three figures seen,
>> With bowed necks, and joined hands, side-faced;
> And one behind the other stepp'd serene,
>> In placid sandals, and in white robes graced:
> They pass'd, like figures on a marble urn,
>> When shifted round to see the other side;
>>> They came again; as when the urn once more
> Is shifted round, the first seen shades return;
>> And they were strange to me, as may betide
>>> With vases, to one deep in Phidian lore. (1–10)

They seem to emit nothing, which is a kind of taunting to one who is unproductive. Their nonofferings are conveyed in their blank features ("serene," "placid," "white," they "pass"). and the scene is told in the passive voice ("were three figures seen," "the urn once more /Is shifted round"). Quickly, they are recognized as threatening: "How came ye muffled in so hush a masque?" he asks in the second stanza. They are threatening because they are foreign and unknown to him—"How is it, shadows, that I knew ye not?" (11)—and he believes they should not be. Helen Vendler compares the scene to that found in *Hamlet*: the figures, she writes, "bear . . . overtones of the haunting ghost of old Hamlet rebuking his son for not yet having entered upon action."[63] Like the deceased King Hamlet, these figures appear in ominous silence, and, like the prince of Denmark, the speaker is a reluctant nondoer, haunted as much as taunted by the visiting phantoms.

However, this early presentation of indolence as a negative condition for the akratic protagonist soon changes. The figures' silence starts to appear differently, less overtly threatening. We might note that we have encountered a range of ways silence has accompanied the writing of akrasia thus far: the "surd" in Davidson, the unempirical in Murdoch, the causal gap in Sterne, the aporia of the two perspectives of FID in Austen, the unavailability of explanation in Rousseau, the mystery of words in Wordsworth. With Keats we see it again, but a bit differently; here, indolence creates a kind of silence in its nonoutput in its fostering of unresolved contradictions. The nonresolution of contradictions comes through, once again, in the state of abeyance. Like in "Ode to a Nightingale," indolence is associated with summer—a state of being that is rich, full, and in a state of potential:

> Ripe was the drowsy hour;
> The blissful cloud of summer-indolence
> Benumb'd my eyes; my pulse grew less and less;
> Pain had no sting, and pleasure's wreath no flower. (15–18)

"Summer-indolence" is a state that combines ripeness and numbness, and it is a state to be yearned for. In stanza 4, the figure of Poesy does not bring a joy "so sweet as drowsy noons, / And evenings steep'd in honied indolence" (36–37). The rich full mode of summer provides benefits in its nonrelease:

> The morn was clouded, but no shower fell,
> Though in her lids hung the sweet tears of May;
> . . . .
> O shadows! 'twas a time to bid farewell!
> Upon your skirts had fallen no tears of mine. (45–50)

Keats is in this sense like a cloud—not a cloud that is without volition, as we saw in Wordsworth, but one that has reached its limit point of saturation with no release.

The poem refuses to stay in the mode of a person or protagonist who contains contradictions, but rather luxuriates in the distanced mode. Earlier, the speaker had called out to the figures, "O, why did ye not melt, and leave my sense / Unhaunted quite of all but—nothingness" (19–20)? By the end, his wish comes true, as they do leave him with a kind of nothingness. However, this is a more positive turn of affairs than we originally would have thought. In stanzas 5 and 6, he is eager to bid the figures "Farewell!" and "Adieu!," and this is not only in spite of the fact that they have done nothing for him, but also because they have done something for him— namely, nothing. Poesy has, to paraphrase W. H. Auden, "made nothing happen." The speaker is left with a generative state of nonoutput—a state of contradictions with nothing to show for it. It is a stance that refuses to value or abide by a behaviorist or empiricist mode of assessment. "Ye cannot raise / My head cool-bedded in the flowery grass" (51–52), he says, and this is a good thing. He asks them to remain flat and uninspiring: "Fade softly from my eyes, and be once more / In masque-like figures on the dreamy urn" (55–56). The poem ends by staying with the richness of the stance of purposive incapacity, weakness of will, willing weakness, a stance that is distanced from the world and content to keep difficulty in place. To not privilege output is to remain with the unsayable, and the poem ends with the choice to stay there. For the artist, there is then a certain privilege in this state of indolence. We might say that the speaker of this poem is less the akratic protagonist and more the author of the play— that is, less like Hamlet, who is two things at once, knowing yet delaying, having lost "the name of action," and more like the bard himself who, as Hazlitt put it, "turned the globe round for his amusement, and surveyed the generations of men, and the individuals as they passed," the exemplary figure of the disinterested artist.[64]

This ironic stance does not elect to solve, resolve, or disaggregate the condition of akrasia. As with Wordsworth, in this condition Keats has found a dynamic elemental to poetry. As a refusal to either explain or encourage, irreducible to metaphysics or morals, it becomes the form of antinomy. How to be and not to be? That is the question. Like for the authors already considered, it is a condition that cannot be brought out with a commitment to precise causal explication, but that can be seen through uses of language more elliptical and peripheral, through absence and antinomy, and through the curvature of words.

EPILOGUE

The Story of Akrasia

A MAN WALKS TRANCE-LIKE into the sleeping quarters of the king, lifts the dagger, and plunges it into the king's sleeping body. He hadn't wanted to do it, not really, but now he sees that things are out of his control. When his wife had spoken to him about the necessity of the act, his adrenaline kicked in. The neural networks began to operate on a closed circuit, and the pathways became fixed. Now he can think of nothing else. Heart pumping and attention focused, his circulatory system guides his legs forward, and, upon arrival at the bed, his arm starts convulsing upward and downward.

A man walks resolute into the sleeping quarters of the king, lifts the dagger, and plunges it into the king's sleeping body. It is a gruesome sight, but he knows that this is the only way. When he had spoken with his wife earlier, he had grown convinced that she was right. He would just need to weather the sight of all that blood, but once that was over, it will have been the right course of action. All signs pointed in this direction. Now he is convinced: what the witches foresaw was not only destiny but also for the best. Let's get on with it, he tells himself.

As is apparent, the story takes on different meanings if the act is considered to be not intentional (determined) or not irrational (in line with belief). A director, actor, or reader might choose to amplify the fated sense of Macbeth's condition—or, alternatively, his sense of firmly held belief. However, there is something appealing about choosing to interpret Macbeth as an akratic character whose act is both intentional and irrational, freely committed and also pursued with a recognition that it is unjustified, undermotivated, and following the weaker reason. This way of performing or reading Macbeth can ask us to take seriously a condition we might recognize in ourselves: that of being endowed with agency we knowingly pretend we do not have and being equipped with knowledge we purposely ignore. Some may protest that this sort of akrasia is not real, but a story is only as good as the telling, and sometimes a good story attuned to the right level of reality can make visible what we previously did not see.

The story of akrasia indeed remains one of our important stories. We can recognize its continued importance in the frequency with which we share anecdotes of our perennial bouts of procrastination, which remind us of the truth found in the comedic language of paradox—"I know what I should do but I'm not doing it"—which feels both phenomenologically right and logically wrong. We can recognize its importance in a more tragic key when we reflect on our stated goals to divest involvement in one or another institution or practice that wreaks devastation on a global scale. This book has tried to argue that, insofar as this story remained important to English authors in the long eighteenth century, a period with new and different frameworks for understanding and explaining human agency, will, and action, it was essential for them to develop ways of writing failure, neglect, self-betrayal, and irreducible conflict between belief and action in ways that do not reduce to a listing of causes in linear time. Recognizing this concern has allowed us to perceive particular epistemological roles for irony, interpretation, and contradiction in a certain period in English literary history. In Sterne, an ironic sentence performs the failures of causal narration; in Godwin and Austen, the ironic ability of free indirect discourse lies in its holding up the falsity of a character's private utterances; in Johnson and Rousseau, the open-ended and unresolved mode of portraying a person asks us to understand through interpretation; and, in Wordsworth and Keats, contradiction means we view a person like a work of art by attending to the dynamics and juxtapositions rather than striving for a reduced or solved solution or "end." All of these to some extent perform failure, in which the failure of language in some way mimics, performs, expresses, or represents the failures of the person.

In the story I have told, authors found new ways to take this failure in akrasia seriously. They have remained committed to the old fiction, which is also new, and not really a fiction: the one in which there is an "and yet" to agency and an "anyway" to action.

ACKNOWLEDGMENTS

Before this was a book it was a dissertation, and before it was a dissertation it was an idea. For his enthusiastic support for the idea and consistent guidance in its development to dissertation and beyond, I thank my graduate adviser and dissertation director, Thomas Pfau. I am very lucky to have benefited from Thomas's deep learning on an array of subjects from the history of philosophy to poetics and narrative theory as well as his practical wisdom on reading and writing in a humanistic tradition. I am also especially grateful to both Nancy Armstrong and Rob Mitchell, each of whom supported my progress throughout the graduate school years in the English department at Duke, introduced me to new ideas and ways of thinking, and provided essential feedback as readers of my dissertation. Vivasvan Soni generously agreed to serve as a dissertation committee member remotely; I thank him for his sharp feedback and encouragement as well as for having provided me in his own work with a prototype for the kind of scholarly argument I had hoped to approximate. Many other faculty and staff members helped me in my years at Duke in ways that may have seemed small at the time but were in fact quite consequential; I thank especially Sarah Beckwith, Toril Moi, Maryscot Mullins, Kathy Psomiades, Charlotte Sussman, and Len Tennenhouse. Life at Duke was sustained by my fellow graduate students; I want to single out for their companionship in brainstorming ideas and navigating life in graduate school Jack Bell, Chris Catanese, Rebecca Evans, and Stefan Waldschmidt.

I am exceedingly lucky to be working in the unfailingly generous English Department at University of Richmond. For their kindness and support since 2017 while I worked toward turning the dissertation into a book, I thank Bert Ashe, Laura Browder, Abigail Cheever, Libby Gruner, Brian Henry, Peter Lurie, Joyce MacAllister, Elizabeth Outka, Kevin Pelletier, Anthony Russell, Louis Schwartz, Monika Siebert, Julietta Singh, Nathan Snaza, David Stevens, and Emily Tarchokov. I am especially grateful to Elizabeth, Monika, Kevin, and Emily for their hospitality and special assistance in times of need, and to David and Louis for working tirelessly on my behalf as department chairs.

I was able to work on the dissertation version of this project thanks to the funding of the Duke Graduate School and the Evan Frankel Dissertation Completion Fellowship in 2015–16. Once arriving at Richmond, the book was written almost exclusively during the summer months of 2018, 2019, and 2020, so I am grateful to the University of Richmond A&S Dean's Summer Fellowship in 2018 and the A&S Summer Fellowships of 2019 and 2020 for making that possible. I then was able to complete revisions in the spring of 2021 thanks to a sabbatical offered by the university. I am indebted to the James B. Duke Memorial Library and the University of Richmond Boatwright Memorial Library for all of their resources over these years. During graduate school and the summers of 2017 through 2021, much of my writing and editing took place in different coffee shops around the globe and was powered by the coffee served there; I am especially thankful to Joe Van Gogh in Durham, Secret Life in Warsaw, various Starbuckses in Santiago de Chile and Beirut, and Sugar & Twine in Richmond.

I owe thanks to several scholarly presses for accepting essay versions of portions of this book at earlier dates, and I am doubly grateful that they have permitted me to reprint versions of them here. Portions of chapters 2 and 4 originally appeared in *The Eighteenth Century: Theory and Interpretation* 58, no. 1 (Spring 2017): 61–77. Copyright © 2017 University of Pennsylvania Press. Portions of chapter 3 were originally published in *Studies in Romanticism* 57, no. 2 (Summer 2018): 301–23. Copyright © 2018 Trustees of Boston University. Published with permission by Johns Hopkins University Press. And several paragraphs from chapter 1 were originally published in a forum in *Studies in Eighteenth-Century Culture* 47 (2018): 235–39. Copyright © 2017 The Johns Hopkins University Press.

Many thanks are owed to everyone at the University of Virginia Press who put in their hours, skills, and brainpower editing my MS Word document and turning it into a physical book. I thank Angie Hogan for enthusiastically supporting this project and for clearly and reliably shepherding it through the various phases. I also thank Morgan Myers for overseeing what has been a remarkably seamless editorial and production process. I want to extend special thanks to the two readers elicited by the Press—Andrew Franta and Sarah Tindal Kareem—for taking the time and energy (in the midst of a pandemic) to read the entire manuscript with thoughtfulness and care. These two were the perfect choices to serve as readers, bringing their expertise and critical acumen to this book; their suggestions (and kind words) were just what I needed. I also thank those who worked on design, production, and marketing, as well as meticulous copyeditor Emily Shelton and indexer Matthew J. Phillips. I am grateful to Jess Keiser for his consistent support for this project as well as to Robert Volpicelli and my brother Anthony Manganaro for reading over and providing feedback on portions of the manuscript at a late stage.

It is strange to thank one's parents for anything when they are responsible for everything, but it is nonetheless meaningful to thank my mom and my dad in this context for both having long supported the seemingly akratic endeavor of pursuing a professional life in art and ideas. I thank them as well as my brother Anthony and my sister Rania, with whom I first learned how to make things. Lidia refuses to be thanked, so as a separate sort of acknowledgment, I dedicate this book to her and to our two, Salem and Bowie.

NOTES

INTRODUCTION

1. Defoe, *Moll Flanders*, 199.
2. Defoe, 160.
3. Defoe, 163.
4. Davidson, "How Is Weakness of the Will Possible?," in *Essays on Actions and Events*, 21–42, 22.
5. Pinch, *Strange Fits of Passion*, 1, 3.
6. Thompson, *Fictional Matter*, 2–3.
7. Macpherson, *Harm's Way*, 4. In Macpherson's "genealogy of realism . . . depersonalization is literalized in the instrumentalizing logic of strict liability: persons are conceived of as mindless things" (16). For a sort of extension of this logic into the Romantic era, see also Stout's *Corporate Romanticism*, which examines the limits of "individualism" (and the relevance of the categories of "person" and "action") given the consequentialist logics of corporate personhood and collective action in the Romantic-era novel.
8. Kramnick, *Actions and Objects*, 2, 3.
9. The difference with *Actions and Objects* is also accentuated by this book's focus on a slightly later literary period (my study begins with Defoe, whereas Kramnick's ends with Richardson). *Actions and Objects* "moves freely between what in retrospect we would call philosophical and literary writing." Kramnick continues, "I take great pleasure in the nonexistence of this distinction in the eighteenth century. . . . These topics obey no boundaries of genre, though they are framed in different ways according to the formal properties and needs of the texts in which they come into view" (11–12). My somewhat later focus, which includes the Romantic period, is more naturally suited to an examination of the growing rift between the domains of "philosophical and literary writing."

10. Kramnick, 4.

11. Kramnick, 35.

12. For a notable example of a study that investigates eighteenth-century literature for what has been conceptually left behind or left out in the period, specifically through a pointed contrast with antiquity, see Soni's *Mourning Happiness* (2010). Soni's book identifies a turn away from the conceptions of "happiness" found in Solon's proverb "Call no man happy until he is dead" and in Aristotelian *eudaimonia* instead toward the notion of happiness as "feeling" or "affect" concretized in the eighteenth century. This change manifests in eighteenth-century narrative form and informs a broader set of (enduring) political commitments. This sort of investigation looks to changes in the eighteenth century as crucially related to our current moment and, in that sense, undertakes a Foucaultian "archeology of the present" that is in the service of elevating the importance of humanistic inquiry; one purpose, Soni writes, is to find in eighteenth-century literature the grounds for "arguing for a nonmathematizable, narrative-based conception of happiness," thereby "mak[ing] the case for the importance of humanistic approaches to the study of happiness" (14). In a somewhat similar vein, one of my aims here is to illuminate how changing conceptual frameworks in that period can help suggest to us a special role for humanistic inquiry in the present—specifically, through modes of writing that express aspects of human life in ways strictly causal explication cannot.

13. For a very helpful and precise investigation of the history of akrasia/weakness of will up to the seventeenth and eighteenth centuries (discussing those periods very briefly), see Saarinen, *Weakness of Will.* See also Hoffmann, ed., *Weakness of Will from Plato,* a collection of essays that offers a range of different approaches to the subject from thinkers ranging through Plato, Aristotle, Augustine, Aquinas, Kant, Schopenhauer, and Nietzsche. It does not provide an overarching narrative about the trajectory of akrasia, though I think one can perceive the increasing difficulty of maintaining the concept's coherence once we reach Kant.

14. MacIntyre, *After Virtue,* 82.

15. James, *Passion and Action,* 257–58.

16. For a related approach to conceptions of the passions, emotion, autonomy, and restraint rooted in antiquity and their relations to Romanticism, see Risinger, *Stoic Romanticism,* which was published while this book was in production. Risinger produces a genealogy of Stoicism, culminating in figures like Wollstonecraft, Wordsworth, Byron, and Emerson, finding in the Stoic tradition not merely detachment or contentment, but also "a radical commitment, an impulse toward world making—at once ethical, poetical, and political—in which justice is predicated on affective restraint" (12–13).

17. François, *Open Secrets*, xvi; Lee, *Failures of Feeling*, 2. In Lee's study we can see a philosophical conundrum brought about by Hobbesian philosophy that can be instructively compared to the puzzle raised by akrasia: "If feeling is moving, and moving is living, how can we account for those who do not move and who are thus, according to a Hobbesian physics, not themselves moved" (10)? This sort of question presents the impulse for Lee's readings of eighteenth- and nineteenth-century novels, which center on a condition that is out of the bounds of Hobbesian metaphysics.

18. A brief survey of the array of recent studies that inventively interrogate the relationships between literature and knowledge in the long eighteenth century (including examinations of empiricism, description, encyclopedism, cataloguing, and systematization) might include Thompson, *Fictional Matter* (2017); Stalnaker, *Unfinished Enlightenment* (2010); Rudy, *Literature and Encyclopedism* (2014); Pasanek, *Metaphors of Mind* (2015); Silver, *Mind Is a Collection* (2015); Smith, *Empiricist Devotions* (2016); Siskin, *System* (2017); Chico, *Experimental Imagination* (2018); and Keiser, *Nervous Fictions* (2020).

19. See Fessenbecker, *Reading Ideas in Victorian Literature*, chapter 2; relatedly, see Fessenbecker, "Fragility of Rationality." For a defense of "reading for the ideas," which privileges content over form, see the introduction to *Reading Ideas*, "In Defense of Paraphrase."

20. This is not to say that one cannot identify explanatory accounts of akrasia from some of the authors considered in this book. Godwin's novels could be said to put forward ideas about human volition that can be compared with his earlier philosophical writing. Likewise, in certain ways, Johnson's musings on himself offer certain kinds of theories on agency. However, the book's interests do not lie primarily in the upshots or explanations we might derive from such accounts, whether found in philosophy or literature; rather, it focuses on how the philosophical problem motivates distinctive types of linguistic expression (and nonexpression). Indeed, this book is more interested in what is *literary* about philosophy than what is *philosophical* about literature.

21. Rorty, "Self-Deception, Akrasia, and Irrationality," 909.

22. Rorty, "Akratic Believers," 175.

23. Rorty, 175.

24. On akrasia of belief and Sartre's bad faith, see Richard Moran's discussion of the conflict Sartre brings out between "the contrasting roles of commitment (*of* oneself) and theoretical knowledge about oneself" in the case of an akratic gambler: "For the gambler to have made such a decision [to stop gambling] is to be committed to avoiding the gaming tables. He is committed to this truth categorically, as the content of his decision; that is, insofar

as he actually has made such a decision, *this* is what it commits him to. For him his decision is not just (empirical) *evidence* about what he will do, but a resolution of which he is the author and which he is responsible for carrying through. But now, at the same time, he does know himself empirically too; he knows his history, and from this point of view his 'resolution' is a psychological fact about him with a certain degree of strength. And it is the psychological strength of this resolution that justifies any theoretical expectation that he actually will avoid the gaming tables. From this theoretical point of view on his (past) resolution (as facticity rather than as transcendence) it appears to him then as an ungrounded, inconstant thing on which to base any confidence about what he will in fact do. . . . He relates to his resolution as something independent of him, like a machine he has set in motion and which now should carry him along without any further contribution from him. He seeks confidence about his own future behavior at the empirical level, but then realizes that any such theoretical confidence is utterly inadequate on its own to settle his mind, because it can only be totally parasitic on his practical-transcendental resolution" (Moran, *Authority and Estrangement*, 79–80). For the section on Sartre and akrasia, see 77–83.

25. One might also identify akrasia's relevance for behavioral economics; see, for instance, the influential model of "slow" and "fast" thinking put forward by psychologist and economist Daniel Kahneman in *Thinking, Fast and Slow*. It is a model of two systems of thinking, one of which operates "automatically and quickly, with little or no effort and no sense of voluntary control," and the other which "allocates attention to the effortful mental activities that demand it" and "are often associated with the subjective experience of agency, choice, and concentration" (20–21). It is in the clash of these two models that one could account for modes of intentional irrationality in ways that can lend to broad theorizations around human behavior in relation to economic theory.

26. Within Victorian literary studies, we can mention, in addition to Fessenbecker's work on Anthony Trollope and George Eliot (discussed above), Miller's *Burdens of Perfection*, which takes up akrasia, skepticism, and perfectionism in Eliot and Charles Dickens (54–83).

27. The philosophical works that have most informed my own understanding of akrasia for the purposes of this book include Davidson, "How Is Weakness of the Will Possible?" in *Essays on Actions and Events*, 21–42; Rorty, "Self-Deception, Akrasia, and Irrationality"; Rorty, "Where Does the Akratic Break Take Place?"; Rorty, "Akratic Believers" and "The Social and Political Sources of Akrasia"; Callard, "Weaker Reason" and *Aspiration*, chapter 4;

Moran, *Authority and Estrangement;* Saarinen, *Weakness of Will;* and Mele, *Backsliding.*

28. See also Miller's discussion of the gendered connotations of akrasia in the context of Victorian fiction in *Burdens of Perfection:* "We usually imagine *akrasia,* or weakness of will, as the result of a battle between gladiatorial contestants: at moments of decision my will valiantly if ineffectually spars with bedeviling forces (desires usually) that are somehow both mine and beyond my control. It is a particularly masculine, martial picture. . . . And while it might appear to be part of a narrow concern with manly self-control, it is there as well in writing about women, as in Sarah Stickney Ellis's remarks early in *The Women of England* concerning their 'morbid listlessness of mind and body,' and their 'eagerness to escape from every thing like practical and individual duty'" (56).

29. Richardson, *Clarissa,* letter 153, 520.

30. I suspect this would involve drawing upon the arguments staged half a century ago by Hirschman in *Passions and the Interests* (1977), which gives an account of how changing ideas around "counteracting passions" with "interests" made possible the logic of capitalism, and one might extend such insights to think about capitalism's ongoing akratic dynamics, and our culture's continual inability to parse belief from practice.

1. AKRASIA AND EXPLANATION IN ENLIGHTENMENT PHILOSOPHY

1. Callard, "Weaker Reason," 68.

2. The essay "The Weaker Reason" presents an argument as to why that type of account (the dominant account of akrasia) is wrong. In a more recent discussion from her book *Aspiration,* Callard argues instead that akrasia is of a species of intrinsic conflict in which an agent holds two evaluative frames (149–76).

3. Callard, "Weaker Reason," 68.

4. Pfau, *Minding the Modern,* 163. For the fuller discussion of Ockham's voluntarism and its legacy, see 160–82.

5. See Greenblatt, *Swerve.*

6. Taylor, *Sources of the Self,* 143–58.

7. MacIntyre, *After Virtue,* 54. For MacIntyre, this elimination of teleology and of the structure in which man-as-he-happens-to-be is related to man-as-he-could-be-if-he-realized-his-essential-nature entails the necessary failure of the Enlightenment project of justifying morality—one which

results in utilitarianism and Kantianism, and eventually a broader set of incoherences.

8. Dupré, *Enlightenment,* 20.

9. Dupré, 20.

10. Plato, *Protagoras,* 358b–d, 348–49.

11. It is not clear that we should call it the Platonic position, as some have done, not merely because we do not want to collapse character and author, but also because of the different accounts of something like akrasia in the *Republic.*

12. Arendt, *Life of the Mind,* 57.

13. "Now we may ask (I) how a man who judges rightly can behave incontinently [*akratically*]. That he should behave so when he has knowledge, some say is impossible," he writes; "for it would be strange—so Socrates thought—if when knowledge was in a man something else could master it and drag it about like a slave. For *Socrates* was entirely opposed to the view in question, holding that there is no such thing as incontinence; no one, he said, when he judges acts against what he judges best—people act so only be reason of ignorance." But Aristotle continues by arguing that Socrates's view is clearly false—"Now this view plainly contradicts the observed facts"—and proceeds to think about how akrasia is possible (Aristotle, *Nicomachean Ethics,* 1145b21–28, 1038).

   Aristotle also makes some distinctions worth noting between "impetuous incontinence" and "weak incontinence": the first involves a person who forgets his principles in acting against his better judgment, and is able to recognize his betrayal afterwards with remorse, whereas the second involves a person who maintains knowledge of his principles while acting against reason. It is the second formulation that is more commonly recognized as akrasia, and it is the more puzzling case. He also makes the distinction between incontinence "in respect of money, gain, honour, or anger," in which case man pursues pleasures that "are not necessary but worthy of choice in themselves," as opposed to cases in which man pursues pleasures that are "necessary" ("concerned with food and . . . sexual intercourse"). Aristotle means to draw our attention to the latter more than the former (1147b23–34, 1042–43). It is worth noting then that Aristotle's discussion focuses mostly on "weak" (rather than "impetuous") incontinence that pertains to bodily pleasures.

14. Aristotle, 1147a34–b3, 1041.

15. Aristotle, 1152a15–17, 1052.

16. Aristotle, 1151a5–10, 1049.

17. "Voluntary" can refer to a broader class of actions, such that actions done

by purposive choice (or what Anthony Kenny translated as "willing" [*boulesis*]) are voluntary, but voluntary actions can include those done out of necessity, under duress, or—as in the case of akrasia—for the sake of appetitive pleasure. Indeed, by making space for "the voluntary," a category between the developing purposive form of judgment/choice (*prohaeresis*) and mere compulsion, Aristotle allows room for the akratic. For an in-depth discussion of the differences between voluntariness and *prohaeresis* in Aristotle, see Pfau, *Minding the Modern*, 79–107. For detailed discussions on how akrasia helps distill the difference between the voluntary and *prohaeresis*, see Kenny, *Aristotle's Theory of the Will*, 13–26 (specifically referring to the *Eudemian Ethics*) and 69–80. For a discussion of Aristotle's distinctive contributions to theorizing "the will," especially contra Plato and the Epicureans, see Dihle, *Theory of Will*, 58–60.

18. Aristotle, *Nicomachean Ethics*, 1146b35–47a3, 1040.
19. Aristotle, 1147a13–14, 1041.
20. Aristotle, 1147b16–19, 1042.
21. Saarinen, *Weakness of Will*, 11. For a detailed discussion of the various ways to interpret Aristotle on akrasia, see also Chappell, *Aristotle and Augustine on Freedom*, 98–118.
22. I borrow this phrase from Amélie Rorty's "Where Does the Akratic Break Take Place?"
23. Aristotle, *Nicomachean Ethics*, 1103b29–31, 953.
24. MacIntyre, *After Virtue*, 52.
25. As Dihle has written, Augustine was reacting to "the predominantly ontological view of both Neoplatonists and Christians, [in which] man partakes of divine nature or reality by his intellect alone. . . . The goal of human life, under this presupposition, was assimilation to God by intellectual activity. . . . Intellectual activity, in its turn, is always primarily cognitive, will only being either the mode of its application . . . or the byproduct of cognition" (123–24). For an account of the positive influence of Platonism on Augustine's thought, see Wetzel, *Augustine and the Limits of Virtue*, 1–16.
26. There is much to be said on Augustine's relationship to Stoicism. I have left out discussions of Stoicism for the sake of concision, but Stoicism plays an essential role for any historical overview of akrasia/weakness of will. The Stoic models of passion, reason, and most of all the Stoic notion of "assent" is often seen as anticipating to the Augustinian concept of "will" (*voluntas*). As for Stoicism as an intermediary between Aristotle and Augustine, it is important to note that, as Pfau has written, "the Aristotelian psychological vocabulary of *boulesis, prohairesis,* and *hekousion* only reaches Augustine in its substantially altered, Stoic inflection" (*Minding the Modern*, 112).

One must also note the vital role that translation plays in "consolidating" the notion of the will: "In the case of the will, translation holds particular significance because it is only be transposing and reconfiguring *hekousion, boulesis, eph'hemin,* and *prohairesis* into classical Latin and early Christian culture that the notion of the will (*voluntas*) came into existence. Once established, it challenged thinkers from Augustine onward to clarify the will's relationship to the intellect and reason" (108).

For Stoicism—Chrysippus in particular—the issue of how a person can succumb to passions was a central concern. Chrysippus posited that we ultimately "assent" to all passions. This means, on the one hand, that giving in to the passions is not a mere matter of compulsion. On the other hand, this model risks collapsing into the Socratic intellectualism that turns akrasia into a matter of the person choosing the passions over reason. As Saarinen writes, for the Stoics, "all passions, like anger, fear, and distress, are already judgements assented to and therefore functions of the reasoning faculty." This is evident, for example, in the discussion by Chrysippus (ca. 280–260 BC) of Ovid's *Medea,* who says, "I see what is better and approve of it; I follow what is worse." This differs slightly from Euripides's version: "I know indeed what evil I intend to do; but stronger than my deliberations [*bouleumata*] is my *thymos* [what makes me move], which is the cause of the greatest evils among mortals" (lines 1078–80). (Both translations are taken from Arendt, *Life of the Mind,* 69.) For a careful discussion of Chrysippus on Ovid's *Medea* and the relation to Augustine, see Saarinen, *Weakness of Will,* 12–27. Saarinen concludes that "Augustine is finally closer to Stoicism than to Aristotle" (23). For Chrysippus, this falls back on the idea that the emotions that "take one over" are emotions to which one has assented. The Stoic model of "assent" offered Augustine ways of thinking about agential weakness not available in Plato, though in Augustine's formulation, the weakness is less cognitive and less explicable.

27. It has been common to describe Augustine as "inventor" of "the will," and in this sense a kind of inventor of "inwardness" and "psychology," paving the way to modernity with the Reformation and priority of "the self"—see, for instance, Taylor's *Sources of the Self.* This view has also seen significant pushback; see a sum-up of dissenting positions in Pfau, *Minding the Modern,* 120.

28. An earlier instance with the subject arises in the fictional dialogue between Evodius and Augustine in *On Free Choice of the Will.* Augustine cites St. Paul and reflects: "If human beings were good, they would be otherwise. But as it is, they are not good, and it is not in their power to be good, either because they do not see how they ought to be, or because they lack

the power to be what they see they ought to be. . . . Who could doubt that this is a penalty? . . . But since it would be foolish to doubt the omnipotence and justice of God, this penalty is just, and it is imposed because of sin. . . . Therefore, the only remaining possibility is that this just penalty is a consequence of the damnation of human beings" (105–6).

29. Augustine, *Confessions*, 2.4.9, 36.

30. Augustine, 2.4.9, 36.

31. Dihle discusses the importance of "stiffheartedness" or "hard-heartedness" as early examples of weakness of will in the Old Testament: "Man has been given the freedom to ignore or even reject the information and the commandment that God conveys to him, thus blinding himself and going astray. . . . [Pharoah] repeatedly refuses to be obedient, although he realizes perfectly well, from the miracles performed and signs given, both the power and the will of Yahveh. The narrative of Exod. 7ff clearly interprets the behavior of Pharoah in terms of volition rather than cognition" (*Theory of Will*, 75–76).

32. Augustine, *Confessions*, 8.9.21, 177.

33. Augustine, 8.5.10, 168–69. Arendt discusses the differences with respect to the case of Paul: "Paul . . . did not discuss it in terms of two wills but in terms of two laws—the law of the mind that lets him delight in the law of God 'in his inmost self' and the law of his 'members' that tells him to do what in his inmost self he hates." Arendt, *Life of the Mind*, 68.

34. Augustine, *Confessions*, 8.10.24, 179. Indeed, believing in the Manichean view is *itself* a sin; as Pfau puts it, "Augustine insists that such attempts at tracing the mind's inner division back to some external and metaphysical cause is tantamount to an evasion of responsible agency and, thus, an instance of sin " (*Minding the Modern*, 119).

35. Augustine, *Confessions*, 8.10.22, 178.

36. This touches upon a much broader and more complicated set of issues surrounding the compatibility between free choice (*liberum arbitrium*), on the one hand, and predestination and God's foreknowledge, on the other. In his (anti-Pelagian) commitment to compatibilism—specifically, between free will and God's foreknowledge—Augustine maintained that free will only operates with the inscrutable assistance of God's free grace. See *City of God*, book 5, chaps. 9 and 10, in which Augustine responds to Cicero's argument against God's foreknowledge while defending free will. Augustine maintains the compatibility of the two: "We embrace both truths, and acknowledge them in faith and sincerity, the one for a right belief, the other for a right life" (10:195). For a concise discussion of Augustine's notion of the will, its distinction from "mere choice," and its significance to his anti-Pelagian

view of predestination and grace, see Wetzel, *Augustine and the Limits of Virtue*, 1–16. It is also essential to distinguish Augustine's capacity for choice from the full-blown voluntarism of later medievalism or of Kant; as Saarinen writes, "the will is no separate mental faculty or part of the soul, *voluntas* denoting the human psyche in its role as moral agent" (*Weakness of Will*, 19). Will, in other words, is not a free-floating faculty separate from the domain of the moral: it is always to be understood and discussed within the terms of the good and the wicked. At the same time, this is not Hobbes's compatibilism: Hobbesian determinism is not the same as God's foreknowledge, and the latter, crucially, does not conflict with free choice.

37. Oakeshott, *Hobbes on Civil Association*, 18.

38. As James has stressed, Descartes stands out as a kind of transitional figure that makes possible the set of moves we see in Hobbes, Spinoza, Locke, and Hume. For Descartes, the conflict now occurs between the soul and the body in the Cartesian framework; the case of volition guided by passion contrary to reason can be mapped onto the dualist framework: Volition resides in the soul, whereas passion resides between the soul and the body. Therefore, as James has put it, "the site of the struggle has shifted from the soul [as in Aquinas] to the pineal gland, and the opposing powers are now the forces exerted on it by the soul and body instead of the two antagonistic appetites of the soul" (*Passion and Action*, 259).

39. Hobbes, *Leviathan*, 81.

40. Hobbes, 120.

41. Hobbes, 128.

42. Hobbes, 128.

43. Hobbes, *Of Liberty and Necessity*, 269.

44. Oakeshott, *Hobbes on Civil Association*, 19. Along with this comes a broader mutation of what counts as moral philosophy; this can be said to begin more with Grotius who "removed natural law from the jurisdiction of the moral theologian . . . and made its theory the responsibility of lawyers and philosophers" (Schneewind, *Invention of Autonomy*, 82).

45. Spinoza, *Ethics*, part 4, P2, 202.

46. Spinoza, 4, D1 and D2, 200.

47. Spinoza, 4, P8, 204.

48. Spinoza, 3, P1, 154. Susan James notes how Spinozian metaphysics incline closer to that of the Stoics: "Spinoza's account of the antecedents of action diverges from the Hobbesian one by taking a further step towards the Stoic view that the passions are judgements" (James, *Passion and Action*, 274).

49. Spinoza, *Ethics*, 4, P17, 208.

50. Spinoza, 4, preface, 197.

51. Spinoza, 4, preface, 197.

52. "Agreeing with Hobbes," James writes, "Spinoza takes it that both these related capacities are determined by her past, and by the resulting assemblage of ideas that is her mind" (James, *Passion and Action,* 276).

53. See Smith's influential discussion of Hume: "The determining factor in Hume's philosophy" is "the establishment of a purely naturalistic conception of human nature by the thorough subordination of reason to feeling and instinct"—a quality that goes against his reputation as skeptical philosopher ("Naturalism of Hume," 150). See also Norton, *David Hume.*

54. Rawls, *Lectures on the History of Moral Philosophy,* 50; cited in Fleming, "Hume on Weakness of Will."

55. Hume, *Treatise of Human Nature,* book 2, part 3, section 1, 257.

56. Hume, 2.3.3, 265–66.

57. Hume, 267.

58. Hume, 267.

59. As Korsgaard puts it in "The Normativity of Instrumental Reason" from *Constitution of Agency,* for Hume, being irrational happens either "when our passions are provoked by non-existent objects, or when we act on the basis of false causal judgments." The problem, as she puts it, is that "making a mistake . . . is not a way of being irrational": "how can there be rational action, in any sense, if there is no irrational action?" she asks (40). "The problem is coming from the fact that Hume identifies a person's *end* as what he *wants most,* and the criterion of what the person wants most appears to be what he actually *does*" (42). For other criticisms of Hume's philosophy of the will, see Pfau, *Minding the Modern,* 283–326; Foot, *Moral Dilemmas;* and Anscombe, "Modern Moral Philosophy," which refers to Hume as "a mere—brilliant—sophist" (3). For a contrary view, defending the possibility of weakness of will for Hume, see Fleming, "Hume on Weakness of Will." Fleming attempts to show how akrasia can be preserved when giving an account of someone as governed by different degrees of passion. See his narrative examples on 605–6. These examples seem to me, however, to finally resort to the crediting the force of a passion, which must at the end of the day be considered the *prevailing* passion, and, in my reading, eliminates the sense of "weakness" or doubleness I understand as essential for an account of weakness of will. Again, this is a matter of storytelling: Does one privilege the sense of conflict/weakness, or does one privilege the causal explanation? I discuss this dynamic further in the next section on Locke. I am very grateful to Sarah Tindal Kareem for pointing me toward Korsgaard and Fleming on Hume regarding weakness of will/akrasia.

60. For a particularly detailed account of the changes in Locke's account of the will between the first and second editions, see Darwall, *British Moralists,* 149–75.

61. Locke, *Essay Concerning Human Understanding* (1690/94); for the 1690 version, see notes 248–51 (book 2, chapter 21, section 29). Also see Darwall, *British Moralists,* 155. In both editions, the will itself is not to be considered free, for what we prefer is ultimately not a matter of choice, Locke tells us. Our freedom lies instead in whether we act or forbear acting upon the will. Freedom lies in the person, not in the will. *"Liberty,* on the other side, is the power a Man has to do or forbear doing any particular Action, according as its doing or forbearance has the actual preference in the Mind, which is the same thing as to say, according as he himself *wills* it" (2.21.15, 241). *"A man in respect of willing, or the Act of Volition, when any Action in his power is once proposed to his Thoughts, as presently to be done, cannot be free"* (2.21.23, 245). As Darwall has written, "The whole thrust of Locke's account in the first edition is that liberty exclusively concerns what happens (or would happen) *after* volition" (154–55).

62. Locke, *Essay Concerning Human Understanding,* 2.21.35, 253.

63. Darwall, *British Moralists,* 157.

64. Locke, 2.21.29, 249.

65. Locke, 2.21.29, 249.

66. Locke, 2.21, 31, 251. As Pfau writes, "what prompts this view is an already implied understanding of the will as nothing more than efficient causation, the mental equivalent of Newtonian force" (*Minding the Modern,* 220).

67. Pfau, 221.

68. Locke, *Essay Concerning Human Understanding,* 2.21.35, 253–54. Later in the chapter, he wraps up this topic, confronting the question *"how Men come often to prefer the worse to the better;* and to chuse that, which, by their own Confession, has made them miserable" (2.21.56, 271). He eventually has a few answers—the first is more in line with Hobbes, Spinoza, and Hume: "from causes not in our power, such as are often the pains of the Body from want, disease, or outward injuries, as the rack, *etc.* which when present, and violent, operate for the most part forcibly on the *will"* (2.21.57, 271). Next he describes them as based in "wrong judgments Men make of future Good and Evil" (2.21.58, 272); Locke then goes on for a while to discuss the causes of wrong judging, which derive primarily from *"Ignorance"* or *"Inadvertency"* (2.21.677, 278). This, then, is the Socratic option again, in which man ultimately acts against the greater good because he acts upon incorrect judgment.

69. Previously, explaining an action by references to causes tended to mean

"showing the event to be explained as an instance of some law-like regularity"—that is, a broader set of dispositions and behaviors, rather than conceiving of a person's reason as a cause for an action. See Malpas, "Donald Davidson."

70. Candlish and Damnjanovic, "Reasons, Actions, and the Will," 659. This essay offers a detailed discussion of the impact of Davidson's causalism in philosophy of action, and its relations to Wittgenstein, Ryle, and Anscombe.

71. It is a connection Kramnick observes as well in *Actions and Objects from Hobbes to Richardson,* citing Davidson in his discussion of philosophy of action from Hobbes to Hume: "'Cause is the cement of the universe,' wrote Donald Davidson, in words that apply equally to the British philosophers of the seventeenth and eighteenth centuries; 'the concept of cause is what holds together our picture of the universe, a picture that would otherwise disintegrate into a diptych of the mental and the physical'" (59, quoting Davidson, *Essays on Actions and Events,* xv).

72. Davidson, 23.

73. Davidson, 29.

74. Davidson, 30. In the footnote, he writes, "I know no clear case of a philosopher who recognizes that incontinence is not essentially a problem in moral philosophy, but a problem in the philosophy of action" (30n14).

75. Davidson, 30.

76. In *Aspiration,* Callard raises similar questions about this passage in order to elaborate on her view of akrasia as a matter of acting on a "subordinate evaluative perspective, the one excluded from deliberation," thus not acting on "the judgment issued by their dominant evaluative perspective" (157). About Davidson's example, Callard writes, "What, then, has the toothbrusher's reasoning left out? What is the evaluative perspective from which brushing his teeth looks good to him? One can fill out the case in a number of ways, but there is, I propose, a very natural answer as to what overcomes the toothbrusher when his 'feeling that I ought to brush my teeth is too strong for me': the force of habit. Habit—as distinct from any kind of unthinking, potentially pathological tendency toward repetition/patterns of behavior—is the ethical point of view that presents something as 'to be done' or as 'a good thing to do' because one usually does it. Having habits means being such as to value your normal modus operandi. But the value of behaving habitually is precisely shut out of the evaluative perspective that aims to calculate for this occasion specifically ('suggest I forget my teeth *for once*')" (166).

77. See also Davidson, "Adverbs of Action," in *Essays on Actions and Events,* 293–304.

78. In a footnote he clarifies the matter somewhat: "Of course [the akratic] has a reason for doing *a*" (that is, in acting against better judgment, the akratic still acts upon a reason, weaker though it may be); "what he lacks is a reason for not letting his better reason for not doing *a* prevail" (42n25).

79. Davidson, 42.

80. Murdoch, "The Idea of Perfection," in *Sovereignty of Good*, 1–44, 8–9.

81. Murdoch, 20.

82. That this example from Murdoch has a bearing on akrasia is an observation originally made in Rorty, "Akratic Believers," 179.

83. Murdoch, *Sovereignty of Good*, 17.

84. Murdoch, 17.

85. Murdoch, 21–22.

86. Murdoch, 22–23.

2. SOME ENCOUNTERS WITH AKRASIA IN EIGHTEENTH-CENTURY PROSE FICTION

1. Defoe, *Robinson Crusoe*, 14.

2. Watt, *Rise of the Novel*, 63.

3. Augustine, *Confessions*, 2.4.9, 36.

4. Bunyan, *Grace Abounding*, 11.

5. Fielding, *Tom Jones*, 351.

6. Watt's full quote reads, "Formal realism is only a mode of presentation, and it is therefore ethically neutral: all Defoe's novels are also ethically neutral because they make formal realism an end rather than a means, to the illusion that the text represents the authentic lucubrations of an historical person. . . . The problem of the novel was to discover and reveal these deeper meanings without any breach of formal realism" (*Rise of the Novel*, 117).

7. For McKeon (*Origins of the English Novel*, 22), these two categories combine when "the formal posture of naïve empiricism [question of truth] tends to accompany a substantive stance of progressive ideology [question of virtue]" (in Richardson) and "extreme skepticism [question of truth] is reflected in an analogous, conservative ideology [question of virtue]" (in Fielding).

8. One example of this is to be found in Samuel Richardson, whose mode of "writing to the moment" drew readers too close to the experience of his villains, thus risking subverting the novel's moral design. Keymer, for instance, writes, "In depicting with such vividness a vicious yet winning character, in organising the novel around his stratagems and plots, and in

filtering large sections of it through his point of view, Richardson brings the reader to perilous intimacy and even complicity with evil, thereby subverting his own design of stabilisation and reform" (*Richardson's* Clarissa, 157).

9. Defoe, *Robinson Crusoe*, 15.

10. Defoe, 3.

11. Hume, *Treatise of Human Nature*, 1.1.2, 11.

12. For a different sort of discussion of "giving an account of oneself," see Butler's *Giving an Account of Oneself*, which emphasizes the inevitably social character of this enterprise: "When the 'I' seeks to give an account of itself, it can start with itself, but it will find that this self is already implicated in a social temporality that exceeds its own capacities for narration; indeed, when the 'I' seeks to give an account of itself, an account that must include the conditions of its own emergence, it must, as a matter of necessity, become a social theorist" (7–8).

13. Defoe, *Robinson Crusoe*, 57.

14. For a discussion of "account" as metaphor for the mind in eighteenth-century literature (specifically, through attention to the poet/memoirist Laetitia Pilkington), see Silver, *Mind Is a Collection*, 250–60. For the wide range of ways that eighteenth-century figures employed metaphors for the mind that pertained to the economic and financial, see Pasanek, *Metaphors of Mind*, which investigates treasure-houses, mints, impressions, and stamping (50–68).

15. Defoe, *Robinson Crusoe*, 7.

16. Defoe, 7–8.

17. In paying attention to moments that resemble akrasia in Defoe, I am in a certain way emphasizing the opposite of what Macpherson finds in Defoe in chapter 1 ("Matrimonial Murder") of *Harm's Way*. Macpherson pays attention to the blame and responsibility laid on persons who are not blameworthy or acts that were not intentional; she observes in Defoe's providentialism "a legal as well as a theological interest in accident"; and what we find are instances (especially in *Journal of the Plague Year* and *Roxana*) of responsibility "against the criteria by which we tend to define individuals—against interiority, against intentionality, even, paradoxically, against agency itself. On this view, 'persons' are characterized by an unknowing instrumentality as profound as a horse's or an infected, nonsymptomatic nursing mother's" (*Harm's Way*, 28, 30). Without disputing the importance of the legal and formal emphasis on accidents in Defoe, I aim to emphasize the formal peculiarities of these other sorts of actions—ones that the characters themselves deem to be blameworthy and about which they (justifiably) experience guilt.

18. Defoe, *Robinson Crusoe*, 8–9.

19. Starr, *Defoe & Spiritual Autobiography*, 82. In this respect, Starr is responding to Watt's characterization of Crusoe's departure as based in the principle of *homo economicus*—that it is necessary to better his economic condition (77n8). Watt is unconvinced: "If, for example, we turn to the actual effect of Crusoe's religion on his behaviour, we find that it has curiously little. Defoe often suggests that an incident is an act of Divine providence or retribution, but this interpretation is rarely supported by the facts of the story. To take the crucial instance: if Crusoe's original sin was filial disobedience—leaving home in the first place—it is certain that no real retribution follows, since he does very well out of it" (*Rise of the Novel*, 80). Later he writes, "The relative impotence of religion in Defoe's novels, then, suggests not insincerity but the profound secularisation of his outlook, a secularisation which was a marked feature of its age" (82).

20. Hunter, *Reluctant Pilgrim*, 20. Kareem offers a different approach to understanding Defoe's relations to, respectively, Puritan spiritual autobiography and the contemporary philosophy of David Hume; she shows how Defoe's *Robinson Crusoe,* which is indebted to the Puritan spiritual autobiography, and Hume's writing both reside in a place of uncertainty and indeterminacy, allowing the capacity of a distinctive type of wonder "in the wake of an epistemological crisis in which distinctions between real and unreal break down" (30). See Kareem, *Eighteenth-Century Fiction,* 75–108.

21. Defoe, *Robinson Crusoe*, 5.

22. Defoe, 9.

23. Grew, *Meditations*, 44 and 46, quoted in Starr, *Defoe & Spiritual Autobiography*, 76. Starr likewise shows how Defoe's religious conduct manual *The Family Instructor* is centrally concerned with the tendency of a young man to be "naturally subject to rebellious impulse" (75–76). In his book *Defoe & Casuistry,* Starr also dwells on Defoe's interest in this "devillish principle" in man—the perversion of the will—which he argues prompts a great deal of casuistry (self-deceiving and reasoning reasoning) in order to defend it.

24. Starr has suggested that we are reading such scenes incorrectly if we are asking for a causal analysis of them. In an aside on "hardness of heart"—which is a notion conceptually adjacent to "weakness of will," except its perversity lies in its stubbornness rather than weakness in spite of knowledge—he argues that this condition needs to be understood in *spiritual* rather than *psychological* terms: "The first thing to emphasize about hardness of heart is that it is in fact a spiritual state, not merely a psychological one. To be sure, its manifestations are of a kind nowadays approached psychologically. But so long as men continued to believe in the reality and

importance of the soul, psychology remained largely a method of analyzing and describing the state of a soul through its outward workings. . . . Even the most painstaking narrations of it may have spiritual assessment rather than psychological realism as their purpose" (*Defoe & Spiritual Autobiography*, 141). This passage helpfully and persuasively insists that, for Defoe, Moll's state signifies a spiritual condition, which is to say, it primarily speaks to her moral state. We are missing the point, Starr seems to suggest, if we look to these scenes expecting to find "psychological realism." However, if that is true, then surely there is more to say about the inconsistency this creates in the context of Defoe's novel. Given that Defoe is certainly *also* interested in "psychological realism" throughout his narratives, doesn't this shift away from a causal-psychological epistemology speak to an interesting ambivalence in his work? If nothing else, it signifies that a condition like hardness of heart or weakness of will requires a noticeable shift away from causal explanation.

25. McKeon sees both Watt's and Starr's views as extreme, referring to "the modern tendency to see Defoe's work as essentially an essay in secular materialism [in] Ian Watt's view" and the aim of "assimilating *Robinson Crusoe* to something like an ideal type of Protestant narrative religiosity [by George Starr and Paul Hunter]." He continues, "Both arguments are made with great skill, but both may appear extreme insofar as they seem unnecessarily obliged to imply a mutual exclusion. As the Weber thesis suggests, in the historically transitional territory of early modern Protestantism, spiritual and secular motives are not only 'compatible'; they are inseparable, if ultimately contradictory, parts of a complex intellectual and behavioral system" (*Origins of the English Novel*, 319). For another discussion on the compatibility of the two, see Richetti, *Defoe's Narratives*, 23.

26. Defoe, *Moll Flanders*, 1.

27. For a detailed discussion of *Moll Flanders* in the context of Defoe's writings on crime, for instance, see Backscheider, "Crime Wave and *Moll Flanders*," based originally on material appearing in Backscheider, *Daniel Defoe: His Life* (Baltimore, MD: Johns Hopkins University Press, 1989).

28. Defoe, *Moll Flanders*, 150–51.

29. For a consideration of the importance of finance and statistics to epistemology in Defoe's fiction, see, for instance, Sherman, *Finance and Fictionality*.

30. Defoe, *Moll Flanders*, 151.

31. Defoe, 151.

32. Starr writes that Moll's condition consists of "a kind of slavery to Satan" as per "seventeenth- and early-eighteenth-century discussions of habitual sin"—namely, "being held fast in the devil's clutches, and having no power

to get out of them." He continues, "It is clear from Defoe's other works that he believed in the existence of the devil" (*Defoe & Spiritual Autobiography,* 153–54).

33. Defoe, *Moll Flanders,* 163.

34. These moments play into the inherent ironic ambiguity of autobiographical narrative, or what Goldie has called "the ineluctable ironic gap (epistemic, evaluative, and emotional) between internal and external perspective" (*Mess Inside,* 43). Chapter 3 discusses these ironies further, specifically in relation to free indirect discourse.

35. Haywood, *Love in Excess,* 185–86.

36. Croskery continues: "It thus poses not only a playful alternative to the Restoration paradigm of male and female sexuality, but it also provides a serious alternative to our own modern psychoanalytic interpretations of the semiotic nature of sexual desire" ("Masquing Desire," 70). For Croskery, Haywood's Humean attitude toward the passions "complicates without compromising her standing in the canon as an effective feminist voice"; and it is important to note that "the primacy of passion as a motivating force does not necessitate, any more than Hume's later claims would do, a loss of moral or political agency" (71, 72).

37. Thompson, *Ingenuous Subjection,* 128. For the entire chapter, "Eliza Haywood's Philosophical Career: Ingenuous Subjection and Moral Phys- iology," see 121–51. Both Croskery and Thompson are responding to a psychoanalytic framework that might understand Haywood's heroines through the "hysteric." Ballaster sees the figure of the hysteric as refusing signification or interpretation while keeping the hysteric herself powerless "over the representational scene her body creates" (*Seductive Forms,* 173). Bocchicchio discusses Haywood's subversive narrative presentations of the "hysterical woman": "Haywood's texts continuously present a repetition of hysterical attacks which in effect 'overproduce' that hysteria, bringing it to the forefront of the narrative. In this way, Haywood's fiction challenges the delimiting iconography that it seems, on the surface, to reproduce: the narrative can articulate, through repetition, the protest that the hysterical character, passive by definition, cannot. . . . The carefully contextualized attacks of her heroines show the hysterical body not to be a 'naturally fem- inine' one, but rather to be the result of cultural forces at work" ("Blushing, Trembling, and Incapable of Defense," 102).

38. Spacks, "Ev'ry Woman," 32–33.

39. Haywood, *Fantomina,* 43, 41.

40. Haywood, 44.

41. Kramnick, *Actions and Objects,* 184. Kramnick describes a "collapse of

thought and action" (186) and identifies that Haywood here "is interested in consciousness but not exactly in personhood" (191). For the entirety of Kramnick's discussion on will, mind, intention, and consent in *Fantomina*, see chapter 5 of *Actions and Objects*, especially 182–93.

42. As Croskery, Kramnick, and others have noted, the question of how to understand the lady's agency ultimately turns on nothing less than how to interpret the nature of the lady's consent prior to the rape, if we understand it as such. See Croskery's discussion of the question of rape in *Fantomina*, 72–78. Kramnick emphasizes "the period's conflicted notion of consent as at once a state of mind and a kind of act" (186) and argues that "the language of mental states is too shifting in time and too inextricable from conflicting social forms to land on one or the other side of consent" (187).

43. "Distraction" and "inattention" are also significant themes to this novel, as has been powerfully brought out by Phillips: as she writes, "Distraction, in Haywood is less a vice than a trait associated with vivacious heedless-ness, inadvertent error, and *gaîté du coeur*" (*Distraction*, 65). See 61–95 for a range of insightful observations concerning Betsy's psychology.

44. Haywood, *Betsy Thoughtless*, 39.

45. Haywood, 41.

46. Sterne, *Vol. 6: A Sentimental Journey through France and Italy* (1767) in *The Florida Edition of the Works of Laurence Sterne*, 6:122.

47. Sterne, *Sentimental Journey*, 6:21.

48. Ricks notes "the wonderfully comic pages [in *Tristram Shandy*] that are given to the other intellectual disciplines: the pages about the law, science (particularly medicine), religion, history, psychology, even psychiatry" (xx) as well as the mockery of the novel form itself: "Sterne belonged to an age which was increasingly tempted to look upon literature as an ultimate good, and he was writing in a form—the novel—which quite rightly thought that it was fitted to accomplish literary tasks in some ways more profound, more true and more complete than any literature that had preceded it.... But Sterne's brilliant tactic was to bring out all the time how severe the limits of words are. The potential arrogance of literature—in its relations to the other arts, to the sciences, to religion, to life—is put wittily before us, and by a man who writes so well that he can hardly be suspected of denigrating a skill which he himself lacks" (xix–xx). See also the discussion of Sterne in Franta's *Systems Failure*: "Narrating a will to order that is inevitably thwarted ... Sterne in turn transforms failure itself into a kind of ordering principle, as its thematization becomes a means of gesturing toward the contingency that narrative cannot finally embody" (43).

49. Sterne, *Vol. 1: The Life and Opinions of Tristram Shandy, Gentleman* (1759–

67) in *Florida Edition*, 1:106. Melvyn New's editorial note points this line to Swift's *A Tale of a Tub*, sect. 9: "But when a Man's Fancy gets *astride* on his Reason, when Imagination is at Cuffs with the Senses, and common Understanding, as well as common Sense, is Kickt out of Doors; the first Proselyte he makes, is Himself." Sterne, *Vol. 3: The Notes* in *Florida Edition*, 3:141. For a more detailed discussion of Sterne's identification between the hobbyhorse with the ruling passion, see Sterne, *Vol. 3: The Notes*, 3:123–24, which discusses 85, lines 20–21, from vol. 1 of *Tristram Shandy*.

50. Sterne, *Tristram Shandy*, 1:2.
51. Sterne, *Sentimental Journey*, 6:151.
52. Sterne, 6:7.
53. Ellis, *Politics of Sensibility*, 21.
54. Cash, "The Sermon in *Tristram Shandy*," 400. To show this, he points to the hobbyhorse in *Tristram Shandy* (400–401). See also New, *Laurence Sterne as Satirist*. For New, "*Tristram Shandy* can best be understood by locating it in the mainstream of the conservative, moralistic Augustan tradition" (1–2). New emphasizes in particular that "*Tristram Shandy* can best be understood through the intentions and conventions of the dominant literary form of that tradition, satire," whereas Cash does not see so programmatic a moral function in Sterne's fictions, though he shares New's view of Sterne's moral orthodoxy. For contrary views, see Brissenden, *Virtue in Distress;* and Lamb, *Sterne's Fiction*. Brissenden has disputed Cash's and New's emphasis on guilt as a central theme in *Sentimental Journey*, which, he argues, is more centrally concerned with Yorick's goodness. The issue, he writes, is "not that benevolence leads to carnality but that carnality leads to benevolence" (*Virtue in Distress*, 219). Lamb too disputes New's view that *Tristram Shandy* functions as a series of jokes that satirize society and thus uphold moral codes in the manner of Swiftian satire, instead emphasizing the nonprogrammatic, multipronged, and deconstructive tendencies of Sterne's writing (see *Sterne's Fiction*, 2–5).
55. Sterne, *Tristram Shandy*, 1:147.
56. See Deuteronomy 4:11 or Psalm 97:2. This connection is made by Melvyn New in the endnotes to the Penguin edition of *Tristram Shandy* (630). New has noted in his editorial work on this text that Sterne in this sermon borrows from a sermon traditionally attributed to Jonathan Swift, "The Difficulty of Knowing One's-Self," which reads, similarly: "Thus nothing is more common than to see a wicked Man running headlong into Sin and Folly, against his Reason, against his Religion, and against his God. Tell him, that what he is going to do will be an infinite Disparagement to his Understanding, which, at another Time, he sets no small upon; tell him

that it will blacken his Reputation, which he had rather die for than lose; tell him that the Pleasure of the Sin is short and transient, and leaveth a vexatious Kind of a Sting behind it, which will very hardly be drawn forth; tell him that this is one of those things for which God will most surely bring him to Judgment, which he pretendeth to believe with a full Assurance and Persuasion: And yet for all this, he shuteth his Eyes against all Conviction, and rusheth into the Sin, like a Horse into the Battle; as if he had nothing left to do, but like a silly Child to wink hard, and to think to escape a certain and an infinite Mischief, only by endeavouring not to see it" ("Difficulty of Knowing One's-Self," 15). Cash has shown how Sterne in *Tristram Shandy* uses and develops Swift's metaphor of the horse in battle that rushes into sin through the trope of the hobbyhorse: "Sterne writes about inner forces which are neither mysterious nor overpowering....A man must 'give himself up' to such a passion; it does not overwhelm him" ("Sermon in *Tristram Shandy*," 400–401).

57. Sterne *Sentimental Journey*, 6:7.
58. Sterne, 6:121–22.
59. Sterne, 6:122.
60. Sterne, *Tristram Shandy*, 2:570–71.
61. For a rich discussion of the limits of the aspirations of "the dream of transparent communication" and thus the limits of a system of order in *Sentimental Journey*, with particular attention to nonverbal communication, see Franta, *Systems Failure*, chapter 2, 45–52. For discussions on sound, touch, and flesh of language in Sterne, which touch upon Sterne's use of the dash, see Tadié, *Sterne's Whimsical Theatres of Language*.
62. Sterne, *Sentimental Journey*, 6:122.
63. Sterne, 6:122.
64. Aristotle, *Nicomachean Ethics* 1147a1–9, 1040.
65. Sterne, *Sentimental Journey*, 6:123.

3. AKRASIA AND FREE INDIRECT DISCOURSE IN ROMANTIC-ERA NOVELS

1. Austen, *Emma*, 159, 160.
2. Miller, *Jane Austen*, 64. Miller elaborates: "What generates the first 'Emma could not forgive her' is Emma's own affective consciousness, intimately accessed and ironically inflected by its free indirect narrative performance. What generates the second 'Emma could not forgive her' is pure narration, a detached consciousness to which Emma's own has ceased to contribute,

having been reduced to a little bit of information useful to the plot. By virtue of repeating the same formula (truly magical), we move from free indirect style—for all its irony, always grounded in an intimate identificatory relation to the image of the person—to mere omniscient narration, more remote in its detachment, and less engagé in its impersonality" (65).

3. Austen, *Emma*, 347.

4. Austen, 351.

5. The claim would go that essential to a "free indirect" mode of discourse, strictly speaking, is a free/detached element of the text that cannot be attributed to a known speaker or narrator, and that the first-person mode, in which the identity of the narrator is known, would necessarily negate that sense of impersonality. However, it is worth pointing out that novels like Godwin's significantly approximate that effect despite the first-person mode. Even though the narrator can be identified, the narrative often functions much like straightforward narration of events as in a third-person omniscient narration and the quiet shifts between narration and character consciousness produce a similar effect. Cohn classifies first-person retrospective instances of "narrated monologues" (her nomenclature for what is typically called FID) as "self-narrated monologues." In cases of "*retrospection into a consciousness*," she writes, "the same basic types of presentation appear, the same basic terms apply, modified by prefixes to signal the modified relationship of the narrator to the subject of his narration: psycho-narration becomes self-narration . . . , and monologues can now be either self-quoted, or self-narrated" (*Transparent Minds*, 14). For an extended discussion on the dynamics of autobiographical memory, with "someone who is internal to a narrative, having a role as a 'character' in the narrative . . . also be[ing] external to it, having also the role of external narrator," thereby approximating "free indirect style," see Goldie, *Mess Inside*, 26–55.

6. Banfield, *Unspeakable Sentences*, 220.

7. Fludernik, *Fictions of Language*, 80. This quote is provided as a paraphrase of observations by Wolfgang G. Müller and Dieter Beyerle: Müller, "Der freie indirekte Stil bei Jane Austen als Mittel der Rede- und Gedankenwiedergabe," *Poetica* 1.7 (1985): 206–36; Beyerle, "Ein vernachlässigter Aspekt der erlebten Rede," *Archiv für das Studium der neueren Sprachen* 208 (1978): 350–66. Fludernik's book lucidly delves into a broad array of research on FID through the twentieth century in various languages. For a discussion of empathy and irony in free indirect discourse, see 72–82.

8. Vološinov, *Marxism*, 156; also quoted in Banfield, *Unspeakable Sentences*, 222.

9. For a summary of alternative views, see Fludernik, *Fictions of Language*,

93–99. Fludernik counts herself among those who "maintai[n] that free indirect discourse is an oral phenomenon and that its rarity in pre-eighteenth-century texts is accounted for by its original reliance on intonation to indicate a 'voice'. Scholars in this tradition recognize numerous instances of proto-free indirect discourse in medieval texts . . . and they point to the currency of free indirect discourse in present-day conversation" (93). Fludernik then goes on to discuss some examples from Chaucer (93–94). For a brief discussion of first-person free indirect speech in eighteenth-century novels *Moll Flanders* and *Clarissa,* see 88; for examples on uses of FID in standard American English, see 84.

10. Banfield, *Unspeakable Sentences,* 254. Elsewhere she writes, "Represented thought [Banfield's name for FID] is restricted to genres which are not orally composed (the epic) or an imitation of an oral communication (the drama and *skaz*)" (241).

11. Pascal, *Dual Voice,* 45. Pascal defends the move away from free indirect "style" (*le style indirect libre*) to "speech": "For some time I myself preferred the name 'free indirect style', since it seemed to me that 'speech' too strongly suggested that we are here concerned with the literary expression of spoken words or articulate thoughts; 'style', the French term, has in this respect a useful ambiguity. But the term 'speech' in these contexts refers not to actual spoken language, but to a mode of discourse, and it is important to use for 'free indirect speech' the same term as for 'direct speech' and 'indirect speech', since they are all in fact so closely bound together" (32).

12. Miller's discussion of FID in *Burdens of Perfection* is adjacent to a chapter on akrasia/weakness of the will in Victorian novels and so can be instructively compared to the present discussion. For Miller, FID can be considered as a technique that stands in response to various forms of skepticism—including the skepticism of knowing other minds—accentuated in the Victorian era. Akrasia stands out as one expression of skepticism due to the conflicts that it creates between first-person and third-person modes of moral reasoning, and FID is capable of furnishing a second-person ("you") perspective that functions as a sort of moral voice for the novel form. FID is, for Miller, "the voice of that philosophical aspect of the novel [called] perfectionist." The passage continues: "For why should the novel grant us as its most outrageous gift the illusion of unprecedented access to the consciousness of others, a gift nowhere more distinctively wrapped than when in free indirect discourse, if not in response to the skeptical anxiety that such access is, in our non-reading existence, nowhere available" (89–90)? For the section on akrasia/weakness of will in Victorian novels, see 54–83; for the section immediately after on FID, see 84–91.

13. Godwin, *St. Leon,* 97.

14. Kelly, *English Jacobin Novel,* 210.

15. Godwin, *St. Leon,* 95.

16. Godwin, 95.

17. Godwin, 98.

18. Godwin, *Enquiry,* book 4, chapter 7, page 172.

19. Philp, *Godwin's Political Justice,* 93.

20. Godwin, *Enquiry,* 4.8.185. Philp writes, for Godwin, "knowing a moral truth, and recognising that it applies in a particular case and that one has the capacity to perform the required action, provide the necessary and sufficient conditions for the performance of that action. . . . Truth alone motivates us" (*Godwin's Political Justice,* 31). As Philp discusses, Godwin's Platonic embrace of the immutable truth and its relation to perfectibility is indebted to the eighteenth-century Rational Dissenters. See 26–34 and 89–95.

21. Godwin, *Enquiry,* 4.6.168.

22. Godwin, 6.5.163–64. Hume's line: "Nor is there any thing more extraordinary in this, than in mechanics to see one pound weight raise up a hundred by the advantage of its situation" (*Treatise of Human Nature,* 2.3.3, 267).

23. Godwin, *Enquirer,* v–vi.

24. Godwin, vi. As Klancher writes, Godwin was to "relinquish the overarching ambition of the original *Political Justice*—the task of philosophical totalization that by 1797 he was reluctantly calling 'incommensurate to our powers'—so that instead of high theory, Godwin now pursued local 'investigations,' open-ended inquiries into 'education, manners, and literature,' which demanded questioning the method, the motive, and the reflexive position of the cultural inquirer himself" ("Godwin and the Republican Romance," 154). Rajan focuses on the open-ended process of "reading" encouraged by *The Enquirer:* "The reader cannot be governed by the announced moral, but must read actively, doing more than simply reproducing the text. . . . For by making writing the production rather than the reflection of an anterior meaning, Godwin also makes reading the production, through 'experiment' or experience, of a text that is still in process" (*Supplement of Reading,* 169).

25. Godwin, *Enquirer,* vii.

26. Philp argues that "the later editions [of *Political Justice*] seem to abandon the rationalism of the first edition in favour of a more Humean scepticism, and some critics have argued that this shift undermines the cogency of Godwin's argument for the inevitability of moral and political improvement" (*Godwin's Political Justice,* 8).

27. Godwin, *Enquiry*, 1.5.43.

28. Aristotle, *Nicomachean Ethics*, 1147a13–14, 1147b16–19, 1041–42.

29. Godwin, *St. Leon*, 266.

30. Godwin, 99–100.

31. See Handwerk, "Mapping Misogyny," 397–98. Nazar also discusses how "Godwin's critique of Rousseau builds on the earlier critique developed by Mary Wollstonecraft in her novels and educational writings," which emphasize how "Rousseau's structuring norm of nature [exposes] its fundamental arbitrariness and injustice to women." Nazar reads the novel as a critique of not merely the "gendering of virtue," but the broader "cast of [Rousseau's] sentimentalism" (*Enlightened Sentiments*, 107, 84). For more on *Fleetwood* in the context of Godwin's career and how it subverts the "literary types found in earlier Jacobin novels" with its focus on an intemperate misanthrope, see Kelly, *English Jacobin Novel*, 250.

32. As Kelly has noted, Godwin had begun translating Rousseau's *Confessions* in 1789 and had recently reread it at the time of writing *Fleetwood* (*English Jacobin Novel*, 243). See also Kelly, "Romance of Real Life."

33. Goldie, *Mess Inside*, 43; see note 5. Although akrasia is not expressly featured in his discussion, it would seem to fit right in. For Goldie's separate treatment of akrasia, see *Emotions*, 84–122.

34. Godwin, *Fleetwood*, 301.

35. Godwin, 314.

36. Godwin, 297.

37. Fludernik, *Fictions of Language*, 73.

38. Cohn, *Transparent Minds*, 117.

39. Godwin, *Fleetwood*, 294–95.

40. Godwin, 325–26.

41. Handwerk, "Mapping Misogyny," 376.

42. Scott review in Godwin, *Fleetwood*, 521.

43. Review from the *Anti-Jacobin Review and Magazine* 21 (August 1805): 337–58, quoted in Godwin, *Fleetwood*, 524.

44. Godwin, 310.

45. Booth has emphasized the moral dimension of the "double vision that operates throughout the book," which combines "our inside view of Emma's worth and our objective view of her great faults" (*Rhetoric of Fiction*, 256). For an interpretation of FID as gossip, see Finch and Bowen, "Tittle-Tattle of Highbury." Ferguson understands the Finch and Bowen article as representative of a style of Foucauldian model of criticism that interprets FID as eliminating individuality on behalf of social consciousness. For Ferguson, *Emma* indeed asks us to see the distinctive formal quality of FID as negoti-

ating those two realms, providing a moral structure while attentive to the particularities of character. For Miller, "Style flaunts its mastery, its ability to enter and then exit a character's state of mind at will, while always retaining, at whatever level of intimacy, the immunity of its impersonality" (*Jane Austen*, 66). In *Dual Voice*, Pascal describes Austen as a "narrator who is prominent as story-teller and moralist, but who is (with rare lapses) non-personal, non-defined, and therefore may enjoy access to the most secret privacy of the characters" (45).

46. Ferguson, "Impact of Form," 171. It is worth emphasizing Ferguson's word "privileged" in order to bring out some important elements of akrasia, not just in discrete moments in this novel, but generally speaking. Insofar as akrasia involves knowingness, it is also tied to one who has the capacity to do differently. This is why akratics in literature tend to be those in positions of privilege (intellectual, economic, or institutional).

47. Austen, *Emma*, 93.

48. Austen, 145.

49. Austen, 268.

50. Rorty, "Akratic Believers," 175–83.

51. Austen, *Emma*, 24.

52. Austen, 24.

53. Banfield, *Unspeakable Sentences*, 197.

54. Cohn, *Transparent Minds*, 117.

55. Ferguson, "Now It's Personal," 530.

56. Banfield, *Unspeakable Sentences*, 210.

57. To this we can also add yet another related sentence elsewhere in the novel: "She could not repent" (176).

58. Murdoch, *Sovereignty of Good*, 17.

4. AKRASIA, LIFE WRITING, AND INTERPRETATION

1. The comic artist behind this strip and the revival of the classical *Nancy* comic since 2018 is Olivia Jaimes (pseudonym).

2. Konnikova, "Getting over Procrastination"; Hall, "Science."

3. Augustine, *Confessions*, 8.7.17, 174.

4. See Schleiermacher, *Hermeneutics and Criticism*. For a discussion of the history and dilemmas of interpretation, see Iser, *Range of Interpretation*.

5. For the most fundamental contributions to hermeneutics, see especially Wilhelm Dilthey, *Introduction to the Human Sciences* (1883) and *The Forma-*

tion of the Historical World in the Human Sciences (1910); Martin Heidegger, Being and Time (1927); and Hans-Georg Gadamer, Truth and Method (1960).

6. Bate, Samuel Johnson, 455. This makes Johnson a key figure in "illustrating the transition to the modern inwardness of the religious life and the problems of elusiveness and self-doubt that attended it." He continues, "His instinctive sympathies were with those forms of Protestantism that had found Augustine the most congenial of the early Church writers precisely because of Augustine's stress of the irreplaceable subjectivity of the religious experience and a theology of grace conceived in terms of the *personal* conversion to God of the reflectively conscious individual."

7. Bate, 300.

8. Bate continues: "In particular, he anticipates the concept of 'repression' as he turns on the way in which the human imagination, when it is frustrated in its search for satisfaction, doubles back into repression, creating a 'secret discontent,' or begins to move ominously into various forms of imaginative projection" (306).

9. Two examples of book-length studies of Rousseau that describe him in this way include Starobinski, *Transparency and Obstruction;* and Damrosch, *Restless Genius*. Starobinski writes, "It took Kant to think Rousseau's thoughts, and Freud to think Rousseau's feelings" (141–42, also quoted in Damrosch, 2).

10. Brooks, *Reading for the Plot*, 32.

11. Brooks, 32–33.

12. See chapter 3, note 31.

13. Boswell, *Life of Samuel Johnson*, 41.

14. Jordan, *Anxieties of Idleness*, 153–54. Jordan's chapter "'Driving on the System of Life': Samuel Johnson and Idleness" offers many resources, anecdotes, and insights about Johnson's idleness (153–77).

15. Plumb, "Commercialization of Leisure," 265.

16. The incipient logic here is one that would be diagnosed most astutely and influentially by Max Weber, but it is also phrased concisely by Adam Smith in *Wealth of Nations* when he characterizes the inverse relationship between revenue and industry: "Wherever capital predominates, industry prevails: wherever revenue, idleness" (book 1, chapter 3, 358).

17. In his study, Spiegelman traces the "progress of the trope" from "sloth" as "monastic vice" ("neglect of ecclesiastical duties") in reference to monks who become indifferent to their obligations to God, and the Stoic notion in which it was the opposite of fortitude, toward the Christian definition that we see in Aquinas (*Majestic Indolence*, 7–9). See 3–20 for the broader account.

18. Spiegelman, 7.

19. See Google Books Ngram Viewer, "procrastination" in "British English" between years 1600 and 2000. A steep uptick begins at around 1740 to reach a peak at around 1825. I cannot speak to the accuracy of Google's model or the reliability of its data set, so it should be taken with a grain of salt. The data is not really the point anyway. https://books.google.com/ngrams /graph?content=procrastination&year_start=1600&year_end=2000&corpus =26&smoothing=3 (accessed July 19, 2021).

20. Spiegelman, *Majestic Indolence*, 9.

21. "Savage was 'always applauding his past conduct, or, at least, forgetting it to amuse himself with phantoms of happiness, which were dancing before him; and willingly turned his eyes from the light of reason, when it would have discovered the illusion, and shown him, what he never wished to see, his real state'" (Alkon, *Samuel Johnson and Moral Discipline*, 119–20).

22. Bate, "Introduction," in Johnson, *Essays*, xi–xxix, xxv.

23. "However serious Johnson's other intentions, he wanted [the *Rambler*] to sell, and a title that would openly proclaim it at the start as a series of moral discourses would have at once cut it off from the popular journalistic proto-type on which he hoped to capitalize" (Bate, *Samuel Johnson*, 289).

24. Johnson, *Idler* no. 31, 18 November 1758, in Johnson, *Essays*, 292.

25. Johnson, *Idler*, no. 59, 2 June 1759, 326. Similarly, in the second essay written for the *Rambler* from March 24, which focuses on the condition of being distracted by concern for the future, Johnson notes how "we forget the proper use of the time now in our power, to provide for the enjoyment of that which, perhaps may never be granted us" (3). Likewise, in the *Rambler* no. 24, Johnson discusses the dangers of the man who "employs himself upon remote and unnecessary subjects, and wastes his life upon ques-tions, which cannot be resolved, and of which the solution would conduce very little to the advancement of happiness; . . . [who] lavishes his hours in calculating the weight of the terraqueous globe, or in adjusting successive systems of worlds beyond the reach of the telescope" (57).

26. Spiegelman describes Johnson as representing a "pivot between the medieval theological status of sloth and its location as a mental infirmity described by proto-psychiatrists from the Renaissance onward" (*Majestic Indolence*, 13).

27. Johnson, *Rambler*, no. 28, 23 June 1750, 65.

28. Johnson, *Rambler*, no. 8, 4 April 1750, 23. Relatedly, on self-deception:

When he calls himself to his own tribunal, he finds every fault, if not absolutely effaced, yet so much palliated by the goodness of his intention, and the cogency of the motive, that very little guilt or turpitude remains;

and when he takes a survey of the whole complication of his character, he discovers so many latent excellencies, so many virtues that want but an opportunity to exert themselves in act, and so many kind wishes for universal happiness, that he looks on himself as suffering unjustly under the infamy of single failings, while the general temper of his mind is unknown or unregarded. . . .

It is natural to mean well, when only abstracted ideas of virtue are proposed to the mind, and no particular passion turns us aside from rectitude; and so willing is every man to flatter himself, that the difference between approving laws, and obeying them, is frequently forgotten. (*Rambler*, no. 76, 8 December 1750, 134–35)

Another strategy, he continues, is to take comfort in the faults of others:

There are, however, great numbers who . . . live at peace with themselves, by means which require less understanding, or less attention. When their hearts are burthened with the consciousness of a crime, instead of seeking for some remedy within themselves, they look round upon the rest of mankind, to find others tainted with the same guilt: they please themselves with observing, that they have numbers on their side; and that though they are hunted out from the society of good men, they are not likely to be condemned to solitude. (135)

29. Johnson, *Rambler*, no. 28, 23 June 1750, 65.
30. We have reason then to be skeptical of assertions on Johnson's "views" on the ontology of the will. Hudson has argued that Johnson's "view of the will was essentially that of Hobbes, probably as revised by Locke": in this view, Johnson understands the will as operating by "antecedent necessity" (caused by whatever was the last desire), which is determined by the strength or weakness of desires as correlated to certain objectives (*Samuel Johnson and Eighteenth-Century Thought*, 90–91). Hudson also writes, "Boswell seemed convinced that Johnson was so deeply disturbed by the case for necessity that he was unwilling to face the question squarely. This inference has led to some modern conjectures on Johnson's secret agreement with Hobbes" (90). Throughout his chapter on Johnson and eighteenth-century ethics, Hudson describes Johnson's moral outlook as "Christian epicureanism," a perspective that understands obligation and causal necessity differently than another dominant moral view of the time, utilitarianism (see 66–99). Bate's characterization of Johnson is more convincing: "Since the result is greater than the mere sum of the parts, any attempt to condense the moral writing (as also the critical writing) into

system or formulas always becomes frustrated. As we anatomize, abstract, categorize, and label (with the best of intentions), we inevitably lose what is essential: the active interplay of qualities—of compassion and anger, of humor and moral profundity, of range of knowledge and specialized focus, of massive moral honesty and specific technical or psychological acumen—that come together so refreshingly and reassuringly in Johnson's conversation and moral writing" (*Samuel Johnson*, 297–98).

31. Alkon, *Samuel Johnson and Moral Discipline*, 86–87.
32. Johnson, *Idler*, no. 27, 21 October 1758, 284–85.
33. Johnson, 285.
34. Johnson, *Rambler*, no. 134, 29 June 1751, 177–79.
35. Johnson, *Idler*, no. 31, 18 November 1758, 291–92.
36. See Bate, *Samuel Johnson*, 292n5.
37. Johnson, *Idler*, no. 31, 18 November 1758, 293.
38. As he also puts it, "The writer of his own life has at least the first qualification of an historian, the knowledge of the truth. . . . He that speaks of himself has no motive to falsehood or partiality except self-love, by which all have so often been betrayed, that all are on the watch against its artifices" (Johnson, *Idler*, no. 84, 24 November 1759, 348–49).
39. Rousseau, *Confessions*, 17, 169.
40. Rousseau, 44.
41. Rousseau, 114.
42. Starobinski, *Transparency and Obstruction*, 183. He writes elsewhere: "His subjective life is not 'hidden,' not buried in psychological 'depths.' It bubbles spontaneously to the surface; emotion is always too powerful to be contained or repressed" (181).
43. Starobinski, 182.
44. De Man, *Allegories of Reading*, 279.
45. Locke, *Essay Concerning Human Understanding*, 43.
46. MacIntyre, *After Virtue*, 82.
47. Starobinski, *Transparency and Obstruction*, 181.
48. De Man, *Allegories of Reading*, 280. De Man also draws upon Raymond, who observes, "It appears that after having stigmatized his misdeed he gradually begins to justify it. The same gliding and swerving motion can be observed more than once in the *Confessions*. . . . He is always led to distinguish the intent from the act" (*Jean-Jacques Rousseau*, 1273–74, quoted and translated by de Man, 282).
49. Rousseau, *Confessions*, 46.
50. Augustine, *Confessions*, 2.4.9, 36.
51. Rousseau, *Confessions*, 45.

52. Rousseau, 169.

53. Rousseau, 352.

54. It has been a crucial text for the deconstructive accounts of speech, linguistic meaning, and intention, particularly in de Man's 1977 essay, "The Purloined Ribbon," which makes up his chapter on "Excuse" in *Allegories of Reading* (1979), and in the antitheory account of Knapp and Michaels. As the ongoing conversations around key episodes in this work reveal, the work invites an ongoing process of interpretation that is built into the subject matter and formal structure of the work itself.

55. Rousseau, *Confessions*, 87.

56. Rousseau, 88–89.

57. Defoe, *Moll Flanders*, 151.

58. Rousseau, *Confessions*, 88. In de Man's treatment of this passage, he posits that "what Rousseau really wanted is neither the ribbon nor Marion, but the public scene of exposure which he actually gets" (*Allegories of Reading*, 285). Damrosch thinks this is too simple: "There was no one thing that he 'really' wanted, and in brooding on memories that wouldn't go away, he brought the past to life in all its fullness" (*Restless Genius*, 438).

59. De Man uses this episode to show how the text decouples "performative rhetoric" from "cognitive rhetoric" (300)—that is, the speaker's knowledge of what happened from what the speaker says happened, the explaining/excusing speech act from the signifying language. The disconnect arises out of the fact that these "two rhetorical codes" "fail to converge" (300), because language is not "an instrument in the service of a psychic energy" but "a machine [that] performs anyway," "prior to any figuration or meaning" (299). Knapp and Michaels argue that de Man's claims as to language's inherent meaninglessness prior to the additions of "signifieds" are incoherent. "It is not true," they write, "that sounds in themselves are signifiers; they become signifiers only when they acquire meanings, and when they lose their meanings they stop being signifiers. De Man's mistake is to think that the sound 'Marion' remains a signifier even when emptied of all meaning. The fact is that the meaningless noise 'Marion' only *resembles* the signifier 'Marion,' just as accidentally uttering the sound 'Marion' only *resembles* the speech act of naming Marion. De Man recognizes that the accidental emission of the sound 'Marion' is not a speech act (indeed, that's the point of the example), but he fails to recognize that it's not language either" ("Against Theory," 734–35). For a pertinent discussion of eighteenth-century intentionalism (specifically, in *Clarissa*) anchored in a discussion of de Man's intentionalist treatment of Rousseau's utterance, see also Macpherson, "Lovelace, Ltd."

5. AKRASIA AND THE POETRY OF ANTINOMIES

1. Empson, *Seven Types of Ambiguity*, vi.
2. Empson, 196–97. He goes on: "Indeed, human life is so much a matter of juggling with contradictory impulses (Christian-worldly, sociable-independent, and such-like)" and this "inconsistency . . . shows that they are in possession of the right number of principles, and have a fair title to humanity."
3. Brooks, *Well-Wrought Urn*, 3–21. I am grateful to Oren Izenberg for sharing thoughts with me on the subject of the relation between akrasia/irrationality and poetry.
4. Keats, *Letters: Vol. 1*, no. 45, 193–94.
5. Kant writes, "THESIS: Causality in accordance with laws of nature is not the only causality from which the appearances of the world can one and all be derived. To explain these appearances it is necessary to assume that there is also another causality, that of freedom. / ANTITHESIS: There is no freedom; everything in the world takes place solely in accordance with laws of nature" (*Critique of Pure Reason*, 409).
6. Kant, *Critique of the Power of Judgment*. See the "First Introduction" (45) and "Introduction" (63–64). Here Kant discusses the divisions of philosophy, the domains of philosophy, and the role of judgment in combining his earlier projects of theoretical philosophy and practical philosophy treated in the *Critique of Pure Reason* and the *Critique of Practical Reason*, respectively.
7. See Wordsworth, *Prelude*, 10:805–903.
8. Potkay, *Wordsworth's Ethics*, 6.
9. Potkay, 7. What we get then is contradiction akin to what Wright has examined in the context of the Victorian novel as the mode of "bad logical forms," which "aren't in need of solutions; rather, they're in need of attention" (*Bad Logic*, 18).
10. Jarvis, *Wordsworth's Philosophic Song*, 3–4. Potkay cites this line by Jarvis (206n17).
11. See Brooks, *Well-Wrought Urn*, 151–66.
12. Keats, "In Drear Nighted December," lines 21–25. All quotes of Keats poems are drawn from the versions in *Poems of John Keats*, ed. Jack Stillinger.
13. Brooks, *Well-Wrought Urn*, 192–214, 195.
14. Mellor, *English Romantic Irony*, 11–12. According to Mellor, for Schlegel, this irony is to be associated with the figure of Socrates who says, "I know nothing."
15. Mellor, 14, 22.

16. Spiegelman, *Majestic Indolence*, 5. As discussed in chapter 4, Spiegelman traces the "progress of [the] trope" of indolence from sloth as "primarily a monastic vice," through "by the time of Aquinas [as] related to *tristitia*, an aversion from man's *spiritual* good" (8) and in Chaucer where it comes to occupy a middle space between the "sins of the spirit—pride, envy, and anger—and those of the flesh—avarice, gluttony, and lechery" (8–9). It was then with Robert Burton in the seventeenth century that "combine[d] the spiritual and the psychological dimensions of 'acedia' and to redefine, under the rubric of 'melancholy,' what was to become known for at least two centuries as the distinctive malady of the English": "Idleness" as "the *malus genius* of our nation" (9). See Spiegelman, 5–20. The changes, Spiegelman notes, are partly cultural: "leisure" becomes "widespread, economically feasible, and morally defensible" and with that new concerns about wasting time (11).

17. For a discussion on the idea of poetry and metaphysical "ease," proposed as a sort of sibling to the poetry of *otium* or Romantic indolence, see Izenberg, "Confiance au Monde."

18. François, *Open Secrets*, 1, xvi, xvii, xviii. See also Khalip, *Anonymous Life,* for its attention to Romanticism's interest in "engaged withdrawal or strategic reticence" (3).

19. Wordsworth, "Preface" (1800), in Coleridge and Wordsworth, *Lyrical Ballads,* 171–87, 178.

20. Additionally, they both shirked from "the automatic gendering of indolence, whether as male (in Thomson) or as female (in Shenstone)" (Spiegelman, 90–91). Here Spiegelman refers to William Shenstone's 1750 "Ode to Indolence."

21. Wordsworth, "Expostulation and Reply" in *Lyrical Ballads,* 2.1–4 and 17–20.

22. This phrase shows up again in *The Prelude* as "cannot chuse but feel" in books 2 and 13, lines 20 and 84, respectively.

23. For this sort of account of Wordsworth, see, for instance, Hirsch, *Wordsworth and Schelling.*

24. Coleridge and Wordsworth, "Preface," in *Lyrical Ballads,* 171–87, 173. Spiegelman notes that this goes along with antiurban sentiment, one that manifests in Wordsworth's description in the preface of *Lyrical Ballads* (177) when he refers to the "multitude of causes unknown to former times are now acting with a combined force to blunt the discriminating powers of the mind, and unfitting it for all voluntary exertion to reduce it to a state of almost savage torpor"; see Spiegelman, *Majestic Indolence,* 14.

   For an in-depth look at various connotations of indolence, idleness, work, play, *otium,* and *negotium* in the poetry of Wordsworth, see Spiegelman,

21–57. Of chief interest to Spiegelman with respect to Wordsworth—which distinguishes his focus from my own—is the freedom of idleness: "Art as a self-sustaining unit and as a process that retains a close proximity to the activities of children and gods, who are alike in their freedom. Such freedom derives from idleness, however momentary, since idle moments provide Wordsworth with the ontological condition necessary for pastoral contemplation in both its serious and its holiday moods" (29). Spiegelman considers *Nutting, Michael, The Idle Shepherd-Boys, Resolution and Independence,* and the Intimations ode, in addition to *The Prelude.*

25. Johnson, *Idler,* no. 32, 25 November 1758, in Johnson, *Essays,* 296.
26. All citations of *The Prelude* are from the 1805 version.
27. This condition at the start of *The Prelude* has been much discussed in Wordsworth criticism. Hartman has called this opening as performing "an experience of aphasia" (incapacity to articulate), and we can consider aphasia as species of akrasia if we regard it not as literal incapacity but as failure despite capacity. See Hartman, *Wordsworth's Poetry,* 38. As Chandler has put it, "Book 1 as we know it employs the paradoxical fiction that a poem can go on at length about its failure to get going at all" (*Wordsworth's Second Nature,* 189). Chandler goes on to argue that the speaker's experience ought not to be understand as a merely private, psychological, or idiosyncratic; the "triumph of mental discipline" is also the triumph of "discipline-as-tradition," or the political ideology Wordsworth inherits from Edmund Burke (199); see 184–215.

   In a more recent staging of this procrastinatory strategy of turning to write about oneself instead of taking on the difficult writing enterprise at hand, we can turn to the 2002 Charlie Kaufman/Spike Jonze film *Adaptation* (2002) in which Charlie Kaufman is our Wordsworth. Instead of writing a film adaptation of the Susan Orlean book *The Orchid Thief,* he endeavors to do something a little more manageable: write about himself trying to write the work.
28. Coleridge, *Biographia Literaria,* 45.
29. Coleridge, *Notebooks,* vol. 1, 832.
30. Coleridge, *Biographia Literaria,* 111. To quote Laurence Lockridge, Coleridge came to believe that "if we were as subject to the mechanical whims of motives and impulses as [the 'mechanico-corpuscular philosophers'] assert, we would suffer a chaotic unpredictability of character, going to bed benign and waking up vicious" (*Ethics of Romanticism,* 49).
31. Coleridge, *Biographia Literaria,* 95, 121.
32. Coleridge, *Coleridge's Poetry and Prose,* 2.45–48.
33. About Kant, Coleridge writes, "In his *moral* system he was permitted to

assume a higher ground (the autonomy of the will) as a POSTULATE deducible from the unconditional command, or . . . the categorical imperative, of the conscience" (*Biographia Literaria*, 154). Lockridge writes about the appeal of the categorical imperative to Coleridge in light of his idiosyncrasies: it "offers the errant opium-eater a seemingly sturdy guide to the moral life" (*Ethics of Romanticism*, 75). While inspired by the thought of Kant (and Fichte), Coleridge would depart from their frameworks in seeing the will as essentially spiritual in origin. In *Aids to Reflection,* Coleridge expands upon Augustine's notion of the will as the sole source of sin: inasmuch as sin "is *evil,*" he writes, "in God it cannot originate: and yet in some *Spirit* (i.e., in some *supernatural* power) it *must*. For in *Nature* there is no origin. Sin is therefore spiritual Evil: but the spiritual in Man is the Will . . . the corruption must have been self-originated" (273). Thus, Coleridge would increasingly embrace an Augustinian notion of the will as "pre-eminently the *spiritual* Constituent in our Being" (75). For a wide-ranging and precise discussion of Coleridge's engagements with the will and their relations to the history of Western philosophy, see Pfau, *Minding the Modern,* 468– 503. As Pfau writes, Coleridge "seemingly endorses the modern, Kantian view of human agents as strictly self-legislating and self-legitimating," but at the same time he also "conceives the will in distinctly Augustinian and Scholastic terms as uniquely spiritual and indexed to the normative (divine) authority of the Platonic *logos*" (471). For another wide-ranging discussion of this trajectory, see also Evans, *Sublime Coleridge.*

34. Moments in *The Prelude* indeed directly address Coleridge: "Throughout this narrative, / Else sooner ended, I have known full well / For whom I thus record the birth and growth / Of gentleness, simplicity, and truth, / And joyous loves that hallow innocent days / Of peace and self-command" (6.269–74). Coleridge would acknowledge the poem's assistance to his personal constitution in "To William Wordsworth": "Thou hast dared to tell / What may be told, to the understanding mind / Revealable; and what within the mind / By vital breathings secret as the soul / Of vernal growth, oft quickens in the heart / Thoughts all too deep for words!" (Coleridge, "To William Wordsworth," in *Coleridge's Poetry and Prose,* 2.6–11). Abrams has written, "The poet's solemn voice seized upon Coleridge as though it were itself a great wind which, like the literal storm in *Dejection,* fanned his torpid spirit . . . into a momentary and painful rebirth" ("Correspondent Breeze," 118).

35. The idea of agency as dependent upon custom and habit arrives out of what Chandler has persuasively called Wordsworth's sense of his "second nature," an idea borrowing from Edmund Burke and that also contains

Burke's suspicions toward reason, autonomy, and self-legislation. Chandler argues that Wordsworth construes his errors in his early ideas of a writing task and in his childhood spots of time lie in his conception of freedom or "the ambitious Power of choice" (1850 version, 1:166): "The time, place, and manners of his poem cannot be singled out with steady choice. They will always be to some extent a function of who he is—and that means of who he has been. He cannot, for example, *choose* to 'settle on some British theme' or to carry on with Milton's work; his theme will inevitably be in some sense British, just as his verse, in some measure, will be Miltonic. The poet's mistake is to think that he can write a poem as Thoreau says we must live our lives—deliberately—that he can determine its course by weighing alternatives at every step" (*Wordsworth's Second Nature*, 194).

36. By the end it would advocate a view of the willful fancy and imagination and its broader "dependency" (8:640) that requires drawing upon the active gifts of nature and habit. See *Prelude*, 8:486, 511–677): "There came . . . / A willfulness of fancy and conceit" (8:520–21) / "willful fancy grafted upon feelings / Of the imagination" (584–85); also 13:66–331. See also the "ennobling interchange / Of action from within and from without" (12:376–77).

37. Potkay, *Wordsworth's Ethics*, 95. Potkay is citing Kivy, *Sound Sentiment*, 2–15, 46–52.

38. Hartman, *Wordsworth's Poetry*, 8–9. For Hartman, the difference between Milton on the one hand and Wordsworth and Keats on the other is that for the latter two "surmise is no longer an exceptional figure of thought but an inalienable part of the poetry. The poem itself is now largely surmise, a false surmise perhaps, but the poet has nothing else to dally with, and the distinction is less between false and true than between surmise and surmise" (10–11). See also Potkay on Wordsworth's use of negatives in *The Excursion* (*Wordsworth's Ethics*, 162).

39. Augustine, *Confessions*, 2.4.9, 36.

40. Augustine, 2.3.8, 35. Original Latin: Augustine, *The Confessions of Augustine: Electronic Edition*, edited and translated by J. J. O'Donnell, http://www .stoa.org/hippo/text2.html (accessed July 19, 2021).

41. Chandler observes the description in this passage of the "huge cliff" that rises up "as if with voluntary power" (1:406–7) as "a reflection of the boy's own misguided will. The more desperately this will is asserted, the greater the force of the adversary. This way lies madness" (*Wordsworth's Second Nature*, 211).

42. Keats, *Letters: Vol. 1*, no. 26, 142.

43. Keats, no. 27, 146.

44. Keats, no. 159, 78–79.

45. Levinson, *Keats's Life of Allegory*, 7. Levinson continues: Keats was not "per-mitted possession of the social grammar inscribed in [the] aesthetic array" of poetry that inspired him (10). Bayley writes, "His personality is not self-renewing—it is not ruthless and egocentric enough" ("Keats and Reality," 112). Ricks discusses Bayley's noble "badness" more in the context of Keats's "adolescence," his ability to evoke and express embarrassment; see *Keats and Embarrassment*.

46. All quotes from Keats's poetry are drawn from *Poems of John Keats*, and line numbers will be provided parenthetically in the body of the text.

47. Keats, *Letters: Vol. 1*, no. 38, 169–70. Bate has called "this act of will sus-tained for seven months," as "something almost unique in modern poetry" (*John Keats*, 193). He also describes the "weeks of difficulty in getting started in *Endymion*, the nervous trips from the Isle of Wight back to Mar-gate, then Canterbury, then home to Hampstead" (180).

48. Wordsworth, *Prelude*, 1:220–22.

49. As Bayley has written, "Even at its most unpropitious, *Endymion* is packed with borrowed life" ("Keats and Reality," 102). The word "packed" aptly characterizes the poem's character as a grab-bag repository for poetic im-agery. Each line offers new opportunities for "poetry," whether Chaucerian, Spenserian, or Thomsonian. It is in the "badness" of "Endymion" that Bayley finds Keats's unique strength: "When he tries to express reality he becomes abstract; when he turns towards the discipline of art he becomes Parnassian" (105), Bayley writes, adding that "with Keats the processes of 'maturity' are those of real impoverishment and sacrifice, of muting and muffling" (112). Similarly, Bate has written that despite the common appraisal of Keats's poetry in terms of its "economy . . . of phrase," "*Endy-mion* is easily one of the most diluted poems Keats wrote. In fact, it is one of the most diluted poems in a century often given to poetic dilution" (*John Keats*, 171). Indeed, as we read, we find continually the attempt to prolong the imagery, to add descriptions onto "one bare circumstance"—qualities that characterize Byron's descriptions of Keats as "vulgar" and what, more recently, McFarland has called (more positively) the "too much-ness" of Keats (*Masks of Keats*, 130).

50. Keats, *Poems of John Keats*, 102. Ricks writes memorably about the em-barrassment staged here, his embarrassment by *Endymion* and "by his self-inflicted obligation to dissociate himself from the poem even while publishing it (such conflicting impulses are endemic in embarrassment)" (*Keats and Embarrassment*, 11). Keats would not repeat this method of composition for the remainder of his life. As McFarland has written, the approach to *Endymion* from "*a priori* design was absolutely at variance with

[the] . . . understanding of the proper genesis of poetry" that Keats is most well known for (*Masks of Keats*, 126–27).

51. Hazlitt, *Complete Works*, 47. Keats would very similarly write about "Men of Genius" that they "are great as certain ethereal Chemicals operating on the Mass of neutral intellect—by they have not any individuality, any determined Character" (*Letters: Vol. 1*, no. 43, 184–85). As Bromwich has observed, it is not merely Hazlitt's ideas that influenced Keats, but his idioms: "Keats understood Hazlitt's ideas till they became second nature to him; but the ideas were always inseparable from the tact of expression; Hazlitt's power, in every way, was *communicated*" (*Hazlitt*, 370). Keats, he continues, "felt bold enough to call on him by December 1818. . . . No other encounter between poet and critic has been so fortunate for literature" (367–69). For an extensive discussion of what Keats's "negative capability" owes to Hazlitt, see also 374–79. For a discussion of Keats's and Hazlitt's first encounter in November 1816, see Wu, *William Hazlitt*, 196–97.

52. Khalip has investigated how Hazlitt's notion of "disinterest" informs a broader "ethics of lyric anonymity" that we find expressed in Keats's "negative capability"; for Khalip, "disinterest" is "the crucial term for divesting ourselves of the premise that we are fully self-possessed individuals" (*Anonymous Life*, 27; see 25–66 for the broader discussion). Khalip also draws from Bromwich, "Genealogy of Disinterestedness," which briefly considers Hazlitt's *Essay* and Keats. Spiegelman, on the other hand, discusses Keats's indolence—not by considering his indebtedness to Hazlitt, but rather through Keats's experience studying physiology as a medical student. Keats, Spiegelman writes, "would have heard his lecturers at Guy's Hospital discuss the mental form of hypochondriasis in melancholy, among the causes of which are 'indolent inactive life' as well as 'intense study'" (*Majestic Indolence*, 101). See also De Almeida, *Romantic Medicine and John Keats*, 286–98.

53. Bromwich, "Genealogy of Disinterestedness," 64.

54. Hazlitt, *Essay*, 1.

55. Hazlitt, 176–77. For careful discussions about the distinctions between Hazlitt's philosophy of thought and action and those of other philosophers—namely, Hobbes, Locke, Berkeley, Shaftesbury, Hutcheson, Hartley, Helvetius, Coleridge, and Kant—see Albrecht, *Hazlitt and the Creative Imagination*, 1–28. The primary difference from Coleridge rests in Hazlitt's dependence upon empiricism; in this sense, "he never thought of Coleridge's transcendentalism as anything but nonsense," and though he looked into Kant he grew convinced that "Kant's system 'was a wilful and monstrous absurdity'" (5). On Hartley, Albrecht writes, "For Hartley,

association coalesces the pleasures of imagination with those of the moral sense; and moral action results when these pleasures activate the 'set of compound vibratiuncles' that Hartley terms 'the will.' For Hazlitt, however, the imagination has a more dominant role. It not only supplies vivid images that enter into the idea of a 'good' but charges them with habitual thought and feeling to 'create' the sympathetic object of voluntary action'" (24).

56. Hazlitt, *Essay*, 137.

57. Hazlitt, 113–14. Bate writes, "In his *Principles of Human Action*, Hazlitt went much further than Adam Smith's *Theory of Moral Sentiments*. His hope was to show that imaginative sympathy was not a mere escape hatch from the prison of egocentricity, but something thoroughgoing, something indigenous and inseparable from all activities of the mind. Sympathetic identification takes place constantly—even if only with ourselves and our own desired future" (*John Keats*, 256; see 256–59 for a fuller discussion). Wu recounts Godwin's central role the publication of the *Essay* (*Hazlitt*, 101–6). As Wu and various other of Hazlitt's biographers have recounted, the *Essay* was not well received upon publication. See also Jones, *Hazlitt*, 18–21; and Grayling, *Quarrel of the Age*, 92–94.

58. Hazlitt, *Essay*, 201–2.

59. Hazlitt, 101–3. This capacity in poetry relates to what Empson has referred to as contradiction as a "use of opposites, where two things thought of as incompatible, but desired intensely by different systems of judgments, are spoken of simultaneously by words applying to both; both desires are thus given a transient and exhausting satisfaction, and the two systems of judgment are forced into open conflict before the reader" (*Seven Types of Ambiguity*, 226). In a related, memorable passage, Empson writes, "A contradiction of this kind may be meaningless, but can never be a blank; it has at least stated the subject which is under discussion, and has given a sort of intensity to it such as one finds in a gridiron pattern in architecture because it gives prominence neither to the horizontals nor to the verticals, and in a check pattern because neither colour is the ground on which the other is placed; it is at once an indecision and a structure, like the symbol of the Cross" (192).

60. Nersessian, *Calamity Form*, 120.

61. Keats, *Letters: Vol. 1*, no. 43, 185.

62. McFarland, *Masks of Keats*, 130.

63. Vendler, *Odes of John Keats*, 28.

64. In its soporific vision of moving figures that seem to move at a great distance from the poet, this stanza recalls a scene described by Hazlitt in an essay called "On Londoners and Country People" in which Hazlitt

describes modern city life as "an endless phantasmagoria": a place where someone is able to see everything and yet feel removed and unmoved by it all. He focuses on the lower-class cockney (in this respect responding to *Blackwood's Magazine*'s characterization of Keats and Hazlitt as of the "Cockney school" of writing). The cockney witnesses the hubbub around him and yet remains "nothing in himself": "The true Cockney . . . sees everything near, superficial, little, in hasty succession. The world turns round, and his head with it, like a roundabout at a fair, till he becomes stunned and giddy with the motion. Figures glide by as in a *camera obscura*. There is a glare, a perpetual hubbub, a noise, a crowd about him; he sees and hears a vast number of things, and knows nothing. His senses keep him alive; and he knows, inquires and cares for nothing farther. . . . He notices the people going to court or to a city-feast, and is quite satisfied with the show. . . . A real Cockney is the poorest creature in the world, the most literal, the most mechanical, and yet he too lives in a world of romance—a fairy-land of his own. . . . He is a shopman, and nailed all day behind the counter: but he sees hundreds and thousands of gay, well-dressed people pass—an endless phantasmagoria—and enjoys their liberty and gaudy fluttering pride" ("On Londoners and Countrypeople," 50–52). For more on how this scene depicts "the exhausted interiority of the modern metropolitan subject as a direct consequence of the commodification of styles, expressive conventions, and a ubiquitous print culture," see Pfau, *Romantic Moods*, 353.

BIBLIOGRAPHY

Abrams, M. H. "The Correspondent Breeze: A Romantic Metaphor." *Kenyon Review* 19, no. 1 (Winter 1957): 113–30.

Albrecht, W. P. *Hazlitt and the Creative Imagination.* Lawrence: University of Kansas Press, 1965.

Alkon, Paul Kent. *Samuel Johnson and Moral Discipline.* Evanston: Northwestern University Press, 1967.

Anscombe, G. E. M. "Modern Moral Philosophy." *Philosophy* 33, no. 124 (1958): 1–19.

Arendt, Hannah. *The Life of the Mind.* New York: Harcourt, 1978.

Aristotle. *Nicomachean Ethics.* Translated by W. D. Ross. In *The Basic Works of Aristotle,* edited by Richard McKeon, 927–1112. New York: Modern Library, 2001.

Augustine. *City of God: Concerning the City of God against the Pagans.* Translated by Henry Bettenson. New York: Penguin, 2003.

———. *Confessions.* Edited and translated by Philip Burton. New York: Everyman's Library, 2001.

———. *On Free Choice of the Will.* Translated by Thomas Williams. Cambridge, MA: Hackett, 1993.

Austen, Jane. *Emma* [1815]. New York: Penguin, 1996.

Backscheider, Paula. "The Crime Wave and *Moll Flanders.*" In *Moll Flanders* [1722], by Daniel Defoe, edited by Albert J. Rivero, 460–71. New York: W. W. Norton, 2004.

Ballaster, Ros. *Seductive Forms: Women's Amatory Fiction from 1684 to 1740.* London: Clarendon, 1992.

Banfield, Ann. *Unspeakable Sentences: Narration and Representation in the Language of Fiction.* New York: Routledge, 1982.

Bate, Walter Jackson. *John Keats.* Cambridge, MA: Harvard University Press, 1963.

——. *Samuel Johnson.* New York: Harcourt Brace Jovanovich, 1975.

Bayley, John. "Chatterton Lecture on an English Poet: Keats and Reality." In *Proceedings of the British Academy,* vol. 48, 92–125. Oxford: Oxford University Press, 1962.

Bocchicchio, Rebecca P. "Blushing, Trembling, and Incapable of Defense: The Hysterics of *The British Recluse.*" In *The Passionate Fictions of Eliza Haywood: Essays on Her Life and Works,* edited by Kirsten T. Saxton and Rebecca P. Bocchicchio, 95–114. Lexington: University Press of Kentucky, 2000.

Booth, Wayne C. *The Rhetoric of Fiction.* 2nd ed. Chicago: University of Chicago Press, 1983.

Boswell, James. *The Life of Samuel Johnson* [1791]. New York: Penguin, 1979.

Brissenden, R. F. *Virtue in Distress: Studies in the Novel of Sentiment from Richardson to Sade.* New York: Macmillan, 1974.

Bromwich, David. "The Genealogy of Disinterestedness." *Raritan* 1 (Spring 1982): 62–92.

——. *Hazlitt: The Mind of a Critic.* Oxford: Oxford University Press, 1983.

Brooks, Cleanth. *The Well-Wrought Urn: Studies in the Structure of Poetry.* New York: Harcourt, 1947.

Brooks, Peter. *Reading for the Plot: Design and Intention in Narrative.* Cambridge, MA: Harvard University Press, 1984.

Bunyan, John. *Grace Abounding* [1666]. In *Grace Abounding with Other Spiritual Autobiographies,* edited by John Stachniewski and Anita Pacheco, 1–94. Oxford: Oxford World's Classics, 1998.

Butler, Judith. *Giving an Account of Oneself.* New York: Fordham University Press, 2005.

Callard, Agnes. *Aspiration: The Agency of Becoming.* Oxford: Oxford University Press, 2018.

——. "The Weaker Reason." *Harvard Review of Philosophy* 22 (2015): 68–83.

Candlish, Stewart, and Nic Damnjanovic. "Reasons, Actions, and the Will: The Fall and Rise of Causalism." In *The Oxford Handbook of the History of Analytic Philosophy,* edited by Michael Beaney, 689–708. Oxford: Oxford University Press, 2013.

Cash, Arthur H. "The Sermon in *Tristram Shandy.*" *English Literary History* 31, no. 4 (December 1964): 395–417.

Chandler, James. *Wordsworth's Second Nature: A Study of the Poetry and Politics.* Chicago: University of Chicago Press, 1984.

Chappell, T. D. J. *Aristotle and Augustine on Freedom: Two Theories of Freedom, Voluntary Action, and Akrasia.* New York: Macmillan, 1995.

Chico, Tita. *The Experimental Imagination: Literary Knowledge and Science in the British Enlightenment.* Stanford, CA: Stanford University Press, 2018.

Cohn, Dorrit. *Transparent Minds: Narrative Modes for Presenting Consciousness in Fiction*. Princeton, NJ: Princeton University Press, 1978.

Coleridge, Samuel Taylor. *Aids to Reflection*. Edited by John Beer. Princeton, NJ: Princeton University Press, 1993.

———. *Biographia Literaria: The Collected Works of Samuel Taylor Coleridge*. Edited by W. Jackson Bate and James Engell. Princeton, NJ: Princeton University Press, 1985.

———. *The Notebooks of Samuel Taylor Coleridge: Volume 1*. Edited by Kathleen Coburn. New York: Pantheon, 1957.

Coleridge, Samuel Taylor, and William Wordsworth. *Lyrical Ballads, 1798 and 1800*. Edited by Michael Gamer and Dahlia Porter. Peterborough, ON: Broadview, 2008.

Croskery, Margaret Case. "Masquing Desire: The Politics of Passion in Eliza Haywood's *Fantomina*." In *The Passionate Fictions of Eliza Haywood: Essays on Her Life and Works*, edited by Kirsten T. Saxton and Rebecca P. Bocchicchio, 69–94. Lexington: University Press of Kentucky, 2000.

Damrosch, Leo. *Jean-Jacques Rousseau: Restless Genius*. Boston: Houghton Mifflin Harcourt, 2005.

Darwall, Stephen. *The British Moralists and the Internal "Ought": 1640–1740*. Cambridge: Cambridge University Press, 1995.

Davidson, Donald. *Essays on Actions and Events*. Oxford: Oxford University Press, 1980.

De Almeida, Hermione. *Romantic Medicine and John Keats*. Oxford: Oxford University Press, 1991.

De Man, Paul. *Allegories of Reading: Figural Language in Rousseau, Nietzsche, Rilke, and Proust*. New Haven, CT: Yale University Press, 1979.

Defoe, Daniel. *Moll Flanders* [1722]. Edited by Albert J. Rivero. New York: W. W. Norton, 2004.

———. *Robinson Crusoe* [1719]. Oxford: Oxford World's Classics, 2007.

Dihle, Albrecht. *The Theory of Will in Classical Antiquity*. Berkeley: University of California Press, 1982.

Dupré, Louis. *The Enlightenment and the Intellectual Foundations of Modern Culture*. New Haven, CT: Yale University Press, 2004.

Ellis, Markman. *The Politics of Sensibility: Race, Gender, and Commerce in the Sentimental Novel*. Cambridge: Cambridge University Press, 1996.

Empson, William. *Seven Types of Ambiguity*. New York: New Directions, [1930] 1947.

Evans, Murray J. *Sublime Coleridge: The Opus Maximum*. New York: Palgrave Macmillan, 2012.

Ferguson, Frances. "Jane Austen, *Emma*, and the Impact of Form." *Modern Language Quarterly* 61, no. 1 (Summer 2000): 157–80.

——. "Now It's Personal: D. A. Miller and Too-Close Reading." *Critical Inquiry* 41, no. 3 (Spring 2015): 521–40.

Fessenbecker, Patrick. "The Fragility of Rationality: George Eliot's Akrasia and the Law of Consequences." *British Journal of the History of Philosophy* 29 no. 2 (2021): 275–91.

——. *Reading Ideas in Victorian Literature: Literary Content and Artistic Experience*. Edinburgh: Edinburgh University Press, 2020.

Fielding, Henry. *Tom Jones* [1749]. Edited by John Bender and Simon Stern. Oxford: Oxford World's Classics, 1996.

Finch, Casey, and Peter Bowen. "'The Tittle-Tattle of Highbury': Gossip and Free Indirect Style in *Emma*." *Representations* 31 (Summer 1990): 1–18.

Fleming, Patrick. "Hume on Weakness of Will." *British Journal for the History of Philosophy* 18, no. 4 (November 2010): 597–609.

Fludernik, Monika. *The Fictions of Language and the Languages of Fiction: The Linguistic Representation of Speech and Consciousness*. New York: Routledge, 1993.

Foot, Philippa. *Moral Dilemmas: And Other Topics in Modern Philosophy*. Oxford: Oxford University Press, 2002.

François, Anne-Lise. *Open Secrets: The Literature of Uncounted Experience*. Stanford, CA: Stanford University Press, 2008.

Franta, Andrew. *Systems Failure: The Uses of Disorder in English Literature*. Baltimore, MD: Johns Hopkins University Press, 2019.

Godwin, William. *The Enquirer: Reflections on Education, Manners, and Literature*. New York: Augustus M. Kelley, 1965.

——. *An Enquiry Concerning Political Justice* [1793]. Edited by Mark Philp. Oxford: Oxford University Press, 2013.

——. *Enquiry Concerning Political Justice*. 3rd ed. Edited by K. Codell Carter. London: Clarendon, 1971.

——. *Fleetwood; or, The New Man of Feeling* [1805]. Edited by Gary Handwerk and A. A. Markley. Peterborough, ON: Broadview, 2001.

——. *St. Leon: A Tale of the Sixteenth Century* [1799]. Edited by William Brewer. Peterborough, ON: Broadview, 2006.

Goldie, Peter. *The Emotions: A Philosophical Exploration*. Oxford: Oxford University Press, 2002.

——. *The Mess Inside: Narrative, Emotion, and the Mind*. Oxford: Oxford University Press, 2012.

Grayling, A. C. *The Quarrel of the Age*. London: Weidenfeld & Nicolson.

Greenblatt, Stephen. *The Swerve: How the World Became Modern*. New York: W. W. Norton, 2011.

Hall, Alena. "The Science Behind Our Urge to Procrastinate." Huffington Post, December 6, 2017. https://www.huffpost.com/entry/science-of -procrastination_n_5585440.

Handwerk, Gary. "Mapping Misogyny: Godwin's 'Fleetwood' and the Staging of Rousseauvian Education." *Studies in Romanticism* 41, no. 3 (Fall 2002): 375–98.

Hartman, Geoffrey. *Wordsworth's Poetry: 1787–1814.* New Haven, CT: Yale University Press, 1964.

Haywood, Eliza. *Fantomina* [1725]. In *Fantomina and Other Works,* edited by Alexander Pettit, Margaret Case Croskery, and Anna C. Patchias, 41–71. Peterborough, ON: Broadview, 2004.

———. *The History of Miss Betsy Thoughtless* [1740]. Edited by Christine Blouch. Peterborough, ON: Broadview, 1998.

———. *Love in Excess* [1719]. Edited by David Oakleaf. Peterborough, ON: Broadview, 2000.

Hazlitt, William. *The Complete Works of William Hazlitt, Volume V: Lectures of the English Poets* [1818]. Edited by P. P. Howe. New York: AMS, 1967.

———. *An Essay on the Principles of Thought and Action, and Some Remarks on the Systems of Hartley and Helvetius.* New York: Scholars' Facsimiles & Reprints, 1969.

———. "On Londoners and Countrypeople." In *The Miscellaneous Works of William Hazlitt,* vol. 2, 50–63. London: Derby & Jackson, 1857.

Hirsch, E. D. *Wordsworth and Schelling: A Typological Study of Romanticism.* New Haven, CT: Yale University Press, 1960.

Hirschman, Albert O. *The Passions and the Interests: Political Arguments for Capitalism Before Its Triumph.* Princeton, NJ: Princeton University Press, 1977.

Hobbes, Thomas. *Leviathan* [1651]. New York: Penguin, 1985.

———. *Of Liberty and Necessity* [1654]. In *The English Works of Thomas Hobbes of Malmesbury,* vol. 4, edited by William Molesworth, 229–78. London: John Bohn, Henrietta Street, Covent Garden.

Hoffmann, Tobias, ed. *Weakness of Will from Plato the Present.* Washington, DC: Catholic University of America Press, 2008.

Hudson, Nicholas. *Samuel Johnson and Eighteenth-Century Thought.* London: Clarendon, 1988.

Hume, David. *A Treatise of Human Nature: A Critical Edition* [1740]. Edited by David Fate Norton and Mary J. Norton. Oxford: Oxford University Press, 2007.

Hunter, J. Paul. *The Reluctant Pilgrim: Defoe's Emblematic Method and Quest for Form in* Robinson Crusoe. Baltimore, MD: Johns Hopkins University Press, 1966.

Iser, Wolfgang. *The Range of Interpretation.* New York: Columbia University Press, 1960.

Izenberg, Oren. "Confiance au Monde; or, The Poetry of Ease." Nonsite, December 2011. https://nonsite.org/confiance-au-monde-or-the-poetry-of-ease (accessed June 28, 2021).

James, Susan. *Passion and Action: The Emotions in Seventeenth-Century Philosophy*. London: Clarendon, 1997.

Jarvis, Simon. *Wordsworth's Philosophic Song*. Cambridge: Cambridge University Press, 2007.

Johnson, Samuel. *Essays from the* Rambler, Adventurer, *and* Idler. Edited by W. J. Bate. New Haven, CT: Yale University Press, 1968.

Jones, Stanley. *Hazlitt: A Life*. London: Clarendon, 1989.

Jordan, Sarah. *The Anxieties of Idleness: Idleness in Eighteenth-Century British Literature and Culture*. Lewisburg, PA: Bucknell University Press, 2003.

Kahneman, Daniel. *Thinking, Fast and Slow*. New York: Farrar, Straus & Giroux, 2011.

Kant, Immanuel. *Critique of the Power of Judgment* [1790]. Edited by Paul Guyer. Translated by Paul Guyer and Eric Matthews. Cambridge: Cambridge University Press, 2000.

——. *Critique of Pure Reason* [1781]. Translated by Norman Kemp Smith. New York: Palgrave Macmillan, 2007.

Kareem, Sarah Tindal. *Eighteenth-Century Fiction and the Reinvention of Wonder*. Oxford: Oxford University Press, 2014.

Keats, John. *The Letters of John Keats, 1814–1821*. 2 vols. Edited by Hyder Edward Rollins. Cambridge, MA: Harvard University Press, 1958.

——. *The Poems of John Keats*. Edited by Miriam Allott. New York: W. W. Norton, 1970.

Keiser, Jess. *Nervous Fictions: Literary Form and the Enlightenment Origins of Neuroscience*. Charlottesville: University of Virginia Press, 2020.

Kelly, Gary. *The English Jacobin Novel, 1780–1805*. London: Clarendon, 1976.

——. "'The Romance of Real Life': Autobiography in Rousseau and William Godwin." In *L'Homme et la nature: Actes de la societé canadienne d'étude du dix-huitième siècle*, edited by Roger L. Emerson, Gilles Girard, Roseann Runte, 93–101. London, ON: University of Western Ontario Press, 1982.

Kenny, Anthony. *Aristotle's Theory of the Will*. New Haven, CT: Yale University Press, 1979.

Keymer, Thomas. *Richardson's* Clarissa *and the Eighteenth-Century Reader*. Cambridge: Cambridge University Press, 1992.

Khalip, Jacques. *Anonymous Life: Romanticism and Dispossession*. Stanford, CA: Stanford University Press, 2009.

Kivy, Peter. *Sound Sentiment: An Essay on the Musical Emotions*. Philadelphia: Temple University Press, 1989.

Klancher, Jon. "Godwin and the Republican Romance: Genre, Politics, and Contingency in Cultural History." *Modern Language Quarterly* 56, no. 2 (June 1995): 145–65.

Knapp, Steven and Walter Benn Michaels. "Against Theory." *Critical Inquiry* 8, no. 4 (Summer 1982): 723–42.

Konnikova, Maria. "Getting over Procrastination." *New Yorker,* July 22, 2014. newyorker.com/science/maria-konnikova/a-procrastination-gene.

Korsgaard, Christine. *The Constitution of Agency: Essays on Practical Reason and Moral Psychology.* Oxford: Oxford University Press, 2008.

Kramnick, Jonathan. *Actions and Objects from Hobbes to Richardson.* Stanford, CA: Stanford University Press, 2010.

Lamb, Jonathan. *Sterne's Fiction and the Double Principle.* Cambridge: Cambridge University Press, 1989.

Lee, Wendy Anne. *Failures of Feeling: Insensibility and the Novel.* Stanford, CA: Stanford University Press, 2019.

Levinson, Marjorie. *Keats's Life of Allegory: The Origins of a Style.* Hoboken, NJ: Blackwell, 1988.

Locke, John. *An Essay Concerning Human Understanding* [1690/94]. Edited by Peter Nidditch. London: Clarendon, 1975.

Lockridge, Laurence. *The Ethics of Romanticism.* Cambridge: Cambridge University Press, 1989.

MacIntyre, Alasdair. *After Virtue: A Study in Moral Theory.* Notre Dame, IN: University of Notre Dame Press, 1981.

Macpherson, Sandra. *Harm's Way: Tragic Responsibility and the Novel Form.* Baltimore, MD: Johns Hopkins University Press, 2010.

———. "Lovelace, Ltd." *English Literary History* 65, no. 1 (Spring 1998): 99–121.

Malpas, Jeff. "Donald Davidson." In *The Stanford Encyclopedia of Philosophy,* edited by Edward N. Zalta. https://plato.stanford.edu/entries/davidson/ (accessed June 28, 2021).

McFarland, Thomas. *The Masks of Keats: The Endeavour of a Poet.* Oxford: Oxford University Press, 2000.

McKeon, Michael. *The Origins of the English Novel, 1600–1740.* Baltimore, MD: Johns Hopkins University Press, 1987.

Mele, Alfred. *Backsliding: Understanding Weakness of Will.* Oxford: Oxford University Press, 2012.

Mellor, Anne K. *English Romantic Irony.* Cambridge, MA: Harvard University Press, 1980.

Miller, Andrew H. *The Burdens of Perfection: On Ethics and Reading in Nineteenth-Century British Literature.* Ithaca, NY: Cornell University Press, 2008.

Miller, D. A. *Jane Austen, or The Secret of Style*. Princeton, NJ: Princeton University Press, 2003.

Moran, Richard. *Authority and Estrangement: An Essay on Self-Knowledge*. Princeton, NJ: Princeton University Press, 2001.

Murdoch, Iris. *The Sovereignty of Good*. New York: Routledge, 1970.

Nazar, Hina. *Enlightened Sentiments: Judgment and Autonomy in the Age of Sensibility*. New York: Fordham University Press, 2012.

Nersessian, Anahid. *The Calamity Form: On Poetry and Social Life*. Chicago: University of Chicago Press, 2020.

New, Melvyn. *Laurence Sterne as Satirist: A Reading of* Tristram Shandy. Gainesville: University Press of Florida, 1969.

Norton, David Fate. *David Hume: Common-Sense Moralist, Sceptical Metaphysician*. Princeton, NJ: Princeton University Press, 1982.

Oakeshott, Michael. *Hobbes on Civil Association*. Indianapolis: Liberty Fund, 1937.

Pasanek, Brad. *Metaphors of Mind: An Eighteenth-Century Dictionary*. Baltimore, MD: Johns Hopkins University Press, 2015.

Pascal, Roy. *The Dual Voice: Free Indirect Speech and Its Functioning in the Nineteenth-Century European Novel*. Manchester: Manchester University Press, 1977.

Pfau, Thomas. *Minding the Modern: Human Agency, Intellectual Traditions, and Responsible Knowledge*. Notre Dame, IN: University of Notre Dame Press, 2013.

———. *Romantic Moods: Paranoia, Trauma, and Melancholy, 1790–1840*. Baltimore, MD: Johns Hopkins University Press, 2005.

Phillips, Natalie. *Distraction: Problems of Attention in Eighteenth-Century Literature*. Baltimore, MD: Johns Hopkins University Press, 2016.

Philp, Mark. *Godwin's Political Justice*. London: Gerald Duckworth, 1986.

Pinch, Adela. *Strange Fits of Passion: Epistemologies of Emotion from Hume to Austen*. Stanford, CA: Stanford University Press, 1998.

Plato. *Protagoras*. Translated by W. K. C. Guthrie. In *Plato: The Collected Dialogues,* edited by Edith Hamilton and Huntington Cairns, 308–52. Princeton, NJ: Princeton University Press, 1962.

Plumb, J. H. "The Commercialization of Leisure in Eighteenth-Century England." In *The Birth of a Consumer Society: The Commercialization of Eighteenth-Century England,* edited by Neil McKendrick, John Brewer, and J. H. Plumb, 265–85. Indianapolis: Indiana University Press, 1982.

Potkay, Adam. *Wordworth's Ethics*. Baltimore, MD: Johns Hopkins University Press, 2012.

Rajan, Tilottama. *The Supplement of Reading: Figures of Understanding in Romantic Theory and Practice*. Ithaca, NY: Cornell University Press, 1990.

Rawls, John. *Lectures on the History of Moral Philosophy*. Cambridge, MA: Harvard University Press, 2000.

Raymond, Marcel. *Jean-Jacques Rousseau: La Quête de Soi et la Rêverie*. Paris: Libraire J. Corti, 1962.

Richardson, Samuel. *Clarissa, or, The History of a Young Lady* [1748]. Edited by Angus Ross. New York: Penguin, 1985.

Richetti, John. *Defoe's Narratives: Situations and Structures*. London: Clarendon, 1975.

Ricks, Christopher. "Introductory Essay" [1967]. In *The Life and Opinions of Tristram Shandy, Gentleman,* by Laurence Sterne, edited by Melvyn New and Joan New, xi–xxxii. New York: Penguin, 2003.

———. *Keats and Embarrassment*. London: Clarendon, 1974.

Risinger, Jacob. *Stoic Romanticism and the Ethics of Emotion*. Princeton, NJ: Princeton University Press, 2021.

Rorty, Amélie Oksenberg. "Akratic Believers." *American Philosophical Quarterly* 20, no. 2 (1983): 175–83.

———. "Self-Deception, Akrasia, and Irrationality." *Social Science Information* 19, no. 6 (1980): 905–22.

———. "The Social and Political Sources of Akrasia." *Ethics* 107 (July 1997): 644–57.

———. "Where Does the Akratic Break Take Place?" *Australasian Journal of Philosophy* 58, no. 4 (December 1980): 333–46.

Rousseau, Jean-Jacques. *The Confessions* [1780]. Translated by J. M. Cohen. New York: Penguin, 1953.

Rudy, Seth. *Literature and Encyclopedism in Enlightenment Britain: The Pursuit of Complete Knowledge*. New York: Palgrave Macmillan, 2014.

Saarinen, Risto. *Weakness of Will in Renaissance and Reformation Thought*. Oxford: Oxford University Press, 2011.

Schleiermacher, Friedrich. *Hermeneutics and Criticism and Other Writings* [1838]. Edited by Andrew Bowie. Cambridge: Cambridge University Press, 1998.

Schneewind, J. B. *The Invention of Autonomy: A History of Modern Moral Philosophy*. Cambridge: Cambridge University Press, 1998.

Scott, Walter. *Edinburgh Review* 6 (April 1805): 182–93. Reprinted in *Fleetwood; or, The New Man of Feeling* [1805], by William Godwin, edited by Gary Handwerk and A. A. Markley, 518–22. Peterborough, ON: Broadview, 2001.

Sherman, Sandra. *Finance and Fictionality in the Early Eighteenth Century: Accounting for Defoe*. Cambridge: Cambridge University Press, 1996.

Silver, Sean. *The Mind Is a Collection: Case Studies in Eighteenth-Century Thought*. Philadelphia: University of Pennsylvania Press, 2015.

Siskin, Clifford. *System: The Shaping of Modern Knowledge*. Cambridge, MA: MIT Press, 2016.

Smith, Adam. *An Inquiry into the Nature and Causes of the Wealth of Nations* [1776]. Edited by Edwin Cannan. Chicago: University of Chicago Press, 1976.

Smith, Courtney Weiss. *Empiricist Devotions: Science, Religion, and Poetry in Early Eighteenth-Century England*. Charlottesville: University of Virginia Press, 2016.

Smith, Norman Kemp. "The Naturalism of Hume." *Mind* 14 (1905): 149–73.

Soni, Vivasvan. *Mourning Happiness: Narrative and the Politics of Modernity*. Ithaca, NY: Cornell University Press, 2010.

Spacks, Patricia Meyer. "Ev'ry Woman Is at Heart a Rake." *Eighteenth-Century Studies* 8, no. 1 (Fall 1974): 27–46.

Spiegelman, Willard. *Majestic Indolence: English Romantic Poetry and the Work of Art*. Oxford: Oxford University Press, 1995.

Spinoza, Benedict de. *Ethics* [1677]. In *A Spinoza Reader: The Ethics and Other Works*, edited and translated by Edwin Curley, 85–265. Princeton, NJ: Princeton University Press, 1994.

Stalnaker, Joanna. *The Unfinished Enlightenment: Description in the Age of the Encyclopedia*. Ithaca, NY: Cornell University Press, 2010.

Starobinski, Jean. *Jean-Jacques Rousseau: Transparency and Obstruction*. Translated by Arthur Goldhammer. Chicago: University of Chicago Press, [1957] 1988.

Starr, G. A. *Defoe & Casuistry*. Princeton, NJ: Princeton University Press, 1971.

———. *Defoe & Spiritual Autobiography*. Princeton, NJ: Princeton University Press, 1965.

Sterne, Laurence. *The Life and Opinions of Tristram Shandy, Gentleman*. Edited by Melvyn New and Joan New. New York: Penguin, 2003.

———. *The Florida Edition of the Works of Laurence Sterne*. 8 vols. Edited by W. G. Day, Joan New, Melvyn New, and Peter de Voogd. Gainesville: University of Florida Press, 1978–2008.

Stout, Daniel. *Corporate Romanticism: Liberalism, Justice, and the Novel Form*. New York: Fordham University Press, 2016.

Swift, Jonathan. "The Difficulty of Knowing One's-Self" [1726]. In *The Works of Jonathan Swift: Volume VIII*, edited by Walter Scott. London: Gale, Curtis & Fenner, 1814.

Tadié, Alexis. *Sterne's Whimsical Theatres of Language: Orality, Gesture, Literacy*. Farnham: Ashgate, 2003.

Taylor, Charles. *Sources of the Self: The Making of the Modern Identity*. Cambridge, MA: Harvard University Press, 1989.

Thompson, Helen. *Fictional Matter: Empiricism, Corpuscles, and the Novel*. Philadelphia: University of Pennsylvania Press, 2017.

——. *Ingenuous Subjection: Compliance and Power in the Eighteenth-Century Domestic Novel.* Philadelphia: University of Pennsylvania Press, 2005.

Vendler, Helen. *The Odes of John Keats.* Cambridge, MA: Harvard University Press, 1983.

Vološinov, V. N. *Marxism and the Philosophy of Language.* Princeton, NJ: Seminar, 1973.

Watt, Ian. *The Rise of the Novel: Studies in Defoe, Richardson, and Fielding.* Berkeley: University of California Press, 1957.

Wetzel, James. *Augustine and the Limits of Virtue.* Cambridge: Cambridge University Press, 1992.

Wordsworth, William. The Prelude *of 1805, in Thirteen Books.* In *The Prelude: 1799, 1805, 1850,* edited by Jonathan Wordsworth, M. H. Abrams, and Stephen Gill, 28–483. New York: W. W. Norton, 1979.

Wright, Daniel. *Bad Logic: Reasoning about Desire in the Victorian Novel.* Baltimore, MD: Johns Hopkins University Press, 2018.

Wu, Duncan. *William Hazlitt: The First Modern Man.* Oxford: Oxford University Press, 2008.

INDEX

Abrams, M. H., 209n34
absence, 7, 57–58, 61, 69, 76. *See also*
  darkness; paradox; silence
account, accounting, 55–56, 62, 71–73,
  76, 79, 120–21, 189n12, 189n14. *See
  also* explanation; narrative
acedia. *See* sloth
action: and adverbs, 45; and belief, 4,
  14, 21–22, 26–28; and blame and
  responsibility, 8–9, 60–65, 68–77,
  81–82, 92–97, 99–103, 123–30,
  140, 145–46, 189n17; and efficient
  causation, 3–4, 32–41; externalist
  models of, 8–9; and imagination, 40, 118–19, 143, 149, 157; and
  intention, 2–3, 8, 11, 21–22, 43–46,
  64–67, 70–78, 110–11, 118–19, 125,
  127–30, 141, 168; moral/teleologi-
  cal frameworks of, 3–4, 11, 23–25,
  28–37, 43, 47–48, 50–51, 53–54, 63,
  65–67, 73–74, 116–17; and necessity, 34–35, 86–88; philosophy of,
  2–5, 8–11, 21–48, 86–90, 141–43,
  156–57, 178n27, 187n74; undermotivated, 5, 9, 18–19, 23, 30, 43,
  71, 79, 147, 149. *See also* akrasia;
  cause; character; habit; inaction;

motivation; philosophy; voluntary;
  will
addiction, 15, 85, 141–42. *See also* akrasia; habit
affect, 4–5, 8, 34–35. *See also* emotion;
  passion; Spinoza, Benedict de
After Virtue (MacIntyre), 10–11, 25,
  28–29, 179n7
agency. *See* action; freedom; voluntary; will
akrasia: ambiguity of, 15–16, 61–62,
  63–70, 167–68; and appetite, 26–
  27, 33–34; Aristotle's account of,
  26–29; Augustine's account of,
  29–32, as bad faith, 14, 177n24; and
  behavioral economics, 178n25; of
  belief, 14, 101, 177n24; and darkness, 74–75, 105, 147–49; Davidson's account of, 43–46; in drama,
  51; in Enlightenment philosophy,
  4–5, 7–8, 32–41, 114–16, 125, 142–
  43, 156–57; and explanation, 21–46,
  55–56, 59, 114–23, 125–30, 142–43,
  156–57, 177n20; and gender, 15,
  179n28, 192n37; Hobbes's treatment of, 33–34; Hume's treatment
  of, 35–36; as inaction, 14, 109–10,

akrasia (*continued*)

111–23, 133, 137–46, 151–55, 158–65; Locke's treatment of, 39–41; and narrative, 1–3, 21–22, 29–30, 37–48, 50–63, 70–71, 76–79, 85–86, 90–98, 104–5, 118–21, 167–69; and poetry, 132–39, 141–51, 151–55, 157–65; and privilege, 200n46; scale of, 16–17; in scholarship, 7–8, 12, 14; and self-deception, 14, 89–90, 96–97, 101–3, 109–10, 113–15, 122, 141, 202n28; Spinoza's treatment of, 34–35; in Stoicism, 181n26; and transparency, 124–25; as voluntary, 27, 180n17; and weakness of will, 13–14. *See also* cause, causal, causation; character; contradiction; darkness; explanation; hardness of heart; indolence; paradox; philosophy; procrastination; sloth; weakness of will; will

Alkon, Paul Kent, 113, 116, 202n21

ambiguity, 15–16, 62, 63–70, 132–33, 145–47. *See also* akrasia: ambiguity of

Anatomy of Melancholy (Burton), 112

Anscombe, G. E. M., 10, 185n59, 187n70

antinomy, 10, 134–37. *See also* contradiction

appetite, 26–27, 33–34. *See also* akrasia: and appetite; Aristotle; desire; Hobbes, Thomas

Aquinas, Thomas, 26, 112, 201n17, 207n16

Arendt, Hannah, 10, 26, 181n26, 183n33

Aristotle, 2–4, 11, 15, 23–29, 116–17, 180n13, 180n17; *Nicomachean Ethics,* 26–29, 180n13. *See also* akrasia; enkratic man

associationism, 75, 142

Augustine, Saint, 3–4, 15, 23, 25–26, 29–32, 60, 107, 125, 127, 129, 147, 158, 181–82nn25–28, 183nn33–34, 183n36; *The Confessions,* 3, 15, 29–32, 60, 107, 147. *See also* akrasia; theology; weakness of will; will

Austen, Jane, 5, 80–84, 99–105; *Emma,* 5, 80–86, 96, 99–105, 199n45

autobiography, 51, 58–59, 92, 192n34. *See also* Augustine, Saint; *Prelude, The;* Rousseau, Jean-Jacques; spiritual autobiography

autonomy, 7, 176n16, 208n33

Bacon, Francis, 4

bad faith, 14, 177n24. *See also* akrasia: as bad faith; Sartre, Jean-Paul

Ballaster, Ros, 192n37

Banfield, Ann, 83–84, 102–3, 197n10

Bate, Walter Jackson, 109, 113, 201n6, 201n8, 202n23, 203n30, 211n49, 213n57

Bayley, John, 153, 211n45, 211n49

behaviorism, 33, 42, 46–47, 164

Bildung, 91–92

Biographia Literaria (Coleridge), 142

Bocchicchio, Rebecca P., 192n37

Booth, Wayne C., 99, 199n45

Boswell, James, 111

Bowen, Peter, 99, 199n45. *See also* Finch, Casey

Boyle, Robert, 7

Brissenden, R. F., 194n54

Bromwich, David, 156, 212nn51–52

Brooks, Cleanth, 133, 136

Brooks, Peter, 110

Bunyan, John, 51

Burton, Robert, 112
Butler, Judith, 189n12

Callard, Agnes, 15, 21–23, 179n2, 187n76. *See also* weaker reason
Candlish, Stewart, 42, 187n70. *See also* Damnjanovic, Nic
Cash, Arthur H., 73, 194n54, 194n56
Castle of Indolence (Thomson), 112, 138, 152–53
casuistry, 76–77, 190n23
causalism, 42–43, 186n69
cause, causal, causation: and blame and responsibility, 8–9, 60–62, 63–69, 71–77, 81–82, 92–97, 99–103, 123–30, 140, 145–46, 189n17; efficient, 3–4, 32–41; explication, 5–6, 32–41, 49–55, 58, 62–63, 71; formal or final, 4; and freedom, 9, 27, 134–35, 183n36; and sin, 58–60, 73–75, 182n28, 208n33. *See also* action; causalism; explanation
Chandler, James, 208n27, 209n35, 210n41
character, 1–3, 39–41, 44–48, 49–105, 118–23, 167–68; conservation of, 52, 98; and development, 104–5; undermotivated, 3, 5, 14, 15–16, 30, 97–98, 119, 168
Chico, Tita, 177n18
childhood, 29–30, 147
Cohn, Dorrit, 95, 196n5
Coleridge, Samuel Taylor, 15–16, 133–35, 141–43, 208n30, 208–9nn33–34; *Biographia Literaria*, 142; *Dejection*, 142; *Lyrical Ballads* (with Wordsworth), 140
compatibilism, 9, 183n36
compulsion, 35, 74–75, 98, 115–16. *See also* akrasia: as voluntary; ignorance

Confessions, The (Augustine), 3, 15, 29–32, 60, 107, 147
Confessions, The (Rousseau), 92, 109–10, 123–31, 205n54, 205nn58–59
consciousness, 1–2, 66, 80–81, 83–84, 95–97, 99–105, 192n41, 195n2, 196n5, 199n45; compromised, 15, 39–40; reflective and non-reflective, 102–3. *See also* subconscious
consent, 193n42
contradiction, 4–6, 132–35, 143, 160–61, 163–65. *See also* antinomy; paradox; poetry
corpuscles, 7–8
Critique of Pure Reason (Kant), 134
Critique of the Power of Judgment (Kant), 134
Croskery, Margaret Case, 64, 192nn36–37, 193n42
custom. *See* habit

Damnjanovic, Nic, 42, 187n70. *See also* Candlish, Stewart
Damrosch, Leo, 201n9, 205n58
darkness (trope), 74–75, 105, 147–49
Darwall, Stephen, 38, 186nn60–61
Davidson, Donald, 3, 41–46, 187n71, 187n76
Defoe, Daniel, 1–2, 49–50, 55–63, 188n6, 189n17, 190nn19–20, 190–91nn23–25, 191n27, 191n29, 191n32; *Moll Flanders*, 1–2, 4, 6, 59–62; *Robinson Crusoe*, 49–50, 55–59, 190n20
Dejection (Coleridge), 142
de Man, Paul, 124–26, 205n54, 205nn58–59
Descartes, René, 11, 24, 103, 184n38

desire, 4–5, 32–34, 36, 63–67. *See also* appetite; Hobbes, Thomas; passion

detachment, 153, 156, 176n16, 195n2, 196n5

determinism, 27, 34, 73, 183n36. *See also* cause, causal, causation; necessity; predestination

Dihle, Albrecht, 180n17, 181n25, 183n31

Dilthey, Wilhelm, 108

disinterestedness, 134, 155–65, 212n52

drama, 51

Dupré, Louis, 25

Ellis, Markman, 73

Emma (Austen), 5, 80–86, 96, 99–105, 199n45

emotion, 7, 72–73, 176n16, 181n26. *See also* affect; Hume, David; passion

empiricism, 25, 33, 46–47, 177n18, 177n24, 212n55; naïve, 188n7. *See also* epistemology; philosophy

Empson, William, 132–33, 213n59

Endymion (Keats), 154–55, 211nn49–50

enkratic man (Aristotle), 26–27

Enlightenment, 3–5, 9–10, 16, 24–25, 32–41, 156–57. *See also* akrasia; Hobbes, Thomas; Hume, David; Kant, Immanuel; Locke, John; philosophy; Spinoza, Benedict de

Enquirer, The (Godwin), 88, 198n24

Enquiry Concerning Political Justice (Godwin), 82, 86–90, 198n20, 198n24, 198n26

enumeration, 56–57. *See also* account, accounting; explanation

Epicureanism, 4; Christian, 203n30

epistemology: Christian, 58–59; empiricist, 25, 33, 46–47, 177n18, 177n24, 212n55; externalist, 8; and humility, 88; and intellectual his-

tory, 4, 10–11, 24–25; literary, 6–7, 20, 23, 39–41, 43–46, 54, 59, 83; materialist, 7–8, 55–56, 59–60, 79. *See also* hermeneutics; knowledge; philosophy

epistolary (genre), 86

essay, 88, 109, 113–23. *See also* Johnson, Samuel

Essay Concerning Human Understanding (Locke), 37–41, 43–44, 125, 186n61, 186n66, 186n68

Essay on the Principles of Human Action (Hazlitt), 156–57, 212nn51–52, 212n55, 213n57

ethics. *See* action: moral/teleological frameworks of; philosophy: moral

Ethics (Spinoza), 34–35

Euripides, 15, 181n26

explanation, 21–25, 28–29, 32–41, 43–46, 52–53, 106–7, 115–16, 120–21, 125, 128–31, 142–43, 177n20; as account, 55–56; as causal explication, 11, 32–41, 49–50, 62–63, 71, 186n69; and expression, 143–44; failure of, 71, 76–79, 106–7, 118–23, 125–31; and silence, 45–46, 61–62, 76–79. *See also* account, acounting; action; cause, causal, causation

"Expostulation and Reply" (Wordsworth), 139–40

Faerie Queen (Spenser), 14

failure, 22–23, 25–32, 39, 41, 45–46, 71, 76–79, 84, 115–17, 124–25, 168–69. *See also* explanation; narration

Fantomina (Haywood), 65–67, 192–93nn41–42

feelings, 7, 11–12, 91–92, 98, 125, 129, 176n12, 177n17, 185n53. *See also* affect; emotion

Seeing the Elgin Marbles," 160–
62; "Sleep and Poetry," 154, 160;
"To Autumn," 159–60; "To My
Brother George," 154, 160. *See also*
akrasia: and poetry; indolence;
negative capability; poetry; procrastination
Keiser, Jess, 177n18
Kelly, Gary, 85, 199nn31–32
Khalip, Jacques, 207n18, 212n52
Kivy, Peter, 144
Klancher, Jon, 198n24
Knapp, Steven, 124, 205n54, 205n59.
See also Michaels, Walter Benn
knowledge: and action, 2–3, 6, 15–16,
26–28; in eighteenth-century
studies, 177n18; and guilt, 15–16;
and interpretation, 6, 108–9; self-
knowledge, 73–74. *See also* action;
akrasia; guilt; interpretation
Korsgaard, Christine, 185n59
Kramnick, Jonathan, 8–9, 67, 175n9,
187n71

laziness, 14, 16, 106, 112–13. *See also*
inaction; indolence; procrastina-
tion; sloth; weakness of will
Lee, Wendy Anne, 11–12, 177n17
leisure, 16, 112, 137–38, 144, 207n16.
See also idleness; indolence; lazi-
ness
Leviathan (Hobbes), 33
Levinson, Marjorie, 153, 211n45
Life and Opinions of Tristram Shandy
(Sterne), 71–74, 194n54
Life of Mr. Richard Savage (Johnson),
113
Life of Samuel Johnson, The (Boswell),
111
life writing. *See* autobiography

literature. *See* autobiography; epistemology: literary; essay; genre;
narrative; novel; poetry
Locke, John, 4, 7, 11, 37–41, 43–44,
114–16, 125, 186n61, 186n66, 186n68.
See also Enlightenment; *Essay Concerning Human Understanding*
Lockridge, Laurence, 208n30, 208n33
logic, 11–12, 22, 30, 45, 55–57, 62. *See
also* contradiction; explanation;
paradox; reason
Love in Excess (Haywood), 63–64
Lucretius, 4, 24; *On the Nature of
Things,* 24
Lyrical Ballads (Coleridge and Wordsworth), 140

Macbeth (Shakespeare), 51, 167–69
MacIntyre, Alasdair, 10–11, 25, 28–29,
179n7
Mackenzie, Henry, 92
Macpherson, Sandra, 8, 175n7, 189n17,
205n59
Man of Feeling, The (Mackenzie), 92
mauvaise foi. See bad faith
McFarland, Thomas, 211nn49–50
McKeon, Michael, 54, 191n25
Medea (Euripides), 15, 181n26
Medea (Ovid), 33–35, 40, 181n26
Mellor, Anne K., 136–37
Michaels, Walter Benn, 124, 205n54,
205n59. *See also* Knapp, Steven
Miller, Andrew H., 178n26, 179n28,
197n12
Miller, D. A., 80–83, 99, 103–4, 195n2,
199n45
Moll Flanders (Defoe), 1–2, 4, 6, 59–62
morality. *See* action: moral/teleolog-
ical frameworks of; philosophy:
moral; virtue

Moran, Richard, 177n24
motivation, 28, 43, 64, 130, 147, 149,
  168. *See also* action; cause; character: undermotivated; intention;
  voluntary; will
Murdoch, Iris, 46–48, 104–5

Nancy (comic), 106–7
narration: and autobiographical
  memory, 92, 94, 192n34; failures
  of, 53, 77–78; first-person retrospective, 2, 59–61, 86, 96–97,
  111; third-person omniscient,
  1–2, 63, 65–70, 99. *See also*
  autobiography; free indirect discourse
narrative: as account, 55–57, 71,
  78–79; and explanation, 21–23,
  29–30, 39–41, 43–46, 110, 118–
  21; and free indirect discourse,
  84. *See also* account, accounting;
  epistemology: literary; explanation; novel
Nazar, Hina, 199n31
necessity, 9, 86–88, 203n30
negative capability, 139, 155, 157–58,
  212nn51–52. *See also* Keats,
  John
Nersessian, Anahid, 158
New, Melvyn, 193n49, 194n54, 194n56
Newton, Isaac, 4, 25
Nicomachean Ethics (Aristotle), 26–29,
  180n13
novel, 6, 13, 50–54, 69–73, 78–79,
  82–85, 92–94, 99, 104–5. *See
  also* Austen, Jane; Defoe, Daniel;
  free indirect discourse; Godwin,
  William; Haywood, Eliza; narration; narrative; Sterne, Laurence;
  individual works by title

Oakeshott, Michael, 32, 34
"Ode on Indolence" (Keats), 152–53,
  160, 162–64
"Ode to a Nightingale" (Keats), 158–
  59, 163
Of Liberty and Necessity (Hobbes),
  33–34
"On Seeing the Elgin Marbles"
  (Keats), 160–62
On the Nature of Things (Lucretius), 24
Ovid, 15, 33–35, 40, 182n26

paradox, 3, 16, 31, 33, 77–78, 86, 121,
  133, 136–37, 168. *See also* contradiction
Pasanek, Brad, 177n18, 189n14
Pascal, Blaise, 25
Pascal, Roy, 84, 197n11, 199n45
passion, 4–5, 7, 34–37, 63–65, 71–
  74, 76, 179n30. *See also* appetite;
  desire; emotion; Hume, David
passivity, 87, 138–39, 144–45, 150–51.
  See also action; inaction
periodization, 12–13
personification, 138, 150, 162
perspective. *See under* narration
Pfau, Thomas, 10, 24, 39, 180n17,
  181–82nn26–27, 183n34, 185n59,
  186n66, 208n33, 213n64
Phillips, Natalie, 193n43
philosophy: of action, 2–5, 8–11,
  21–48, 86–90, 141–43, 156–57,
  178n27, 187n74; Aristotelian, 3–4,
  25–29; Augustinian, 3–4, 29–32;
  Epicurean or Lucretian, 4–5, 24;
  Humean, 7–8, 35–37; and literature, 4–12, 37–41, 43–48, 50–53,
  78–79, 86–90, 135–36, 141–43,
  175n9, 176n12, 177n18, 177n20;
  moral, 10–11, 28–29, 34, 184n44,

187n74; and narrative, 21–23, 29–30, 39–41, 43–48, 110, 118–21; Platonism, 26, 29, 32, 180n11, 181n25; of power, 34; Scholasticism, 3–4, 25–26, 208n33; Stoicism, 29, 176n16, 181n26, 184n48. *See also* action; akrasia; Davidson, Donald; Enlightenment; Godwin, William; Hobbes, Thomas; Hume, David; Locke, John; Murdoch, Iris; reason; Spinoza, Benedict de

Philp, Mark, 87, 198n20, 198n26

Pinch, Adela, 7

Plato, 4, 26, 29, 32, 180n11, 181n25

Plumb, J. H., 112

poetry, 132–65; and contradiction, 132–33, 136, 138–39, 158–65; and figuration, 162–63; and thinking, 135–36. *See also* Keats, John; Wordsworth, William

Potkay, Adam, 135, 144, 210n38

predestination, 87, 183n36

Prelude, The (Wordsworth), 134–35, 140, 143–51, 208n27, 209–10nn34–36, 210n41

procrastination, 5, 106–7, 111–16, 118–23, 139–42, 144–45, 149–51. *See also* idleness; inaction; indolence; Johnson, Samuel; Keats, John; passivity; Wordsworth, William

prohaeresis (purposive choice), 27, 180n17. *See also* Aristotle; voluntary

Protagoras (Plato), 4, 26

psychoanalysis, 109–10. *See also* subconscious

Rajan, Tilottama, 198n24

Rambler (periodical), 109, 113–21. *See also* Johnson, Samuel

Rawls, John, 35

Raymond, Marcel, 204n48

realism, 175n7; formal, 54, 188n6, 190n24

reason: and appetite, 33; as cause, 42, 186–87nn69–70; disengaged, 24; means versus ends, 25; and passions, 7, 35–36, 73; practical, 14, 23, 26–28, 32, 35, 85, 134, 206n6; as strong or weak, 22–23; theoretical, 26, 28, 134, 206n6. *See also* action; judgment; knowledge; philosophy; weaker reason

Recluse, The (Wordsworth), 140–41

Richardson, Samuel, 16, 54, 175n9, 188n8

Ricks, Christopher, 153, 193n48, 211n45, 211n50

Risinger, Jacob, 176n16

Robinson Crusoe (Defoe), 49–50, 55–59, 190n20

Romanticism, 12–13. *See also* Coleridge, Samuel; Keats, John; Wordsworth, William

Rorty, Amélie, 14–15, 101, 181n22, 188n82

Rousseau, Jean-Jacques, 91–92, 107–11, 123–31, 205n54, 205nn58–59; *The Confessions,* 92, 109–10, 123–31, 205n54, 205nn58–59; in English literature, 111. *See also* autobiography

Rudy, Seth, 177n18

Saarinen, Risto, 28, 176n13, 178n27, 181n26, 183n36

Sartre, Jean-Paul, 14, 177n24. *See also* bad faith

Schlegel, Friedrich, 136–37. *See also* irony

Schleiermacher, Friedrich, 108. *See also* hermeneutics

Schneewind, J. B., 10, 184n44

Scholasticism. *See under* philosophy

Scott, Walter, 97

self-deception, 14, 113–16, 122, 202n28. *See also* akrasia: and self-deception

self-governance. *See* autonomy

sentence (grammar), 53–54, 70–71; ironic, 6, 70–71, 78–79, 80–84, 95–96, 98, 102–4. *See also* grammar; irony

Sentimental Journey, A (Sterne), 5, 71–79, 195n61

Shakespeare, William, 14, 51, 93, 152, 156–57, 162–64, 167–68; *Hamlet*, 51, 93, 152, 162–64; *Macbeth*, 51, 167–69

silence (theme), 13, 45–46, 56–58, 76–79, 84, 163

Silver, Sean, 177n18, 189n14

sin, 29, 58–59, 60–61, 73–75, 129, 147–48, 182n28, 183n34, 208n33

Siskin, Clifford, 177n18

"Sleep and Poetry" (Keats), 154, 160

sloth, 112–13, 137, 201n17, 202n26. *See also* idleness; inaction; indolence; procrastination

Smith, Adam, 201n16, 213n57

Smith, Courtney Weiss, 177n18

Smith, Norman Kemp, 185n53

Socrates, 4, 26, 180n13. *See also* Plato

Soni, Vivasvan, 176n12

Spacks, Patricia Meyer, 64–65, 68, 99

Spenser, Edmund, 14, 138–39

Spiegelman, Willard, 112, 137–38, 201n17, 202n26, 207n16, 207n24, 212n52

Spinoza, Benedict de, 4, 11, 34–35, 184n48, 185n52

spiritual autobiography, 51, 58–59, 190n20. *See also* autobiography

Stalnaker, Joanna, 177n18

Starobinski, Jean, 124–25, 201n9, 204n42

Starr, G. A., 58, 190n19, 190–91nn23–25, 191n32

Sterne, Laurence, 5, 70–79, 193n48, 194n54, 194n56; *Life and Opinions of Tristram Shandy*, 71–74, 194n54; *A Sentimental Journey*, 5, 71–79, 195n61

St. Leon: A Tale of the Sixteenth Century (Godwin), 82–83, 85–86, 90–91

Stoicism, 29, 176n16, 181n26, 184n48

Stout, Daniel, 175n7

subconscious, 53, 78, 109. *See also* consciousness

Swift, Jonathan, 193n49, 194n54, 194n56

Tadié, Alexis, 195n61

Taylor, Charles, 24, 182n27

teleology, telos, 4, 24–25, 28–29, 32. *See also* action: moral/teleological frameworks of; explanation

theology, 14, 24, 25–26, 29–32, 201n6, 202n26. *See also* philosophy: Augustinian; philosophy: Scholasticism

Thompson, Helen, 7, 64, 177n18, 197n37

Thomson, James, 112, 138–39; *Castle of Indolence*, 112, 138, 152–53

"To Autumn" (Keats), 159–60

Tom Jones (Fielding), 52

"To My Brother George" (Keats), 154, 160

"To My Sister" (Wordsworth), 139

transparency, 124–27, 130–31, 195n61
Treatise of Human Nature (Hume), 35–37, 55–56, 73

unconscious. *See* subconscious
undermotivated: action, 5, 9, 18–19, 23, 30, 43, 71, 79, 147, 149; character, 3, 5, 14, 15–16, 30, 97–98, 119, 168. *See also* motivation
uneasiness, 4–5, 38–41. See also *Essay Concerning Human Understanding*; Locke, John; motivation

Vendler, Helen, 162–63
virtue, 10–11, 53–54, 75–76, 199n31
voice. *See* free indirect discourse; narration
volition. *See* action; voluntary; will
Vološinov, V. N., 84
voluntarism (in theology), 24
voluntary, 22, 27, 33, 88–90, 180n17; imperfectly, 88–89. *See also* action; *prohaeresis;* will
voluntas. See will

Watt, Ian, 50, 54, 188n6, 190n19, 191n25. *See also* realism: formal
weaker reason (Callard), 22–23, 27–28, 58, 84, 179n2. *See also* akrasia; Callard, Agnes; reason
weakness of will, 3, 13–14, 30–31, 58–59, 73–76, 107–8, 113, 118, 129, 157–58, 176n13, 183n31, 190n24;

in Augustine, 29–32; in Davidson, 42–46; distinguished from akrasia, 13–14; distinguished from willing weakness, 158; histories of, 176n13. *See also* akrasia; Davidson, Donald; indolence; sloth; will
Wetzel, James, 181n25, 183n36
will, 13–14, 24, 29–32, 33–41, 58–61, 73–74, 81–82, 86–90, 115–16, 139–43, 146, 180n17, 181–82nn25–28, 183n33, 183n36, 186n61, 203n30, 208n33; antinomy of (in Kant), 134–35; in Augustine, 29–32, 181–82nn25–28, 183nn33–34, 183n36; divided, 31–32; in Godwin's philosophy, 86–90; in Hobbes, 33–34; in Hume, 35–36, 185n59; in Locke, 37–41, 186n61, 186n68. *See also* action; Augustine, Saint; voluntary; weakness of will
William of Ockham, 24
Wordsworth, William, 5–6, 133–36, 138–41, 143–51, 207n24, 208n27, 209nn34–35, 210n36, 210n38, 210n41; "Expostulation and Reply," 139–40; *Lyrical Ballads* (with Coleridge), 140; *The Prelude,* 134–35, 140, 143–51, 208n27, 209–10nn34–36, 210n41; *The Recluse,* 140–41; "To My Sister," 139
Wright, Daniel, 12, 206n9
Wu, Duncan, 212n51, 213n57

tion, and the Invention of the

ʝ and the Theater Arts
ED BY LAURA KOPP

ntinental Presumptions Gave Rise to the

ʃapacious Desire in the Eighteenth Century
AUNSCHNEIDER

ans Reborn: Anglican Monopoly, Evangelical Dissent, and the
ʒ of the Baptists in the Late Eighteenth Century
JEWEL L. SPANGLER

Ending the French Revolution: Violence, Justice, and Repression from
the Terror to Napoleon
HOWARD G. BROWN

Wild Enlightenment: The Borders of Human Identity in the
Eighteenth Century
RICHARD NASH

Poems of Nation, Anthems of Empire: English Verse in the Long
Eighteenth Century
SUVIR KAUL

If the King Only Knew: Seditious Speech in the Reign of Louis XV
LISA JANE GRAHAM

No Tomorrow: The Ethics of Pleasure in the French Enlightenment
CATHERINE CUSSET

The Unfinished Manner: Essays on the Fragment in the Later
Eighteenth Century
ELIZABETH WANNING HARRIES